# Nativism Overseas

D1114611

SUNY Series, Women Writers in Translation

Marilyn Gaddis Rose, Editor

# Nativism Overseas

## Contemporary Chinese Women Writers

Edited by
Hsin-sheng C. Kao

State University of New York Press

Cover Illustration by Barbara Travis

Chinese Calligraphy by T. Sun

Published by
State University of New York Press, Albany

© 1993 State University of New York

All rights reserved

Printed in the United States of America

No part of this book may be used or reproduced
in any manner whatsoever without written permission
except in the case of brief quotations embodied in
critical articles and reviews.

For information, address State University of New York Press,
State University Plaza, Albany, N.Y. 12246

Production by M. R. Mulholland
Marketing by Nancy Farrell

**Library of Congress Cataloging-in-Publication Data**

Nativism overseas : contemporary Chinese women writers / [edited by]
    Hsin-sheng C. Kao.
        p.    cm.  —  (SUNY series, women writers in translation)
    Includes bibliographical references.
        ISBN 0-7914-1439-6 (acid free paper).  —  ISBN 0-7914-1440-X (pbk.
    : acid-free paper)
    1.  Chinese literature—20th century—History and criticism.
    2.  Chinese literature—Women authors—History and criticism.
    3.  Chinese fiction—20th century—Translations into English.
    4.  Chinese fiction—Women authors—Translations into English.
    I. Kao, Hsin-sheng C.  II. Series.
    PL2303.N38   1993
    895.1'52099287—dc20                                                92-14643
                                                                              CIP

10 9 8 7 6 5 4 3 2 1

To Leslie

# Contents

# Acknowledgments

I am most grateful to the five writers under study in this volume: Chen Ruoxi, Yu Lihua, Nie Hualing, Li Li, and Zhong Xiaoyang. I express my gratitude for their generous permission to translate and publish these stories in English, for their enthusiastic support and constructive responses during this project, and for their reading and commenting on the translations and essays in this volume.

I am equally indebted to my contributors: Samuel Hung-nin Cheung, Michelle Yeh, and Shiao-ling Yu. As my most objective critics, they have patiently and continuously supported my endeavors. Their lucid, well-informed, and critical appraisals, as well as their literary sensibility and affinity with each chosen writer's work, grace this entire volume.

No work can exist without the personal support that precedes it. I owe my gratitude and respect to Angela Jung Palandri for the earliest inspiration and encouragement of my research, and for our endless discussions concerning this project's conceptual framework and direction.

I also wish to thank those individuals who in various other ways have helped me complete this volume: Sarah Cohen for deepening my understanding of exile literature, especially Jewish exile writer Isaac Bashevis Singer; and C. T. Hsia, Yvonne Sung-sheng Chang, Dominic C. A. Cheung, Charlotte Furth, Charles Hartman, Leo Ou-fan Lee, K. C. Leung, and Yu Lihua for sharing my enthusiasm for modern Chinese literature and remaining my indispensable friends. Likewise, I am indebted to Robin W. Stevens for her editorial assistance and critical comments and for her painstaking and scrupulous efforts to improve the manuscript.

For institutional support of my project, I would like to express my thanks to the State University of New York at Albany, the California State University at Long Beach for a number of research grants, and to the Pacific Cultural Foundation for the writing grant.

Grateful acknowledgments are made for permission to translate the following Chinese stories into English:

Short story "Chengli chengwai" by Chen Ruoxi, copyright © 1983 by Chen Ruoxi. Translation from Chinese source into English by permission of the author.

Excerpts from "Haiwai zuojia he bentuxing" by Chen Ruoxi, copyright © 1988 by Chen Ruoxi. Translation from Chinese source into English by permission of the author.

Short story "Jiemei yin" by Yu Lihua, copyright © 1989 by Yu Lihua. Translation from Chinese source into English by permission of the author.

Excerpts from *Qianshan wai, shui changliu* by Nie Hualing, copyright © 1985 by Nie Hualing. The English excerpt "Many Things to Tell, but Hard to Tell," from the novel *Far Away, A River,* copyright © 1989 by Nie Hualing, is published with the permission of the author.

Short story "Jinxiang" by Li Li, copyright © 1988 by Li Li. Translation from Chinese into English by permission of the author.

Short story "Liangxiao" by Zhong Xiaoyang, copyright © 1987 by Zhong Xiaoyang. Translation from Chinese into English by permission of the author.

# A Note on the Text

Except for proper names and places, the *Pinyin* romanization system has been adopted throughout this book. In the *Selected Bibliography*, both the *Pinyin* romanization and Chinese characters are given.

All translations in this book from the writings of Chen Ruoxi, Yu Lihua, Nie Hualing, Li Li, and Zhong Xiaoyang are translated from the Chinese originals for the first time by the contributors, as are the citations and quotations from Chinese sources. Unless otherwise indicated, all other passages, comments, and translations in this book are mine, and of course whatever error is found in these pages is a responsibility of my own.

*H. C. K.*
*Los Angeles, California*

# Preface

Several years ago, I embarked upon this project at the suggestion of my mentor and dear friend, Angela Jung Palandri, a theorist on modern Chinese women's writing. During one of our many conversations, she urged me to consider the need to direct serious critical attention toward the creative expertise and aesthetics of the large body of overseas Chinese women writers who have enriched contemporary Chinese literature with some of its most enduring, multifaceted themes and narratives. Steady interest in Chinese women's studies is a fact; she reminded me, however, that there are only a few scattered criticisms or translations available to sustain this enthusiasm. Her insightful suggestions have been most constructive with regard to the shaping of this project, and I am thrilled to respond to her calling with the completion of this edited volume of research and translation.

In essence, the word overseas (*haiwai*) conveys the idea of a physical separation and geographic absence from one's home soil, culture, society, people, and roots. Literally, going overseas means going yonder, over "the China seas," which in itself has had a long history. However, as far as its relationship with the West is concerned, only in the middle and late nineteenth century did a large number of Chinese, mostly from the lower working classes, immigrate to the United States and other Western countries in order to escape poverty or hardship. It was not until the late fifties and early sixties that a sizable group of Chinese intellectuals and professionals left their homeland for America in pursuit of freedom and opportunity to carry on their search for what they idealized as their traditional culture. Since that time a new type of literary writing has come into existence.

This type of writing has its origins in the writers' quests for personal identity. Living abroad, they have experienced the dynamic processes of conflict between assimilation and resistance. This conflict or tension has compelled them to choose an independent and autonomous attitude toward the act of creative writing. This is not to say that before then there was no such kind of literary production. In fact, during the first half of the twentieth century in the United States, a number of works were produced by writers of Chinese descent, both written and published in English. Writers such as Lin Yutang, Chiang

Yee, Han Suyin, and more recently Maxine Hong Kingston, Frank Chin, and Amy Tan, are a few famous examples.

However, the Chinese overseas writers that emerged during the second half of this century are different from the above-mentioned Chinese-American writers. The difference lies not only in their writing in the Chinese language instead of English, but also in their efforts to remain identified with contemporary and historical Chinese culture. They also continue to publish in Chinese journals, periodicals, and newspapers in China, Taiwan, and abroad. Many of these writers originally came to the United States as overseas students or professionals. Thus, because of their unique nature, the works written by them are collectively called "Chinese student overseas literature" (*Liuxuesheng wenxue*), "Chinese overseas elite/intellectual literature" (*Haiwai zhishi fenzi wenxue*), and finally, "Chinese overseas literature" (*Haiwai wenxue*).

Compared to works written by many Chinese-American authors, works of the fifties and sixties by Chinese overseas writers stress the themes of rootlessness and the search for self-identity, as well as the concepts of assimilation and rejection, inclusion and exclusion, and internal and external exile. Overseas literature has continued to thrive from the seventies onward, though it does not necessarily have the same form, scope, and literary themes as its predecessors. These more recent works have been enriched by the import of political issues and the broadening of many writers' philosophical outlooks through interactions among diversified schools of thought, human psychology, and social transformations. Thus, these works have evolved as an assiduous exploration of Chinese reality. Taken in their totality, they attempt to react or focus upon Chinese issues, and their contents reflect a distinctive Chinese sociopolitical consciousness as they employ a wide range of narrative strategies and techniques.

*Nativism Overseas: Contemporary Chinese Women Writers* is an anthology of critical essays and newly translated short stories on five representative women writers: Chen Ruoxi, Yu Lihua, Nie Hualing, Li Li, and Zhong Xiaoyang. Though their works are varied in their stylistic intensity and thematic scope, they nonetheless tie together discussions of some of the most compelling issues broached in overseas Chinese literature today. The issues deliberated upon include nativism and expatriation, the poetics of displacement and redemption, the aesthetics of exile within and without, and multicultural polarities and assimilation processes.

The opening article, the "Prologue," is a translation of Chen Ruoxi's discussion of nativism and Chinese overseas writers. It was purposely chosen to both set the tone for the essays and translated stories and to help build the conceptual framework within which the nature of this volume's thematic stresses can be understood. In this article, Chen Ruoxi gives her own definition of the term Chinese overseas writer, attempting to articulate its historic and literary interpretation. At the same time, she persuasively responds to questions posed by various critics by situating the questions in relation to her own personal convictions. Not only is her essay a straightforward philosophical observation of the relationship between overseas writers and their homeland, but it is also a forceful piece that chronicles overseas writers' ties with their native land, justifying their place in the mainstream of today's Chinese literature.

Chen Ruoxi's short story "In and Outside the Wall" assembles a provocative range of perspectives from the two sides of China, symbolized by the antitheses *in* and *out*, and by the word *wall*, implying the Great Wall or China herself. These perspectives raise important questions about the relationship between fiction and reality, and Chen Ruoxi uses her fiction to resolve the fear of overseas Chinese regarding the political division that exists between China and Taiwan and the resulting identity crisis. Thus this story shows the internal and external Chinese sociopolitical struggles of the seventies, which were as urgent as they were controversial.

One of the hallmarks of Chinese overseas writing is the pleasure it takes in its own poetic form while still remaining within the general corpus of Chinese literature. Yu Lihua's writing is most exceptional in this regard and has been included in this collection for two specific reasons. First, from the literary historian's point of view, Yu Lihua is considered a foremost spokesperson for Chinese intellectuals in the United States, and her works are popularly regarded as precursors to the overseas Chinese literary movement as well. Second, from a critical point of view, Yu Lihua is noted both as a particularly vigorous explorer of the boundaries of fictional style and as a theoretical proponent of overseas Chinese literature. Ever since her arrival in America in 1953, her satirical and gloomy visions of this "land of plenty" have not been aimed merely at demythification, but also at rendering a more credible, and at times scathingly pathetic, portrayal of historical reality.

Yu Lihua's writings consciously entwine the concepts of nostalgia, alienation, and the effects of assimilation into American life, and express the fusion and clashes of the two cultures and traditions that nurture her characters. My article, "Yu Lihua's Blueprint for the Development of a New Poetics: Chinese Literature Overseas," specifically addresses the interplay and profusion of these two different traditions, comparing the dichotomies ensconced in the collective layers of the overseas Chinese psyche. On a thematic level, such as in the story included in this collection, "Two Sisters," this interplay usually manifests itself as a taut allegorical device that probes into human complexities and actions, the passage of time, and cultural influences. It is in this sense that the adjective *two* in the story's title can be read, not as a mathematical number, but rather as a dichotomized metaphor that emphasizes the thematic irony in the comparison of the two worlds symbolized by the two sisters.

For author Nie Hualing, the reality of war, death, repression, hypocrisy, and intolerance are not grotesque metaphors for the literary imagination. Instead, she has grown up among them. Having been closely connected with and suffered personally from the devastations of twentieth-century Chinese history, Nie Hualing has become one of the very few and best Chinese writers to bring literature and history into conjunction. Her advocacy of the mobilization of history to serve as an ideological cause has encouraged her to write with complex ideological consciousness and engaging intensity. In an interview conducted by Peter Nazareth of *World Literature Today* (Winter 1981), she outlines her basic premise: "To be Chinese in the twentieth century is to suffer all the wars, revolutions and family tragedies, but the Chinese survived. Of course there are reasons for that survival, but I think one of the reasons is the primitive life force of the Chinese" (p. 12).

In her essay entitled "The Themes of Exile and Identity Crisis in Nie Hualing's Fiction," Shiao-ling Yu discusses Nie's works in terms of the political and social turmoil her characters undergo as they attempt to adjust psychologically and emotionally to an alien sociopolitical and geographic environment. It is their "life force" that allows them to survive and nourish their wounded selves. From the short story "A Day in Wang Danian's Life" to the novel *Lotus*, Shiao-ling Yu explores Nie's infinitely complex web of human interrelationships, the interplay between the individual and history, and the conflict between personal desire and social responsibility.

"Many Things to Tell, but Hard to Tell," an excerpt from Nie's epic-like novel *Lotus*, gives the reader an opportunity to see the intricate interplays between self and family, and action and reaction to history. It is a high-spirited exposé of the marginalized identity crisis experienced by the young half-American and half-Chinese heroine, Lotus, and the results of the historical chaos caused by the Chinese Cultural Revolution. In the story, Lotus equates the sense of self with one's motherland and the source of paternal lineage; however, the denial she receives from her American paternal grandmother and her

Chinese countrymen ontologically breaks her away from her relatives and homeland and from her social ties and cultural continuity, symbolizing a break with the collective history of which she is supposed to be a part. Throughout the novel, the double narrative moves the story artfully back and forth through two distinct kinds of reality: the reality of Lotus's parents of the late forties, a reality "there" in China, and the reality of Lotus in the seventies, the reality "here" in her and her inner world. The intertwining and fusion of these realities exhibits Nie's literary sophistication and masterful skills.

On the whole, what distinguishes many overseas Chinese writers from native Chinese writers, besides their geographic separation, is the former's obsession with their cultural roots. It is a new mode of consciousness, not experienced simply *by* overseas Chinese, but also *of* them and *about* them, standing apart from their own tradition and its audience. Writers like Bai Xianyong, Cong Shu, Guo Songfen, Li Yu, and Liu Daren fall back on this timely kind of experience to make their literary impact. They are all student-intellectual emigrés from Taiwan who write in response to the ever-increasing fervor over China's recognition and identity. Li Li is one of those writers who shares with them a sense of cultural and personal mission and a devotion to "Chineseness" as a starting point. Her writings vary thematically from the trials and tribulations of the Diaoyutai incident, to the joy over China's admission to the United Nations, to an understanding of the anguish over their own survival, and to the commitment and acceptance of the writers' Chinese roots. She refers to her native roots as the "Chinese knot" (*Zhongguo jie*), an ever-present and deeply felt cultural connection linking each of her characters' inward journeys to the search for cultural identity. It is through this "Chinese knot" that Li Li's characters find their most basic and enduring source for self-fulfillment. In the essay "The Divided Self and the Search for Redemption: A Study of Li Li's Fiction," Michelle Yeh explicates this connection, along with the concept of the "divided self," through her detailed analysis of Li Li's short stories. Yeh demonstrates that beneath the surface of Li Li's characters exist layers of doubt and insecurity over the permanence of existential reality itself. This insecurity is intensified and condensed into a dichotomized existence, in which Li Li's characters are constantly torn by their perception of time, by their memory of a China torn apart into two separate political entities, and by their maladjustment to the conflict between two cultures, the East and the West. Nonetheless, the characters in Li Li's fiction rise above the struggles on a moral or spiritual plane, and transcend these troubling political, ideological, and gender-based dichotomies.

Although the concept of internal or metaphorical exile in literature is sometimes not as widely accepted as external exile because of the lack of true physical separation or uprootedness, it is nonetheless a historical reality and an existing condition of man on this earth. Thus I have chosen to include Zhong Xiaoyang for her astute ability to connect with her native Chinese heritage and explore the realms of existential exile, even though she is not in fact classified as an exile or overseas writer in the physical sense.

It is perhaps one of the most challenging tasks for a writer to write about the alienation of the inner self, a sphere that is most private, intangible, elusive, and intense. The dichotomized boundaries between home soil and foreign land can be internalized either as the self perceived in a temporal and spatial time frame, or as the polarized contrasts between here-there, I-thou, or the differentiation between this and that. The oscillation between these extremities forces the exile to mediate the inner transaction represented by the world of presentation and the world of perception. This creates an infinite set of existential clashes and anguish, hopefully leading to the birth of ontological awareness and resolution.

All of these aspects can be found at the center of Zhong Xiaoyang's works. The youngest of our five selected women writers, Zhong is currently residing in Hong Kong, and is considered by some the Zhang Ailing (Chang Ai-ling, or Eileen Chang) of this generation. Although Zhong's alienated heroes and heroines are capable of love and living, they are perpetually trapped in their isolation, waging a battle against the apprehension of death-in-life. In Samuel Hung-nin Cheung's essay "Beyond the Bridal Veil: The Romantic Vision of Zhong Xiaoyang," he discusses the prevailing tone of pessimism in Zhong's stories which concern themselves mainly with the ardent efforts of youth in the often unfulfilling pursuit of love. Cheung points out that Zhong repeatedly tries to convey to the reader the banality of everyday life, in which her characters attempt to conceal from themselves the meaninglessness of their existence. These characters are neither capable of growing to explain the meaning of existence, nor capable of comprehending the significance of self-definition, though they are adept at indulging in private pleasures and the illusiveness of their fantasies. In their best introspective moments, they are only capable of revealing their awe at the "inexplicable mystery of life" and their despair with the "futility" of purposeful striving.

"The Wedding Night" typifies the gloomy vision of Zhong as it is revealed through the fear and suspicions felt by two nameless newlyweds. The exchange of marriage vows and the sharing of the romantic bridal chamber do not in any way sanctify their matrimonial union. Just like exiles stepping onto foreign soil, the bride and groom suffer feelings of physical and ontological displacement in this bridal chamber. The double-voiced accounts rendered by the bride and groom narrators, along with the double construction of historical and factual nuances, suggest the equivalence of internal alienation and the flight from the old and familiar, a salient characteristic of the disjointed exile. Occasionally, these two protagonists "almost" perceive a Joyce-like epiphany, but unfortunately, the multiplicity of the world of appearances overwhelms and drowns their senses and perceptions. In this respect, Zhong is the least optimistic, both in tone and ideology, of the five women writers discussed here.

In sum, putting these five writers in the context of contemporary Chinese literature, we are able to find a consistent voice in line with the literature of exile and self-discovery and of nativism. Their writing asks us to redefine the complex issues of human existence and significance. The multifaceted topics examined by these writers—be it the sociopolitical consciousness of Chen Ruoxi, Yu Lihua's focus on roots, the historical continuity of Nie Hualing, Li Li's cultural knot, or the alienated self of Zhong Xiaoyang— show a social consciousness, a knowledge of essence, culture, and self, and an awareness of their own individual contributions to the continuity of Chinese history.

# Prologue:
# Chinese Overseas Writers and Nativism[1]

## Chen Ruoxi

### Definition of "Chinese Overseas Writer"

I first came across the term *overseas writer* in 1975 when *China News Supplement* (*Zhongguo shibao fukan*) editor-in-chief, Gao Xinjiang, invited me to submit a manuscript. He sent me a bundle of blank manuscript sheets with the words *Overseas Column* (*Haiwai zhuanlan*) printed on the top. As it turned out, he was labeling all writers living outside of Taiwan and mainland China "overseas writers" and even publishing our works in a separate column of the supplement. The only exception he afforded me was the double status of being both a Taiwanese writer and an "overseas writer."

At first, I looked askance at this term *overseas writer*. Always adhering to the principle "Born a Chinese person, die a Chinese ghost," I have never veered from the intention to write in Chinese, about Chinese people, and for Chinese readers. Understandably, I was quite dismayed at being categorized as an outsider from "over" the China "Sea" when my native Taiwan lay nestled well within the confines of that bit of ocean. Nonetheless, as time passed, I began to reconsider the practical value and objective reality of the notion of the term *overseas writer* and gradually made peace with the idea.

At the beginning of the eighties, the Hong Kong Joint Publishing Company introduced a book series entitled *Overseas Literary Collections*,[2] to which I gladly added my novels.[3] Over the past two years, the terms *overseas writers* and *overseas literary collections* have cropped up on the mainland with increasing frequency, sometimes appearing beside "Taiwan-Hong Kong Writers" and sometimes including the latter category. In 1987, I and several other women writers founded the Overseas Chinese Women Writers Friendship Association.[4] At that time, the definition I put forth for *overseas* was "any area outside of the Chinese territories." To my knowledge, this criterion has yet to encounter any objection, and is perhaps at present the most widely accepted definition of the term.

## The Current Profusion of What Has Long Existed

The term *overseas writer*, though it is often considered a phenomenon of the seventies, can be traced back to the late Ming and early Qing dynasties. According to historical documents, there were two literati during the late Ming dynasty, Zhu Shunshui and Chen Yuandai, who fled to Japan and left their mark on the field of poetry there. When Japan invaded China in the late 1930s, many writers fled to Southeast Asia. They were active in literary circles in Singapore, Malaysia, and Hong Kong. Some, such as Yu Dafu, were even buried in foreign countries.

At that time, the term *exiled writers* (*liuwang zuojia*) was more commonly used. This was probably attributable to the refugee status of many of the writers and the inevitable sense that this was a transitory phenomenon.

After World War II, China's civil war began, and soon there was a face-off across the straits. Following these events, the number of overseas writers outside both the mainland and Taiwan skyrocketed. By the early seventies, they had scattered around the globe, and there was no faraway place they could not be found. However, the largest concentration relocated on the American continent, with the United States serving as the main base. Most, of course, came from Taiwan, but among them were many who originally came from the mainland. These writers, already long renowned, continued to use Taiwan as their center for publication and were active in Taiwan's literary circles, sometimes even bringing about a situation in which the guests were playing host to the hosts. Thus, a decade ago, Taiwan's two main newspaper supplements were accused by native writers of having "become overseas writers' territorial holdings."

Unlike writers banished from the Soviet Union, the majority of these writers were not prohibited from returning to their homeland, nor did they suffer from political oppression there. Their decision was akin to that of many Taiwanese students who choose to study abroad. In a country rife with troubles and unpredictable changes in government, many who leave the country to further their studies often stay abroad, contributing to what is commonly known as "brain drain" (*xueliu*).[5] The impetus for settling down in one of the European countries, the United States, or Canada is primarily the attraction of material prosperity and democratic freedom.

Today, the number of overseas writers is still growing. The end of the seventies marked the end of a decade of political upheavals in mainland China. As the Cultural Revolution's isolationist mentality began to crumble, a new openness to the outside world developed. Since then, the tide of emigration and overseas study has risen steadily. On the heels of such a great exodus of talent, many literary figures decided to settle overseas as well, and it is anticipated that those numbers will continue to swell by the day.

To adapt to their new environment, the majority of people who migrate overseas adjust their ambitions, giving up their ideals and changing careers. However, of the writers who settled down overseas permanently, most refused to adjust in this way. Though they had to take menial jobs in order to survive, they persisted in writing, and it became their greatest emotional outlet. In one incident, over thirty years ago, an overseas science student committed suicide because of his inability to adjust to his new environment in the United States. This kind of thing has happened frequently; yet among writers there has not been a single known case reported. Writing, it would appear, is a great pacifier of the psyche.

Many overseas Chinese intellectuals do, however, share an internalized psychological conflict. Although they do not wish to grow old and die in a foreign country, they are still unable to tear themselves away from their current situation. This is known as the "Chinese emotional knot." Typically very lonely people, they often compare themselves to travelers or wanderers, feeling isolated to the extent that after gaining citizenship in their host country they still hold on to a "resident visitor" mentality. Because of their traditional homeland-centered attitude, no matter how good things are for them, they still feel, "I know it's beautiful here, but it's not my home." Chinese people are eternally entangled, heart and soul, in their place of origin. Homesickness is as old as the sky and as enduring as the earth.

Overseas writers do not enjoy these feelings of loneliness. They are fortunate in that, with a flick of a pen, they can transform the deepest homesickness into an essay and send it back to their homeland to be published. Homesickness thus evolves into a cornucopia of creative works, with even the process of submitting the manuscripts serving as a tenuous maintenance of ties with their homeland.

Not only do their works form a special category in their home-land, but their usefulness is unique as well. For example, during the seventies, a large number of overseas students were just beginning to return to Taiwan. Some of them returned to temporary teaching posi-tions; others settled down there permanently. Long before this tumul-tuous wave began, overseas writers had already assumed a responsibility that overseas students should have shouldered but never did. Both directly and indirectly, they introduced American and European ideas to Taiwan through their literature. From the May Fourth Movement on, these writers played the role of transmitters of Western learning to the East. The use of their literature as a bridge between East and West is one of the many reasons their works have been so successful and lasting in the homeland.

Overseas writers enjoyed another run of good fortune after the mainland opened its doors. By virtue of their third-country citizen-ship, they were permitted to shuttle back and forth freely between the straits. Their impressions shone through their writing, and as their literature was published in both China and abroad, their works took on a mediating function. In this age of political division in China, it is apparent how useful these writers have been as a bridge between poetics and the reader.

We cannot emphasize enough the function these works have served in discourse and mediation. In China, freedom of speech is a right the people are still fighting to attain. There is a saying, "Foreign monks love to chant verses." A greater amount of government criticism will be accepted or endured by the government if it comes from the pens of overseas writers. There has been a steady stream of Chinese writers serving time in prison for their works.[6] Overseas writers serv-ing prison terms, however, are a rarity. The main reason, of course, is that they hold foreign passports. Overseas writers often hear such accusatory gibes as "clinging to the West for self-respect" or "The moon is rounder overseas." However, in that moment when the cell door is shut, the public outcry and moral support overseas writers are able to generate make up for much of the perception that they have deserted their colleagues at home.

This unique function, taken on by an innumerable throng of overseas writers, has no precedent in Chinese history or in the history of the world. It is no wonder that, in the seventies, the editors-in-chief of Taiwan's literary supplements finally settled on the title *Overseas Writers* (*Haiwai zuojia*).

## What Is Nativism?

For a writer to be called an "overseas writer" requires more than mere geographical separation from Taiwan or the mainland. It also involves a feeling of separation in the psyche. Yet the reason overseas writers can be grouped together and are able to fill a single place in two separate literary scenes is that their works all share certain special characteristics. They all revolve around China, Chinese people, and Chinese things. Likewise, the contents of their works are often very similar to those written by native writers. Because it has this Chinese nativistic character, many people consider overseas Chinese literature to be peripheral Chinese literature. Some flatly assert that overseas literature, as well as the much-ballyhooed "Taiwanese literature" of recent years, is all an integral part of Chinese literature.

No matter how future history draws the lines, overseas and native Chinese literature are thoroughly intertwined. It would not be exaggerating to say that the connection is one of flesh and blood. It was the possibility of popular exposure in the land of their heritage, where everything from printing to publication was available, that gave overseas writers a conducive environment in which to write in the first place. The greatest concentration of overseas writers, for example, exists in the United States and includes many well-known Chinese writers. Yet, of all their Chinese works, virtually none have been published in the United States.

If nativism is the essence of overseas literature, then what exactly does nativism really consist of? How does one carry on nativism? This has become a point of great contention among writers. In the mid-eighties, the *China News* (*Zhongbao*) invited a number of representative Chinese-American writers to attend a conference in New York entitled "The Nativism of Chinese Overseas Writers."[7] Though the participants talked up a storm without reaching any definitive conclusion, their discussions clearly demonstrated the importance of nativism abroad.

## Homeward Longings

It is my belief that nativism comes part and parcel with an overseas writer's motivation to write. Why do people write? The answers writers give are often eloquent and lofty. In 1985, the French magazine *Liberté* took an international survey of four hundred writers to ask why they write. Some comments were "Because I like it," "So I don't die, to survive," and "For human liberty, and to fight inequality, corruption, poverty, and ignorance."

When I received a phone call for the survey, I likewise gave a very proper reason. Thinking about it afterwards, though, my reasons for writing are really very primitive. Quite simply, it is impossible for me not to write. If I refrain from writing, I just don't feel right.

Early in my college career, one of my professors took an informal survey of our class. It turned out that a large number of the manuscripts students submitted were done to earn money. Some were done in hopes of critical acclaim or to satisfy the desire to be published. Very few harbored any sense of mission to mirror reality, recreate society, or other such things. This is not to say that overseas writers do not have these motivations for writing; however, I do not believe that they are the primary reasons.

My son used to think that having a writer for a mom was really something to be proud of. One day he asked me, for all the time I spend hunched over working at my desk, how much money did I earn? Once he found out that for a whole day of climbing shelves I earned about as much, on average, as a manual laborer makes in an hour, he couldn't contain his disbelief and howled, "Mama! Are you crazy? If I were you, I'd rather die than be a writer!"

Aside from Chinese writers, even American-born writers have to have an insane determination to attempt taking up writing as a profession. According to a report published in an English-language newspaper a few years ago, the average writer's annual income in the United States was $5,000, less than the poverty line. For many writers, it is essential to take a second job just to survive.

This situation is very much like that in Taiwan. Writers by profession, who live solely on their writing income, only started to surface some ten years ago. Now professional writers are gradually growing into a significant group. However, the Chinese mainland is another matter entirely. There professional writers work for a fixed salary. They have writers' relief organizations to take care of their basic needs. They belong to a privileged class; if they go several years without producing any work, they still get to keep their jobs, as always. Apart from the problem of political movements, the treatment of Chinese writers makes one immensely envious.[8]

Things are different for writers overseas. Overseas Chinese writers all have amateur status. Although they live in what people believe to be the land of plenty, the United States, and although the number of Chinese-language publications here is exceeded only by China and Hong Kong, the knowledge that publishing is a losing enterprise here has so far kept any class of professional Chinese writers from developing. Certainly, there are a few unusual cases of writers living off their writing income, but often they have to write insincere political commentaries under assumed names, submitting their manuscripts to publications who receive financial support from unspecified sources.

Overseas writers here are a minority: few in number, small in voice. Overseas writers do not fantasize that their works will stir up political reform in the homeland. They hardly envision themselves on such a mission. Some writers with a burning social consciousness often eye improving overseas Chinese communities, admonishing them for being rootless drifters, and calling for a greater struggle toward political power and achievement. These kinds of writers are few.

To my knowledge, most people write because they cannot help it. They write to console the homeward longings in their own bosom. People always have feelings for the place where they grew up, and once they leave, they begin to miss it. These feelings can be heavy or light, sometimes hidden and sometimes expressed, but they are always revealed sooner or later. Literary types are sentimental, and when it comes to their hometown and homeland, their thoughts and feelings cut even more deeply. Their feelings become so intense that it is like carrying a "profound regret that lingers unceasingly." Many writers spend the first two years overseas writing about the old days they miss, and then move on to comparing the new land with the old. However, this "old" never gets cut away and left behind. Simply stated, without homeward longing, there would be no overseas literature. It is the very essence of nativism.

## Nativism as the Mark of Culture

There are some writers who write in a foreign language but whose works cannot take leave of the people and affairs of China. For example, Lin Yutang wrote a series of expository writings in English contained in *My Country and My People* (1935) that are widely recognized as a great contribution to the dissemination of Chinese culture.[9] There is also Chiang Yee, who wrote the travel journal *The Silent Traveler in San Francisco* (1964), also in English.[10] These volumes of writing drew much attention among English readers, helping the Western world understand Chinese culture and the Chinese peoples' philosophy of life. Cultural essentialism was thus merely a different form of nativism in these works.

Chinese people who are born and raised overseas are also deeply influenced by Chinese culture. Many writers do not realize this, and often proudly proclaim that they are free of "homeward longing" and don't need to carry the cross of four thousand years of Chinese history on their backs. They embrace the land of their birth and upbringing, describe life in that country, write in that country's language, and participate in that country's literary circles. To put it briefly, they will have nothing to do with Chinese literature. However, in reality, though they may not be seeking their roots, they cannot cut the umbilical cord of culture. In the seventies, Maxine Hong Kingston rose up into the American literary scene, writing novels depicting the experiences of the older generation of Chinese-Americans. The mark of Chinese culture in her work remains its distinguishing characteristic.

If we examine the reasons foreign-born overseas writers rise in the American literary scene, it is not hard to see that, besides their abilities with the language and the literary craft, what draws people to them the most are the Chinese elements in their work. Jewish writers, born and raised in the United States, are even more this way. The Jewish writer and Nobel laureate Saul Bellow wrote almost every one of his stories about Jews living in America. Japan is also no exception. Chen Shunchen, a best-selling writer on the Japanese market who is of Taiwanese descent, made a special point to travel to the Chinese mainland in search of writing material.

It should be pointed out that culture emerges in literary works in many ways. Honorable traditions have never been able to compete with strange customs for drawing people's attention and interest. For example, Maxine Hong Kingston's *The Woman Warrior* decried the feudal backwardness of old China's marriage traditions. During the fifties, the novel *Flower Drum Song* by K. Y. Lee achieved popularity for a while. Their works usually centered on the themes of conservatism, the generation gap, and life in Chinatown.[11] There are also many other works that touch upon erotic fetishes for hairstyles, bound feet, concubines, and others. One can imagine why, based upon the traditional notion that "foul odors in the family are not to be fanned outside," these writers have received a great deal of censure. Fortunately, on the heels of China's progress and rise in stature, this sort of shameful portrayal is becoming much less common.

The Evolution of Nativism: New Land and Homeland

Since nativism is intimately involved with the creative work of writers, the relative strengths and weaknesses of nativism take on great significance for their work. Homeward longing is the impetus for writing, but as the original departure from village and country recedes day by day into the distant past, memories inevitably fade. A person cannot live in the past; a writer, especially not.

A writer is most at home writing about familiar people and things. Overseas writers, having chosen a new land and settled down there permanently, inevitably develop feelings for the place as time passes and gradually become familiar with their surroundings. Through this process, nativism expands to take on a double meaning, one for the new land and one for the old.

For example, as the duration of overseas Chinese writers' residence in the United States grows, they turn increasingly to the sensations and conditions of Chinese-American society for their basic material. Some writers keep their emphasis on the Chinese mainland or Taiwan; some describe both sides of the Pacific, flying back and forth like space people. In the end, though, the proportioning of the material is just a way of giving order to the fusion of the new and old land.

Being an overseas writer has its advantages and disadvantages. Living abroad, one's field of vision is wider and one has greater freedom of expression. This no one denies. However, after leaving the homeland far behind, one cannot help but feel estranged from it after a while. Even if one maintains intimate connections with the homeland and returns to visit regularly, one's life still necessarily draws farther and farther apart from it. A common sentiment shared by many overseas writers is that, as this gulf widens, they feel they are rendered helpless, futilely reaching for something that is lost or disappearing.

Since the release and publication of their literary works often take place in the homeland, overseas writers have yet another difficult bottleneck to break through. The billion or more people on both sides of the straits have a limited appetite for literature that describes the life of Chinese abroad. Curiosities from strange lands can always draw big crowds, and such things will probably always have a market. However, ultimately their contents depart from reality and lose the cutting edge of realism, so people cannot easily relate or sympathize with them. Overseas literature has never lacked in quantity, but it has also never exactly been the mainstream on either side of the straits. It is because of these particular circumstances that only in the last twenty years has terminology like "literature of Chinese students overseas" (*liuxuesheng wenxue*), "literature of the wanderers" (*youzi wenxue*), or finally "overseas literature" (*haiwai wenxue*) come into current use.

These drawbacks have not caused overseas writers to falter. Not only have the numbers of overseas writers not fallen, but they have actually continued to rise. Considering the peculiar muddled nature of Chinese history and politics, I feel that we can now anticipate a long period in which overseas writers will continue to flourish, and those writers will maintain their function as both voices of public opinion and bridges between the divided camps.

Overseas writers should feel optimistic, and even pleased with themselves. It is common knowledge that literature is the study of people. Writers may live in different regions or in completely disconnected realms, but the focus of all literature remains people. One need only write well of people, and people will be moved and affected by one's work. Literature that breathes life within its lines to Chinese people residing on all corners of the globe is Chinese literature. Thus, "Chinese overseas literature" is, I believe, simply Chinese literature itself.

## Notes

1. "Chinese Overseas Writers and Nativism" ("Haiwai zuojia he bentuxing") was translated by Hsin-sheng C. Kao with the permission of the author and publisher, and is published here in English for the first time. The original appeared in *Hong Kong wenxue* (September 1988): 18–21. All notes listed hereafter are provided by the translator.

2. This collection contains over forty publications, including anthologies of fiction, poetry, and prose, as well as many individual works. Writers included are Cau Youfang, Chen Ruoxi, Cong Shu, Fei Ma, Guo Songfen, Lan Ling, Li Li, Li Oufan, Liu Shaoming, Ma Lingshi, Nie Hualing, Qian Ge, Qin Song, Shi Shuqing, Shui Jing, Wang Yu, Liu Daran, Ye Weilian, Ye Zi, Yi Li, Yu Lihua, Yu Liqing, Yuan Zenan, Zhang Cuo, Zhao Shuxia, Zheng Chouyu, Zhuang Yin, and others.

3. This refers to her three novels: *Tuwei* (*Breaking Out*, 1983), *Er Hu* (*The Two Hus*, 1986), and *Zhihun* (*Paper Marriage*, 1987).

4. In July of 1989, Chen Ruoxi and her colleagues expanded this association and founded an international organization called "International Chinese Women Writers Overseas Organization." Chen was the first president (1989–91) of this organization, and Yu Lihua is currently the president (1991–1993).

5. Literally meaning "learn to stay abroad," Chen is referring to the many overseas Chinese who try to find any legal way to stay in this adopted new land rather than return to China.

6. This refers to Taiwanese writers who were opponents of the Guomindang. Writers such as Chen Yingzhen, Wang Tuo, and Yang Qingshu were arrested in 1979.

7. This refers to the symposium entitled "The Nativism of Chinese Overseas Writers," sponsored by *Zhongbao* (*China News*), on December 16, 1985, in New York. The participants included Chen Ruoxi, Cong Shu, Hong Mingshui, Li Yu, Tang Degang, Yang Mu, Zhang Cuo, and Zhang Xiguo. Chen's speech was called "Gutu yu xintu" ("Homeland and New Land").

8. In reference to Chinese writers' livelihood, professional salaries, and manuscript payments from 1949 to the 1980s, see Perry Link, *Roses and Thorns: The Second Blooming of the Hundred Flowers in Chinese Fiction, 1979–80* (Berkeley and Los Angeles: University of California Press, 1984), pp. 25–29.

9. Lin Yutang (1895–1976), the son of a Presbyterian minister, earned himself a M.A. from Harvard (1920) and a Ph.D. from the University of Leipzig (1923). During the 1930s and 1940s, he was regarded as the most prominent and prolific Chinese writer in the United States. He was the author of more than fifty books with a wide range of subject matter, including novels, essays, translations, and biographies.

10. Chiang Yee was both a painter and a writer. Besides *The Silent Traveler in San Francisco* (1964), he also wrote *The Silent Traveler in Lakeland* (1937).

11. For a comprehensive analysis of Chinese-American writers and their works, especially works about the older-generation Chinese-Americans in Chinatown, see Liu Shaoming's "Tangrenjie de xiaoshuo shijie" ("The Fictional World of Chinatown"), in his *Shangdi, muqin, airen* (*God, Mother, and the Beloved*) (Taipei: Siji, 1981), pp. 97–121.

Chen Ruoxi

陈若曦

# Chen Ruoxi

Chen Ruoxi (b. 1938), also Chen Jo-hsi, is the pen name of Chen Xiumei, who also has published in English under the name Lucy Chen. She was born in a rural area of Taipei, Taiwan, to a working class family that had been for five generations Taiwanese. An extremely intelligent child, in 1951 she took the entrance examination and was admitted to the most prestigious Taiwanese girls' school, The First Middle School of Taipei for Girls. In 1957 she entered National Taiwan University, where she majored in English literature. That same year she made her literary debut in the *Wenxue zazhi* (*The Literary Review*), which subsequently published half a dozen of her short stories written during her undergraduate days in Taiwan. During her junior year, Chen Ruoxi and a few of her literary friends, Bai Xianyong (Pai Hsien-yung), Li Oufan (Leo Ou-fan Lee), Liu Shaoming (Joseph S. M. Lau), Ye Weilian (Wai-lim Yip), and others, co-founded the *Xiandai wenxue* (*Modern Literature*); she served as one of its editors. After receiving her B.A. in 1961, Chen Ruoxi worked for a year before deciding to further her education in the United States. In 1962 she commenced studies in English literature at Mount Holyoke College. That same year, she published her first book in English, entitled *Spirit Calling* (*Zhaohun*).

The following year, Chen Ruoxi transferred to Johns Hopkins University, where she studied English literature and creative writing. It was there that she met Duan Shiyao (Tuann Shih-yao), a graduate student from Taiwan who was studying engineering. They were married in 1964, and she received her M.A. in 1965. Shortly after her husband finished his Ph.D., the couple, fired by patriotic zeal, left the United States in October of 1966 to repatriate to the People's Republic of China. Unfortunately, their dream of serving the motherland during its reconstruction was shattered by the upheavals of the Great Proletarian Cultural Revolution.

The couple remained in Beijing waiting for teaching assignments from 1966 to 1968, and in 1967 Chen Ruoxi gave birth to their first son. It was not until 1969 that she was assigned to teach English at the Hydraulic College in Nanjing, and in 1970 she gave birth to their second son. Finally, after seven traumatic years in China, the family was granted permission to leave. They arrived in Hong Kong in November 1973.

In 1974, the family moved to Vancouver, British Columbia, where Chen Ruoxi worked in a bank and resumed her writing after nearly a decade of silence. Most of her stories about the Cultural Revolution were written between 1974 and 1978. Then, in 1979, she accepted a position as a researcher for the Institute of Chinese Studies at the University of California at Berkeley, and made Berkeley her permanent residence. During the last few years, Chen Ruoxi has devoted herself to writing and has occasionally spoken as a guest lecturer at several universities in the United States, Hong Kong, Taiwan, and the People's Republic of China. Currently, she is the chief editor of *Square Quarterly (Guangchang)*, a magazine for Chinese exile literature.

Chen Ruoxi's best-known story collection, *The Execution of Mayor Yin and Other Great Cultural Proletarian Revolution Stories* (1976), has been translated into eight languages. She has published seven other collections of her short stories, five novels, seven prose and essay collections, and several volumes of critical writings and translation.

# In and Outside the Wall[1]

## Chen Ruoxi

The Chinese scholastic delegation was planning to visit a California university for two days, at which time they would also give a public lecture to be introduced by Professor Yu Yi of the university's history department. This would be the first time China had sent a delegation to visit the United States since the reestablishment of Sino-American diplomatic ties.[2] Thus, the event caused quite a stir. From the moment the news appeared in the newspaper, the Yus' telephone never stopped ringing. Both colleagues and friends alike called frequently inquiring about the guests' itinerary, subtly indicating their desire to meet the delegation members in person.

Professor Yu specialized in ancient Chinese history and was renowned for his thorough research and erudite publications. Barely over forty years of age, he was already well known in academic circles throughout the United States. Last year, he had traveled to China to explore excavation findings discovered during and after the Cultural Revolution. During his visit he met the delegation's two most prominent scholars, sociologist Bi Wenpu and literary writer Qin Zheng. This was probably the reason the university had assigned him the task of making arrangements for their visit.

The seven-member delegation included the leader of the delegation, Hou Li, four scholars, an interpreter, and a reporter. Their visit was scheduled to fall on a Friday and Saturday. Yu Yi lined up the formal arrangements, such as the public lecture, campus tours, a reception and banquet, for Friday and Saturday mornings. On Saturday afternoon, he planned a tour of the library, followed by an informal dinner at his own home.

The university readily consented to the arrangements he had made, and his wife, Shi Wenhui, was delighted to hear the good news.

Over the past few years, "China fever" had become quite the rage, and everyone competitively bragged about their visits to China. After nearly thirty years of waiting, Yu Yi had finally taken advantage of a scholastic exchange trip and visited his parents on the mainland. Wenhui was Taiwanese and had no roots in China. Because of this, she was less knowledgeable about the mainland than others, which made her feel somewhat incompetent conversing with some of her friends. Thus she thought it was a real privilege to have the opportunity of entertaining these famous scholars in the privacy of their home. Upon hearing the news, she was so excited she could do nothing but twirl around her living room in joy.

"Who else should we invite to dinner?" she asked, suddenly ending her exuberant dance around the room. Tilting her head, she immediately began to prepare a guest list.

"I really don't think we should include anyone else," Yu Yi calmly responded, as if he had already been brooding over this matter himself.

He continued, "An opportunity like this is hard to come by, so we should make the best of it. Haven't you always adored Qin Zheng's writing? You should take advantage of this rare opportunity to talk with him in person. Although he's called 'Qin the Elder' in China, he doesn't look old at all. He's an energetic and vigorous man. Personally, I'd like to talk to Bi Wenpu and hear his views on some current issues, particularly the government's 'Four Modern-izations'[3] policies and the democracy movement that was suppressed so quickly after it emerged."

Realizing that Yu Yi had a point, Wenhui understandably swal-lowed her grand ideas about the dinner party without any resistance.

"They probably won't be able to talk freely unless we separate the interpreter and reporter from them." Having seen and heard Taiwan-ese and American news reports, she intuitively knew that these two delegation members had been assigned to keep an eye on Bi and Qin. It would be better to exclude them from the dinner gathering.

"Well . . ." Yu Yi thought it over for a moment. Suddenly his eyes lit up as he stumbled upon the perfect solution. "There won't be any problem at all! I'll find another cultural organization to invite them to dinner or arrange some other activity."

After eliminating the two guests from her list, Wenhui began to think over the dinner menu. She could not decide whether she should serve them Chinese or Western food.

"Either will do, but it'd be better to serve a few light dishes," her husband offered helpfully. "This is an older delegation. Qin the Elder is nearly seventy, and Bi is about the same age. The geologist, Jian, is around sixty, and the youngest one, Fu, is thirty-seven, the same age as you. I heard that he is Bi's disciple. He's doing research at the Chinese Academy of Sciences. The head of the delegation, Hou

Li, is just over fifty and is a director at the Academy of Sciences. There's no educational background listed, so he's probably a Party administrative cadre."

"Isn't this what they usually call a homogenous trio, the blending of the old, the middle-aged, and the young?"

Wenhui was quite pleased by her ability to apply this Communist jargon. She reminded herself to check out some new books about China from the library so she could learn more for her dinner conversations.

Yu Yi shook his head and sighed, "This 'trio combination' is nothing but top-heavy. It's actually led by the elderly. The Cultural Revolution turned China into a cultural wasteland, and it's going to take time to restore and reconstruct the country again. Now, this handful of senior citizens has become a national treasure. Even at their age, they have to travel abroad. It must be tough on them! On the other hand, Bi, for example, is very much alive and well. He goes abroad quite often. This indicates that the policies are much more flexible now. Although his knowledge of sociological functions is outdated, the materials and information he gathered during his research on the Yao tribe in the Yunnan province is invaluable. I really hope I get to discuss his findings with him."

In order to give Yu Yi a chance to fulfill his wish, Wenhui decided to find some way of separating the head of the delegation, Mr. Hou, from the scholars. However, her primary concern was still deciding what to serve her guests for dinner.

"Yu Yi, these men traveled here from the East Coast giving lectures, going on tours, and attending formal and informal banquets and meals. How can they endure all of this! I need to cook something light, not too greasy. Do you have any idea what I should make?"

"The lighter it is, the better. When I visited Bi last year, he was a vegetarian." Again he reminded her, "Wenhui, promise me you won't invite other guests. If there are too many people, it'll be reduced to a mere social gathering and a complete waste of time. This is a rare opportunity to talk to them without any hindrances." Lost in his wishful thinking, he left poor Wenhui alone to decide on the menu.

Yu Yi was known for his single-minded devotion to research and had the reputation of never involving himself with social trivialities. When not teaching, he always locked himself in his office and seldom answered the phone. He posted a sign on his office door: "By Appointment Only!" Even his students, on whose teaching evaluations he depended for tenure and promotion, did not dare knock on his door without an appointment. Those who knew his temperament would call his wife first, especially when they had to ask him a favor. Wenhui was easygoing and always eager to help others. They were a very close couple, and Yu Yi never stood in the way of anything she wished to do. As private as the Yus were, though, somehow the news leaked out that they would be entertaining the visiting scholars in their home. Much to their dismay, the phone began to ring continuously.

Yin Qin was the first person to call and make a request. Getting right to the point, he asked, "Big Sister Shi, how can you refuse to invite me even if you're not inviting anyone else?" Sounding as if he had every reason in the world to be invited, he continued, "Not only did we come from the same town, we were classmates as well! I'm in the middle of writing an article on the function of imagery in poetry, and I plan to cite Qin Zheng's *Fortress Besieged*[4] as a reference. Now that he's going to be here, I can consult with him in person. Maybe he could help me add a little polish to my article."

Yin Qin and Wenhui came from the town of Lugang in Taiwan and had both graduated from the Department of Foreign Languages and Literatures at the National Taiwan University. When Yin Qin was still in college, he was already recognized as a gifted poet. Two years ago, he was hired by the same university as Yu Yi to teach Chinese literature. Since that time, he had spent a lot of time with the Yus. Indeed, it was difficult for Wenhui to refuse someone who came from both the same hometown and school.

"It'd be alright if you're sure you aren't afraid of meeting 'Communists'!" Wenhui responded with hearty laughter.

Yin Qin, a self-proclaimed patriot, had made frequent trips to Taiwan. He had a doctorate in comparative literature and could teach classical Chinese literature in the States, or, when he obtained a guest lecturer position, he could teach Anglo-American literature in Taiwan. He truly reaped the benefits of his profession under all circumstances. Like a fish in water, he was very happy and content.

He loved Taiwan and his poetry reflected his passion. He wrote about the lost, drifting feelings of an exiled wandering soul in a foreign land, vividly depicting the sentiments of longing for one's home soil. His poems were so moving that the youth in Taiwan often respectfully called him the Qu Yuan[5] of the twentieth century. Consequently, he became the poet laureate of patriotic native poetry and was widely admired. He shared the same dislike of the Communist regime as the Taiwanese government and faithfully read Taiwan's official newspaper, the *Central Daily News*. Thus, he was accustomed to addressing mainlanders as "the Communist bandits."

"Big Sister Shi, please spare me," he laughingly begged for mercy. "Taiwan has become much more flexible. They've adopted a more relaxed attitude toward those who travel to both places. In fact, Taiwan encourages people to travel to both countries and to compare the regimes accordingly. I would like to visit the mainland myself!"

This was indeed news to her. Wenhui could vividly recall just a few years ago when she had heard his patriotic declaration: "The Han people refuse to co-exist with Communist bandits." Thinking about it now, how could she really blame him or others for the change of heart? After all, would any Chinese person refuse an opportunity to visit the mainland?

"Really, Yin Qin, you ought to visit China. With such keen senses and a high level of sensitivity, a poet like you could write a book or two about what you see and hear and get it published. You can get a tourist visa rather quickly now. I understand they even give priority to Taiwanese passport holders. If you really want to travel there, let's get a few people and go together."

"Well, I don't want to travel as an ordinary tourist. It would be like those old American ladies who go on around-the-world tours! No, either I'll go there by invitation, so I can see things ordinary tourists wouldn't see, or I won't go at all. But, I have to find such an opportunity first."

*So, that is his intention.* Wenhui had stumbled upon his long-term motives and could not help but be impressed.

"Yin Qin, I'm sure you'll have many chances. Both countries will probably try their best to lure you! That would be great! I know Yu Yi would like to see China and Taiwan have tourist and cultural exchanges first."

"That's right, that's right! That's exactly what I'm talking about!"

It was so rare to hear Yin Qin agreeing with someone else's opinion that Wenhui felt very flattered.

"Well . . ." Yin Qin cleared his throat, sounding very serious, and continued, "Yu Yi and I could start this exchange program. To be quite honest with you, this type of mission clearly belongs to the two of us."

His initial modesty was now replaced with arrogance, and his voice was fully tainted with a tone of authority and self-confidence. Even hearing him over the phone, Wenhui could imagine him sitting there holding his pipe in his mouth and nodding his head back and forth in earnest.

"Well then, what time is it going to be on Saturday? How about if Emily comes over early so she can help you?"

"That would be great! Emily can help me prepare a few vegetarian dishes. The guests will be here at seven o'clock, so it would be ideal if you came over half an hour early."

"We'll be there."

Yin Qin's wife, Emily, was American. She had converted to Hinduism when she was in college and subsequently became a vegetarian. Because of this, she knew how to cook some fancy meatless dishes. Wenhui was worried about not being able to make any authentic Chinese vegetarian food, so she thought she might as well learn a couple recipes from Emily to give their guests some variety.

Emily called back immediately and insisted on preparing two exquisite dishes ahead of time and bringing them to the dinner with her. Wenhui was very pleased and felt that she had not invited Yin Qin and Emily for nothing.

Since his wife had already invited one American to the dinner, Yu Yi decided that he would invite his favorite American student, Wallace, as well.

Having just recently obtained his doctorate, Wallace was currently teaching at a private college. He specialized in Chinese Moslems. He wanted to write a book and was seeking a research grant and other similar opportunities to help support his field research in the Gansu and Ningxia provinces. Yu's invitation made him feel extremely flattered to have the opportunity to meet Bi Wenpu, and indebted to Yu Yi, his mentor. He immediately announced that he would dedicate his first book to Professor Yu.

Though the stream of phone calls continued to pour in, Wenhui was fiercely determined to refuse the rest of them. Instead, it was Yu Yi who could not handle the pressure of so many requests.

The news of the guests' plan to visit the library had also already leaked out. The library was the biggest one on the West Coast and had the largest collection of Chinese works. Yu Yi's old classmate, Qi Wen, was in charge of the Chinese collection. Usually, he never worked on weekends, but for this particular occasion, he volunteered to open the section containing the rare Chinese collections for the distinguished guests. He was so excited that he called Yu Yi again and again, displaying a tremendous show of enthusiasm for the event.

Having worked in the library for so many years, Qi Wen was often called the founding senior librarian. Two years before, he had accompanied Library of Congress officials on a two-week tour of several metropolitan cities in mainland China. Ever since his return, he had complained that his tight schedule had not allowed him the time to gather local materials. His Chinese division already possessed quite a few contemporary historical materials. However, one of the collection's weaknesses was the lack of journals, magazines, and periodicals from the Sino-Japanese War period. Qi Wen anxiously hoped that through his introductions to these high-ranking Chinese officials he might be able to establish direct contact with the Beijing Library and obtain permission to collect reproduced materials. After hinting around and finally pointing out his purpose to Yu Yi, it became evident that Yu Yi had no choice but to invite him to the dinner, too.

Mrs. Qi was a gourmet cook. Her roast duck with chestnuts was far superior to that of any Chinese restaurant in Chinatown, and she told Wenhui she would bring one for the dinner. Naturally, Wenhui was quite pleased, for now there would be both poultry and vegetarian dishes.

However, the most difficult task was dealing with Xiao Jinsheng, the famous Leftist at the university. He taught Chinese in the East Asian Studies Department and had already visited China four times. During his last trip, he had the honor of shaking hands with Premier Hu Yaobang and Party leader Hu Qiaomu. Because of this, he had become overbearing and arrogant, acting as if he were the overseas spokesman for the Chinese Communists. Ironically, he had no prior knowledge of the Chinese scholars' visit to the university until after he learned about it from the newspapers.

He immediately called Yu Yi's residence. "Hey, Brother Yu, how could you be so tight-lipped about this visit?"

A former journalist, Xiao Jinsheng customarily began conversations with his colleagues or friends by asking in his shoptalk style, "What's the news?" However, this time he was completely out of touch with the latest news. He was infuriated about it, but since he had a favor to ask, he swallowed his pride and called his acquaintance Yu Yi "Brother."

Yu Yi calmly defended himself by saying, "How could I? Actually, I just heard the news from the school myself."

"Well, it's marvelous that they're coming to visit our campus! I invited them when I was in Beijing last time. That's right, I spoke with Qin the Elder during my visit in 1974. Indeed, he really lived up to his reputation and made wisecracks whenever he spoke. However, I dared not mention his name in my previous interview. Because . . . because the 'Gang of Four'[6] was in power!"

"True, everything can be blamed on the Gang of Four!" Yu Yi responded briskly.

"Everything's alright now though! Didn't you know he visited Europe last year? Now this year he's visiting the United States. It's a prime example of the fact that senior intellectuals are once again well respected in China. This time I'd really love to have a good chat with him. Have you made any plans for Saturday? Let me show them some hospitality. I'll invite the delegation over for dinner."

"Thank you, but they're already invited to my home for dinner. There are too many people who want to meet them. My humble home is too small and crowded to invite everyone. Perhaps during their next visit, you can be the host."

Xiao Jinsheng was not to be discouraged even after being flatly rejected. He proposed to co-host the banquet the next day, and again he was politely turned down by Yu Yi.

Wenhui was impressed by her husband's firm stance. He was not afraid of offending the favor of the Chinese Communist government. This act alone demanded courage. In contrast, many of Xiao Jinsheng's students enrolled in his classes solely because they wanted to go to China. And, even though many of Xiao's colleagues felt it was contemptible to get too friendly with him, they still restrained themselves from antagonizing him.

In reality, Xiao Jinsheng was not such a bad person. The problem was that he constantly shifted his alliance and was overly zealous about everything. Formerly, he had been a reporter for an official Guomindang newspaper stationed in the States and was forcefully anti-Communist. In the early seventies, he quit his reporting job and abruptly switched his allegiance to mainland China, flattering everything the Communists did. He appealed to everyone "to learn from Comrade Jiang Qing." His tireless energy was not second to anyone who had shouted slogans such as "Long Live Madame Jiang." After the downfall of the "Gang of Four," he again changed sides, severely criticizing Jiang Qing. It did not matter who was in power or what policy was in effect; it all became agreeable to him. His ever-changing image even caused some self-proclaimed Leftists to shake their heads and sigh in exasperation. Consequently, he was dubbed the most notorious overseas member of the dubious "Wind Party." Even his American colleagues unanimously agreed that he was the one that most deserved this nickname.

Wenhui unfailingly supported her husband in this matter. She felt uneasy about inviting Xiao Jinsheng to the party. He might not only dominate the party, but could also antagonize their guests. Since she had no intention of becoming a Leftist, she thought it was just as well to avoid him completely.

However, on the eve before the delegation's arrival, Yu Yi came home from school and said to Wenhui sheepishly, "Xiao Jinsheng is really as stubborn as a bull. He stayed in my office without any intention of leaving until I agreed to let him throw a cocktail reception for the delegation. He claimed that all the preparations had already been made. I really didn't know how to dissuade him. After all, we're all Chinese! There's no need for public dissent over this matter, and we certainly don't want to make the Americans laugh at our tug-of-war. Anyway, he finally won. He said the reception would take place before dinner, from six to seven. Of course, we're invited."

"We're not going!" Wenhui shouted, raising her eyebrows high in anger.

"Take it easy, Wenhui! Don't get angry with a person like him. He's desperately trying to save face."

Yu Yi continued, "Our department Chair recently returned from Beijing. According to him, Xiao Jinsheng has somehow been recognized by the American media as an authority on China and is more widely recognized than our own university. He couldn't figure out why everyone inquired about Xiao Jinsheng whenever he mentioned the name of our university there. He even told us about this Chinese faculty member who, whenever he talked about the United States, would repeatedly mention the names of only two people, Jimmy Carter and Xiao Jinsheng. So you see, although Xiao is hot in Communist China, he has been ignored here by American universities. This kind of treatment ought to really teach him a lesson."

Wenhui still was not placated and asked, "How could a cocktail reception last an hour? Now, I really don't know when we should start dinner. Xiao Jinsheng is really manipulative!"

"That's why I thought we'd better attend the reception. That way we'll make sure the guests get to our house on time," Yu Yi replied.

Since things had already been organized to such a degree, there was nothing Wenhui could do but comply with the new plans as they stood.

Wenhui had originally planned to accompany the delegation on the library tour. Now, because of the added reception, she was forced to abandon her plans. Instead, she spent the entire Saturday afternoon at home cooking. Fortunately, Mrs. Qi came over early to help. The two of them labored over the preparations until after five o'clock, right before Yu Yi arrived home.

"You two must have worked so hard today! Is everything more or less under control?" Yu Yi asked as he walked into the kitchen.

"We didn't bake the duck yet. It won't taste good if it gets cold," responded Wenhui, breathing a sigh of relief as she started to untie her apron.

Mrs. Qi was busy shredding turnip, not showing any intention of stopping. She urged them, "You two just go ahead! Leave everything here to me. I guarantee dinner will be ready at eight."

"Why do we have to be so punctual to Xiao Jinsheng's reception? Let's sit down and have some tea first." Wenhui was already determined not to get there on time, so she proceeded to boil water for tea.

After a long tiring day, Yu Yi also needed to rest a little, so he sat down at the small kitchen table. Since punctuality was one of his virtues, Yu Yi removed his watch and put it on the table. Sitting upright, he faced his watch, as if he was afraid their conversation would distract him from remembering the time.

"What were their comments on the library's Chinese collections?"

Mrs. Qi was also a librarian, but she did not work in the Chinese division. Still she anxiously wanted to know the visitors' impressions.

"It was great! They said that it could compete with Yale, and that each collection has its own unique qualities. After seeing over a dozen volumes of photocopied newspapers printed by the Red Guard during the Cultural Revolution, the senior cadre, Old Hou, said that if Chinese people wanted to research the Cultural Revolution, they would have to come here to get the materials."

After hearing this, Mrs. Qi felt very flattered. In her eyes, praising the Chinese collections was equal to praising her husband, and she felt she rightly deserved to share this honor.

"Yu Yi, did you show Bi Wenpu and Qin Zheng their own books there?" Wenhui asked her husband.

"Yes, we did. Bi was very humble. When he was told that one of the shelves contained all of his works, he would not even go near it. He shook his hands and responded in English, 'They're nothing, they're all garbage!'"

"Are you kidding?" Both women were very surprised.

"Qin, however, was quite pleased to see his own books. Every one of them is exquisitely bound, with the titles printed in gold. He took Fortress Besieged from the shelf and in it were two borrowing slips, completely filled with checkout and due dates. When he was told what a popular novel it was, Qin persistently exclaimed that it was a product of playful creation, written in his youth, and not worth mentioning. Although he sounded modest, his face beamed, betraying his delight. This 'playful' work, as he called it, could earn him literary immortality. Unfortunately, as gifted a writer as he is, he hasn't written in thirty years!"

The three of them sighed, lamenting the loss of so many productive years.

Wenhui was an ardent fan of Qin's and admired him enormously. The day before, not only had she attended his public guest lecture, but she had even taped it. Thinking about it now, she was still very impressed.

"What a speech he gave yesterday! His command of the English language really moved the Americans who were there, not to mention his great sense of humor. At the reception that followed the lecture, the reporters interviewed all of the delegation members. Qin responded to every question so beautifully that he ended up acting as their sole spokesperson."

Upon hearing the word *reception*, Yu Yi grabbed his watch from the table and glanced at it as he put it on. Interrupting Wenhui, he said, "We don't have much time. You'd better change your clothes now. We have to be there a little early so we can bring them back here on time."

After being reminded a couple times, she finally went upstairs to change.

Wenhui never had any children, so her tiny and delicate figure was perfectly preserved, giving her a youthful appearance. She could usually wear anything she wanted to, but today was different. Facing her closet full of clothes, she just couldn't make up her mind as to what would be the most appropriate choice. It was tough to decide which dress was elegant enough for the reception and at the same time suitable for hostessing a dinner banquet. Because the guests of honor were from China, Wenhui knew it was improper for her to wear anything too fancy. She wanted to give them an unpretentious, conservative impression, especially since she planned to visit the mainland someday. Besides, Mrs. Xiao was known for wearing heavy makeup and extravagant clothes. Wenhui did not want to contend with her on the same level. She thought it would be wise to dress simply and tastefully, inadvertently challenging Mrs. Xiao from a different angle.

Finally having made up her mind, she immediately loosened her hair and started to brush it skillfully. Ordinarily, whenever she attended parties, she preferred to comb her hair into a high coiffure with a topknot. Today, she simply wrapped it into a loose bun behind her head. Last summer, during her trip home to Taiwan, she had purchased a custom-made, crimson Chinese-style dress with both the collar and sleeves hemmed in black satin. The simple elegance and grace of the dress was perfect for this evening. Other than darkening her eyebrows, she did not wear any makeup or jewelry.

After completing her preparations, Wenhui gazed at herself in the mirror. Startled by her own reflection, she was suddenly reminded of her grandmother's picture hanging on the wall back home in

Lugang. Much to her surprise, they were the spitting image of one another.

*That's alright,* she told herself, *those of you who have undergone the Cultural Revolution can now see a bit of native Taiwanese culture.*

With his hands clasped behind his back, Yu Yi was nervously pacing back and forth. Becoming increasingly impatient with waiting, he raised his head abruptly and caught a glimpse of Wenhui coming down the stairs. Holding a black satin handbag, she was dressed like a Taiwanese matron. For a moment, he was completely flabbergasted.

*Women's fashions!* he gasped to himself in astonishment.

"Yu Yi, what do you think of my dress?" Wenhui asked her husband enticingly, turning around to show him the new outfit.

"Well . . . it's very different! Come on, we're late! You need to drive the other car so we can bring the guests home."

They were only fifteen minutes late, but the Xiao residence was already packed full of people. The host and hostess cheerfully greeted everyone with smiles, while their two daughters moved around the room offering the guests plates of hors d'oeuvres.

It was the second time Wenhui had visited the Xiao's house. Five years ago, out of sheer curiosity, she and Yu Yi had come over to see the slides Xiao Jinsheng took during his trip to China. All she could vaguely recall of that day was him wearing a lumpy blue, cotton-padded Chinese jacket and frequently making references to "Chairman Mao" in his conversation, something she had found very irritating.

This time, Xiao Jinsheng wore a spick-and-span, smoothly ironed Western-style suit, and his graying hair was slicked back greasily. With his beaming countenance and image, he could have easily been mistaken for the host of a wedding reception. About the same age as her husband, Mrs. Xiao was just over fifty. However, because she took good care of herself, she did not really look her age. She was wearing a floor-length, black satin *qipao,* a Chinese-style gown that split up the sides. In addition, she adorned herself with a jade bracelet and pearl necklace that made her sparkle and shine. Privately, Wenhui was glad that she had not worn a *qipao.* Otherwise, she would have felt inferior in comparison.

Both the Xiao daughters were studying Chinese at the university. The younger one studied under her father and spoke fluent Mandarin. They had gone to China last year and were considered junior "China experts."

The eldest daughter was graduating from college in the summer and was currently negotiating a job in Beijing. It was said that she would earn a salary equivalent to that of a specialist, higher than the Communist party chairman, Hua Guofen, received. When this news was revealed at the party, it became the envy of the guests. A few of them even inquired how they might apply for a similar position themselves. Consequently, she joined the honored guests in becoming the center of attention.

Since Yu Yi and Wenhui had already met the guests the day before, they exchanged greetings and then strolled into the Xiao's living room. To their astonishment, in just the last few years, the Xiao residence had almost become a showroom of Chinese artwork, displaying a vast array of beautiful and fine things. There were paper cuttings, ivory artifacts, wooden carvings, and Hunan embroidery. The most eye-catching pieces were the authentic paintings and calligraphy rendered by masters of contemporary Chinese art. Works such as Li Keren's landscapes, or portraits by Chen Shifa and Guan Liang, were all personally autographed for Xiao Jinsheng. Since the Yus were connoisseurs of Chinese paintings, they could not help but openly express their admiration.

One American professor, who was also a Chinese art enthusiast, said to Yu Yi, "Any one of these paintings could be auctioned at a high price. Art collectors would surely compete for them."

"Oh, no, these aren't for sale!" Without them noticing, Xiao Jinsheng had suddenly appeared next to them and stood there grinning.

Li Keren's landscape painting reminded Wenhui that this was the painter who had suffered harsh criticism from the "Gang of Four" because of his publicized interview with Xiao Jinsheng. She pointed at the painting and said to her host, "Mr. Xiao, this is really a priceless art treasure!"

Unable to detect her double meaning, Xiao beamed broadly, "Indeed it is! I was the first one to interview him. Now, he's very famous!"

"I heard that Han Suying is also an ardent collector of Chinese paintings. Is it true that she has so many paintings she could have her own art exhibit?" Yu Yi asked his host.

"Indeed, everybody says so."

The American professor was extremely fond of Li Keren's work. Pointing to it, he told the host, "This painting of yours is worth at least twenty thousand dollars."

Upon hearing that, Yu Yi remarked, "Mr. Xiao, if you take a few more trips to China, you could become a millionaire."

"Hardly!" Speaking with his perfect Beijing accent, the host humbly dismissed the remarks with a wave of his hand.

"How can I compare with Han Suying? The Chinese government has bestowed her with many treasures. She is indeed a true millionaire! My collection is insignificant compared to hers!"

As he lamented over the size of his collection, he suddenly clapped his hands and said, "I have a panda specimen in my study. Would you like to see it? The glass case I ordered hasn't arrived yet, so I haven't been able to exhibit it."

The guests politely expressed their interest, and some of them followed him into his study.

Wenhui had already made a special trip to the National Zoo in Washington, D.C., to see the pandas donated by the Chinese government. However, she wanted to see one again since a specimen was right here within reach. Yet, Yu Yi did not show any intention of moving at all. Before she could pull on his sleeve, he was already shaking his head disapprovingly.

"We shouldn't look at it, Wenhui." Hiding his mouth behind his champagne glass, he whispered, "I read an article recently saying that due to environmental pollution, another blunder of the 'Gang of Four,' they've discovered that over two hundred pandas have died. The worry now is that pandas might eventually become extinct. Animal lovers are desperately trying to save them. How could anyone even think of making a panda specimen—this is undoubtedly an exploitation initiated by the 'Gang of Four'!"

Upon hearing this, Wenhui completely lost interest.

Standing not too far from them was the honored guest, Mr. Bi. He was surrounded by other guests who were seeking his opinions on issues ranging from the government's current "Four Modernizations" policies to the effects of contemporary sociology on the future of China. He responded to each question in excellent English. With a slow but firm tone, he exuded complete confidence in the future of China. Very interested in this subject, Yu Yi immediately joined the group.

Wenhui, on the other hand, was not too concerned with politics. Holding a glass of wine, she stood aside and studied Bi, a man she knew had suffered many hardships.

Through her husband, she knew quite a bit about Bi Wenpu's life. What moved her the most was his integrity. Over the past thirty years, he had devoted himself to improving the life of Chinese peasants, he had bravely protested the suppression of intellectuals by the Chinese government, and he had even challenged the government's decision to abolish sociology departments in colleges. These heroic deeds resulted in him being labeled a "Rightist," and people nicknamed him the "spokesman for bourgeois society." He was harshly criticized and sent away to agonizing isolation. During the Cultural Revolution, he was imprisoned in a cattle shed. After undergoing such brutal treatment, it was amazing that he still had the patience to explain China's national policies. Oblivious to his own suffering, he gave people a calm and peaceful impression. Looking at the snowy-white hair on this old man's head, Wenhui was felt her respect for him grow immediately.

"Mr. Bi," asked an American professor, "what is your greatest achievement since the Anti-Rightist Movement?"

The old man responded with a smile, "Well, all the labor I've done over the years has greatly improved my health!"

Continuing, he told the professor how the newly established departments of sociology and psychology in Beijing provided a promising future for academic research, and that American scholars were invited to participate in cultural exchange programs with China.

Compared to Bi, Qin the Elder looked extremely young, appearing to be in his early fifties, with a sturdy body and vigorous spirits. He was also the most popular member of the delegation. He spoke Mandarin eloquently with a southern accent. Wherever he went, he was always surrounded by people. The Americans had a habit of always asking very direct questions, but with his wit and quick humor, he was good at handling the tough and sometimes embarrassing ones. Consequently, there were rarely any red-faced moments; instead only the sound of frequent laughter could be heard.

Wenhui noticed Mr. Hou standing uncomfortably in one corner of the living room. Short and chubby, with a tightly knit poker face, he had a very shrouded and secretive appearance. He was wearing a gray military-style tunic buttoned up to his collar that not only straightened his posture, but also made him look dignified with his temples covered by white hair. An Asian-American studies professor was speaking to him in proper Mandarin. After the American walked away to get a drink, a look of relaxation washed over Mr. Hou's face, as if he had just been relieved of performing some difficult task.

Wanting to know something about this cadre, whom she was supposed to keep an eye on tonight, Wenhui walked over to talk to him.

"Mr. Hou, you must be tired after all the running around you've done the last few days."

"Not at all!" he responded politely.

"What's your impression of America?"

"Well . . . good! . . . I mean it's very good!" he said somberly, as if his shoulders were weighted down with the trust of a billion people. Each word he spoke appeared to have been chosen with the utmost care. Changing the subject immediately, Wenhui talked to him about the reception and the food. As soon as he realized who Wenhui was, he promptly extended his thanks to her for their hospitality and even managed to flash a smile.

"Oh, please come visit Beijing! I would be happy to show you around. Where are you from?"

"Lugang," she replied.

Seeing the blank expression on his face, Wenhui quickly told him where Lugang was located and added, "I'm Taiwanese."

"Oh, so I see," he said with sudden understanding. Amicably, he asked, "Are most Taiwanese people of aboriginal descent?"

"What?" Wenhui exclaimed. She was so shocked she could not help her tone of voice. However, seeing the look of sincerity on his face, her agitation immediately turned into sympathy.

"Many Taiwanese people are also of Han descent," she patiently explained. "The aborigines are one of the Taiwanese minorities."

"So they are! I'm terribly sorry. . . . Well, we haven't been too involved with Taiwan in the past, so our understanding of it is relatively limited. . . ."

Suddenly, his expression became quite serious. "We're all from the same family, Taiwan and the PRC. We sincerely hope Taiwan will be reunited with the Motherland soon. Our current emphasis is on reconstruction efforts, particularly the 'Four Modernizations' policies, and speeding up our goal of reunifying China."

Wenhui could not digest this official, matter-of-fact tone of voice. She politely reminded him, "Don't you believe there should at least be a mutual understanding before launching reunification talks? My own personal knowledge of mainland China is rather limited. However, I've found that the mainland is also relatively uninformed about Taiwan."

"Well, that was an error created by the extreme Leftist policies from the 'Gang of Four' era. Those mistakes are in the process of being rectified now."

"I sincerely hope so! Somehow, I haven't seen any visible improvement yet." Unconvinced that China's ignorance of Taiwan was single-handedly contrived by the 'Gang of Four,' Wenhui wanted to argue with him further on this issue. However, just then Yu Yi came over and began to chat with Mr. Hou.

"Wenhui," he said, "it's seven o'clock. Time to go!" She nodded. The couple excused themselves from Mr. Hou and went together to bid their host farewell.

"But, it's still so early!" Xiao Jinsheng protested. "I'm afraid we didn't take very good care of you all!"

After his repeated attempts failed, Xiao Jinsheng finally conceded and said, "Let's all take a picture together. It's such a pity that the correspondent and the interpreter from the *China News Agency* were unable to be here tonight."

Silently, Yu Yi and Wenhui exchanged a glance of mutual understanding.

Xiao Jinsheng had already hired a professional photographer for the occasion. He immediately organized the guests into two rows in the center of the living room. After getting everyone in place, he stood in the middle of the front row, with Bi the Senior on his left and Qin the Elder to his right. To ensure that there would be at least a couple good-quality photos, he had a few pictures taken. Some of the guests requested extra prints for themselves, and Xiao Jinsheng generously consented to them all.

"Of course, of course, everyone will receive a picture. I'll even send a set of the pictures to publisher Zhu at the *China News Agency* in Beijing."

At the mention of the *China News Agency,* their eyes lit up immediately. Visualizing themselves appearing in the *People's Daily* made many of the guests starry-eyed with excitement.

Yu Yi and Wenhui silently exchanged another look, reflecting their lack of awareness concerning Xiao and his devious plans.

The Xiao family congenially escorted the delegation members to the door. The Yu's drove their cars over, and they and their guests left amid many parting blessings of "Bon voyage" and "See you in Beijing."

As she was about to drive away from the crossroad, Wenhui glanced back into the rearview mirror. Realizing that the Xiao's were now out of sight, she breathed a deep sigh of relief. She felt tired, yet mixed with that was an unspeakable kind of satisfaction—as if she had just won a battle and was returning home with the prize.

The other guests had already arrived at their house and were waiting anxiously. After entering the living room, Yu Yi introduced the guests of honor to everyone. The two elder men, exhausted from standing during the reception, immediately buried themselves in the soft, thick sofas. They declined the offer of cold drinks and asked for hot tea instead.

"We are in the company of good friends, and this is just an ordinary meal," Yu Yi politely explained to the guests of honor. "So, please, don't worry about being formal. If you feel uncomfortable, just kick off your shoes and make yourselves at home. The more relaxed everyone is, the better."

To demonstrate his sincerity, he took off his own tie and jacket, and Qi Wen and Wallace immediately followed suit.

Yin Qin, who had never cared too much about his appearance, was perhaps the most relaxed person there. Wearing a pair of worn-out slacks, he sat on the floor with his pipe in his mouth.

Yin Qin's wife, Emily, had shown respect for the honored guests and was dressed in antique-looking formal Chinese attire. It was probably an opera costume purchased from some obscure alley in Taiwan. The black satin blouse and skirt were covered entirely with embroidered flowers and birds. The outfit was really dazzling to the eyes. She wore a pair of custom-made embroidered shoes, and her hair was brushed into a high coiffure with a topknot. From her earlobes dangled two huge round copper earrings that oscillated back and forth like a swing. Mrs. Qi wore a Chinese *qipao*. Wenhui was truly pleased that the three of them had all worn Chinese dresses. It almost looked as if they had planned it that way, but it was even better because they had not.

While Yu Yi talked with the guests and served tea, Wenhui and Mrs. Qi went into the kitchen to start cooking. Little Fu, the youngest delegate, rolled up his sleeves and offered them his assistance. Finally, after Wenhui had politely declined his help several times, he rejoined the other guests in the living room.

Mrs. Qi kept her promise. At eight o'clock sharp, the roast duck was placed on the dinner table. Plates full of mushrooms with oyster sauce and vegetarian Buddha's Delight were served steaming hot.

The host invited Bi the Senior to begin dinner by serving himself first, after which he returned to the living room to eat. Seeing that Bi had nothing but vegetarian dishes on his plate, and not one piece of duck, Wenhui congratulated herself on her successful dinner plan.

"This food is great!" Yin Qin exclaimed as he entered the living room with his plate piled high and a glass of wine. Declining a chair, he instead sat on the floor facing Qin the Elder and began to eat.

"Mr. Qin, Yin Qin writes modern poetry," Wenhui said, introducing her old classmate. "In Taiwan, people often compose music to accompany his poems. Subsequently, his poetry has become quite popular in music halls and night clubs. In our area, his poetry is considered to be the best."

Wenhui had not thought up the latter part of the compliment herself. She remembered overhearing Yin Qin boasting about it once while he was drunk. As he heard Wenhui compliment him in his own words in front of this literary giant, his blush betrayed him before the warm flush of wine could cover his face and alleviate his embarrassment.

"Spare me, please, Big Sister Shi," he pleaded with her. "You should never have said that, I'm the one who's always starving!"

Qin the Elder cast a brief look at Emily and smiled befittingly. He probably just assumed that since Yin Qin had married an American woman, he was not yet accustomed to eating American food.

Wenhui let out a good-humored chuckle. Emily was famous for her dislike of cooking, so she always kept a variety of fruits and nuts on hand. Whenever Yin Qin complained of hunger, she would throw him a handful, as if she were feeding a bird.

"Mrs. Yin is Hindu, so she's a vegetarian," she informed Mr. Qin.

Qin the Elder nodded sympathetically, simultaneously trying to comfort Yin Qin. "Vegetables are good for your health. Until the last couple years, I used to always have high blood pressure. But there's been such a low supply of meat and cooking oil in Beijing, we've all literally become vegetarians. It's a good thing, though, because my blood pressure has really gone down since then. Now, I feel healthier than ever."

His words were convincing. Looking at him, you could not help but notice his healthy skin coloring and high energy level. Indeed, he was the picture of health!

The mention of food shortages reminded Wenhui of the Democracy Wall[7], also called "Beijing Spring." There had been news reports on television about peasants who had signed petitions demanding that there be enough food to keep them from starving. She asked Qin, "How did they end up solving the problem with the food shortages?"

"Well, the executive branch set up many reception stations, and they handled each case individually." After saying this, Qin stole a look at Mr. Hou, who was sitting on a sofa chair. Old Hou nodded his head, expressing his concurrence.

"If you don't mind, I'd like to ask a question. Initially, Deng Xiaoping showed public support for the 'Big-character' posters[8] and the Democracy movement, but then they arrested a large number of the people who wrote the posters. Do you know why that happened?"

For a while, Wallace's question was greeted only by silence.

Finally, the geologist, Old Jian, cleared his throat and said in a carefully controlled tone, "It's good to have democracy, and it is reasonable to demand democracy. However, if one exploits that beyond reason, or even goes astray, it becomes unfeasible. In order to speed up the 'Four Modernizations,' we cannot afford to do without the leadership of the Party, nor can we allow the practice of anarchism, similar to what we experienced during the Cultural Revolution."

With the exception of Little Fu, the delegation members all spoke up at once, expressing their accord.

With an air of seriousness, Old Hou announced, "Many of the self-proclaimed human rights advocates are actually counter-revolutionaries with concealed motives. Our government had no choice but to arrest them. We're pursuing a proletarian democracy, but what they seek is a bourgeois democracy that depends upon imperial-ism. These two ideas contradict each other completely."

In just a couple sentences, Old Hou had put a quick end to the discussion on "Beijing Spring." He sounded as though he were reading an editorial from the *People's Daily*, with a definite authoritative tone. Not only did Wenhui find it annoying, the others could also feel the stiff air lingering in the room like the stale smoke from a gun. For what seemed like eternity, the room remained silent.

Yin Qin, who always shied away from political issues, seized the moment to discuss literature with Qin the Elder. He expressed his burning desire to go to China and interview the poets Ai Qing and Zang Kejia. Qin nodded his head agreeably.

"You should talk to Old Hou about that. He could help you by personally conveying your intentions to his superiors."

Immediately acting on his suggestion, Yin Qin went over and sat next to Old Hou after heaping his plate with a second helping of food. His wife, Emily, took his vacated seat next to Qin and asked in English, "Did you suffer persecution during the cultural Revolution?"

"Not really," he responded frankly. "Fortunately, I was assigned to participate in translating Chairman Mao's selected works. So, as a consequence, I wasn't too involved with the revolutionary movement and was lucky enough to escape the cultural holocaust. As for the May Seventh Cadre School,[9] it didn't mean anything. Almost everyone went there, and I was no exception."

He spoke in such a light and pleasant manner it made him sound like he was reminiscing about some sort of relaxed leisure activity instead of the toils of forced hard labor.

"That was quite fortunate indeed," Emily nodded, and her big bronze earrings jingled rhythmically as if they were dancing.

"I didn't suffer much," he said. Pointing to the old scholar sitting at the other end of the sofa, he continued, "Bi the Senior is a better example of someone who suffered gravely at the hands of the persecutors."

As Emily looked at Bi, Wallace was just asking him about the customs and practices of the minority Yao tribe. The elder scholar was chewing each bite of his food slowly, trying to respond to Wallace's questions, but actually more engrossed with his food.

As soon as he stopped eating for a moment, Emily interrupted and asked him, "Did you also suffer from persecution during the reign of the 'Gang of Four'?"

"They accused me of being a reactionary academician, so I was imprisoned in a cattle shed and sentenced to seven years of hard labor."

"Do you think there's any possibility that a movement like the Cultural Revolution could happen again?"

Without blinking an eye, he answered, "Yes, there is."

Such an honest reply came so unexpectedly that, once again, the room fell into silence.

Wenhui desperately wanted to separate Old Hou from the other guests. Noticing his plate was empty, she went up to him and said, "Comrade Hou, there's still a lot of food left. Please help yourself to seconds!"

She accompanied Old Hou to help him fill his plate, and Yin Qin, having finished eating, got up and followed them into the dining room.

Their dining room wall was covered with photos of old Chinese pagodas. Barely touching his newly filled plate, Old Hou started to examine the pictures instead.

"This is Yu Yi's collection," Wenhui explained to him. "You've probably seen all of these ancient places, haven't you?"

"I've been to places like the Six Harmony Pagoda and the Giant Goose Pagoda. During the Sino-Japanese War, I worked with the Chinese underground and lived near Thunder Peak Pagoda for over six months."

*So, Old Hou is a veteran of the Sino-Japanese War.* Wenhui immediately felt an increasing amount of respect for him.

"I'm also very fond of Chinese pagodas. They reflect untainted simplicity and guilelessness, and harmonize beautifully with the natural scenery," Yin Qin echoed.

"There are all kinds of pagodas in China! By all means, please come see them. Perhaps you can even come do research on them. Our government would sincerely welcome you and be glad to assist you in this regard. We welcome all of you to visit China."

Wenhui decided to help her classmate further along and said, "Actually, Yin Qin does want to do research in China. I'm sure it would be most helpful if you could give him a recommendation."

"Oh, what kind of books are you writing? Could you give me one or two to take back with me?" Hou responded encouragingly.

Moved by his sincerity, Yin Qin ventured, "If you give me your address, I'll mail a set of my publications to you. They're either poetry or literary criticism. And, please, give me your honest opinions on them when you're done!"

"You're too modest! My youngest son is also studying literature at Beijing University. He is very fond of poetry and enjoys writing it himself. If there's a chance, I'd like him to learn from you!"

At the mention of his son, Old Hou's tone of voice became tender and soft. Much to Wenhui's surprise, she had discovered that this dignified, serene-looking old Communist was in fact a very loving father.

The self-centered and arrogant Yin Qin suddenly became very modest for the first time, "Oh, please, don't flatter me so much!"

At that moment, Wenhui was struck with an idea and exclaimed, "There's a complete set of Yin Qin's writing in Yu Yi's study. Comrade Hou, would you like to see them?"

Since he didn't express any objection, Wenhui took them both to the study, which was conveniently situated at the other end of the house. After inviting them to sit down, she found the books and put them in front of Old Hou.

"Take your time and discuss the books while you eat your dinner. I'll bring you some tea."

Going back to the kitchen, Wenhui plugged in the electric kettle, washed the teapot, and made a fresh pot of Wulong green tea. By the time she returned to the living room with the teapot and cups, it was apparent that the conversation had taken a new turn. Surrounding the two elderly gentlemen, the host and guests had all crowded around the long sofa, some even sitting on the floor. The atmosphere had changed completely. It had become serious and still, as if they were attending a formal meeting, not a dinner party.

"Last year, my daughter went to study in England," Qin the Elder was saying to Yu Yi. "Now, my two nephews also want to study abroad. I'd like them to come to the United States. Is there any way to get them here?"

Yu Yi paused for a moment and then replied, "At the very least, they could apply to study in America!"

Qi Wen nodded his head, expressing his accord, "The easiest way to come here is to apply to study. The Chinese government has already started to permit overseas studies, and the requirement to have a relative living abroad no longer applies. As long as someone can guarantee the student's education and living expenses, the Chinese government will let them go. Of course, the first priority is to pass the TOEFL exam at the American Embassy."

"Really? Why didn't we know about this?"

Several of the guests from China looked at each other with mixed expressions of surprise and joy.

"This was announced in several leading newspapers. Our library still has the clippings to confirm it." Mrs. Qi, who had been quiet up until then, suddenly volunteered the information.

Qin the Elder was deeply affected by this and said, "News of this nature should be announced to everyone openly. Studying overseas has been a long-standing tradition. Unfortunately, this practice was twisted and destroyed by the 'Gang of Four' during the last few years! People are not allowed to make any plans on their own behalf, not even an education. If they did, they would be accused of being self-serving, and the stigma attached to that would also fall on their head."

Bi the Senior tried to comfort him, "Take it easy, the policy is in the process of changing. A vast country like ours can't operate with a closed door policy. Eventually, I believe the door for overseas study will truly be open."

Yu Yi also revealed another bit of information he had read in the newspaper. "I've read reports that the American Embassy has already administered several TOEFL exams."

"What is this TOEFL?" asked Little Fu, who had no idea what the term meant.

"It's an English test, the Test of English as a Foreign Language."

"How does one take this test?"

"All you have to do is ask about it at the embassy." A matter like this seemed simple to Yu Yi, yet could mean many difficulties for his guests.

At first, Old Jian shook his silvery head and said, "We can't get into a foreign embassy that easily."

Bi the Senior gloomily thought about it, too, looking somewhat as though he was at his wits' end.

"Ever since the arrest of that woman, Fu Yuehua, no one dares make too much contact with foreigners."

Upon saying this, Little Fu felt as if he were suffocating, and quickly unbuttoned the top of his Chinese uniform so he could breathe.

Only Qin the Elder was not completely disheartened and said, "I think it's best for the fathers write to the American Embassy requesting information. That way, if something went wrong, the responsibility would only fall upon the father. In the meantime, the most urgent thing is to learn English well."

"Studying English is such a frenzied fad now," Little Fu said, "even dictionaries and grammar books have become scarce. No matter how expensive they are, people will still pay the price for them."

"This fad is just like the one in Taiwan!"

Wenhui's analogy brought a roar of laughter from those who had come from Taiwan. They told the mainlanders how people had made a fortune by setting up English tutoring schools, and advised them to follow the same path.

Bi the Senior anxiously wanted to get his grandsons out of China, but he was worried they would be unable to pass the TOEFL exam.

"If they came here with tourist visas, could they stay on to attend school?" he asked Yu Yi.

"I think it was okay before, but it's probably more difficult now. Let me get back to you after I talk to a lawyer first."

"I have a distant relative in Oklahoma who wants to help us. As soon as my grandsons are able to come to the States, he's willing to help with everything. Unfortunately, precious time was taken from these kids during the first few years of the Cultural Revolution. They were either sent to the mountains or assigned to the countryside for a few years. After it was over and all this time passed by, they completely forgot what they studied. I doubt they can pass the TOEFL now."

Holding his knees, Wallace sat on the carpet quietly and listened attentively to the conversation. From time to time, he would whisper a brief translation to Emily who sat next to him.

Realizing that Bi the Senior was so worried, she volunteered, "My uncle's a lawyer. He specializes in immigration law, so I'll ask him a few questions on your behalf, and there won't be any charge. If you need him to handle the case, I'll ask him to give you a discount!"

The visitors were not familiar with terminology such as *lawyer* or *fee*, so for a moment they were at a loss for words. Yu Yi explained to them that securing a lawyer's assistance at the appropriate time could help solve problems more efficiently. He also told them not to worry about the fees, for money was not a real concern. Even Wallace expressed willingness to help, all of which eased Bi's anxiety immensely.

"Bi, as soon as you get more information on this, please do let me know," Old Jian requested.

Now that the discussion had at last become fruitful, Wenhui immediately sprang back into her role as hostess. "Please, have some tea. This is Wulong green tea from Dongting, and we also have Longjing tea from Hangzhou. I'll go make another pot."

When she went to the kitchen to boil the water, Mrs. Qi followed her in to help.

"Although they kept on saying how wonderful China is, it seems the fact of the matter is that many of the people inside China desperately want to get out of there. . . ."

"Shhh!" Wenhui put a finger to her lips, pointing at the study with her other hand. Mrs. Qi understood immediately and did not say anything more.

After Old Hou returned to the living room, the discussion again became subdued. The two Americans did most of the talking and asked many questions about China. Qin the Elder acted as their interpreter, while Old Hou responded to most of the inquiries himself. The other members of the delegation could only nod their heads to echo their accord.

At around eleven o'clock, the reporter from the *China News Agency* called. After talking to him, Old Hou told his host that they had to leave.

"Since we're leaving for Beijing tomorrow, we'd best be off to pack our suitcases now. Everyone has had an exhausting day and needs some rest. We're very grateful for the hospitality you've shown us the past couple days. We really hope to see you all again soon in Beijing!"

Everyone felt sad that it was already time to leave, and they all exchanged addresses. No one dared ask Old Hou for his address; however, he generously volunteered his office address and telephone number to the Americans.

The host and hostess saw them off at the front door. After helping everyone into the car, Old Hou again thanked Yu Yi on their behalf. He also extended his gratitude to Wenhui. "Mrs. Yu, I'll never forget tonight's dinner. You must come visit us in Beijing! We will be waiting for you."

He also shook hands with her, much in the same manner that Mao Zedong shook Richard Nixon's, his two big hands clasping her tiny ones.

After the delegation members departed, Wallace and the Yins also left. Since the Qis were family friends, Yu Yi thought about asking them to stay for a nightcap. However, when he noticed Wenhui's pale face and stiff expression, he reached over to hold her and said, "Wenhui, you must be tired. Is something wrong?"

"All of a sudden I seem to have developed a headache, but it's nothing, though. I'll be alright in a while."

"You two should get some rest. We'll get together some other time." The Qis were very considerate people and left immediately.

Once the door was closed, Yu Yi turned around to look at Wenhui. She opened her hands and clasped inside was a small slip of paper.

"What's that?" he asked.

"When Old Hou shook my hand, he slipped this note to me."
They went to the light at the table and carefully unfolded the note.

There were only a few lines of writing in pencil:

My son wants to come study in the United States. I hope you can
help him. When you have an opportunity to visit Beijing, please
contact the following address . . . . Thank you very much.


## Notes

1. "In and Outside the Wall" ("Chengli chengwai") was translated by Hsin-sheng C. Kao with the permission of the author and
publisher, and is published here in English for the first time. This
translation is based on the story's appearance in the collection entitled
*Chengli chengwai* (Taipei: Shibao wenhua, 1983), pp. 51–84.

2. During President Carter's administration, Sino-American diplomatic ties were formally established on January 1, 1979.

3. This term refers to former premier Deng Xiaoping's policy to
modernize China's industry, agriculture, science and technology, and
national defense by the year 2000. This modernization plan was first
announced by the late premier, Zhou Enlai (1898–1976), to the Fourth
People's Congress (January 13–17, 1975). It has been a dominant policy
since the late 1970s.

4. The original Chinese title is *Wei cheng*, a novel written by the
erudite scholar Qian Zhongshu in 1947, who is also the author of *Tanyi
lu* (1948) and *Guanzhui pian* (1978).

5. Qu Yuan (340?–278 B.C.) is the reputed author of *Chuci* (*The
Song of the South*). According to the biography that appeared in Sima
Qian's *Shiji* (*Records of the Grand Historians*), Qu Yuan was in the service
of King Huai. Later he was wrongly accused by another high-ranking
retainer. After King Huai's death, his eldest son inherited the throne
and banished Qu to the distant south. As a sign of protest against his
loyalty and patriotism being slandered, Qu committed suicide by
drowning himself in the Miluo River.

6. The "Gang of Four" (*Sirenbang*) refers to the four radical leaders
of the Cultural Revolution, headed by Mao's wife Jiang Qing. The
other three high-ranking members were Zhang Chunqiao, Yao

Wenyuan, and Wang Hongwen. Along with Jiang, they were all ousted in October 1976.

7. The Democracy Wall is also called *Minchu qiang*. Usually posters or articles are written with a Chinese brush in large characters, at least three inches or more, on newspaper or colored paper and posted on the wall for the purposes of public criticism, attacking the government, and criticizing the ills of society.

8. It is also called *Dazibao*, posted on the Democracy Wall. See the previous note for details.

9. The May Seventh Cadre School (*Wuqi ganxiao*) derived its name from the directive issued on that day in 1966 by Mao Zedong, in which he called for the reeducation of the intellectuals by sending them down to the countryside to engage in physical labor. These "schools" were established throughout the country during the decade of the Cultural Revolution.

Yu Lihua

於梨华

# Yu Lihua

Yu Lihua (b. 1931) was born in Shanghai to a middle-class intellectual family. In her teens she and her family moved to Taiwan, where she received her education, graduating with a B.A. in history from the National Taiwan University in 1953. Subsequently, she came to the United States to study journalism at the University of California, Los Angeles, where she obtained her M.A. in 1956. She has been a faculty member of the East Asian Studies Department at the State University of New York, Albany, since 1968, and is currently the president of the International Chinese Women Writers Overseas Organization.

A fastidious writer with a keen sense of observation and creative sensitivity, Yu Lihua has been recognized as the leading spokesperson for Chinese intellectuals in the United States, and has played a prominent role in the development of overseas Chinese literature. Unique in her own way, Yu Lihua's receptivity to stylistic experimentation and linguistic innovation is reflected in all of her works. In them, she has not only captured the new literary sensibility in writing, but above all has freed her style from the trite creative writing rules that vitiated so much of Chinese contemporary aesthetic thought. Rich and varied, her works exhibit an immense beauty and visual density.

Thematically, Yu Lihua places her stories within the context of a historical and social structure and ideology. Her examination and revelation of the common plight and sentiments of overseas Chinese are recognized as the true reflection of the development of Chinese overseas literature of the past four decades. The corpus of her works can be categorized into three stages: the first deals with the concept of rootlessness; the second, with identity crisis and self-search; and the last, on the more introspective themes of homecoming and reconciliation.

Yu Lihua is bilingual and well versed in Western literature. As a graduate student, she won the prestigious Samuel Goldwyn Creative Writing Award (1957) and many other literary awards in Taiwan, including the Jiaxin and Distinguished Writer's Award.

Widely recognized for her continuous stream of publications, Yu Lihua has assembled an amazing bibliography: fifteen volumes of novels, novellas, short story collections, and prose. She is also the author of several volumes of critical writings and translations.

# Two Sisters[1]

## Yu Lihua

The room was quiet when Wenyi awoke, and only the dark imprint of her husband's head rested on the pillow mat beside hers. Dezhi had already left for work.

It was past two o'clock! She must have finally fallen asleep. Most of the night she had tossed and turned, probably because she was so excited, a rather rare incident in recent years. She stretched out her body from head to toe. *My, how wonderful it felt to stretch*, she thought.

Slowly getting out of bed, she glanced at her sapphire-blue rayon dress hanging outside the closet. Dezhi had told her he thought she should wear it when she picked up her older sister, Wenying, from the airport. Brushing her tangled hair back with her hand, she put on her soft-soled slippers and pulled open the drapes. Yawning with pleasure, she stretched again.

As she was about to call Jinma, her servant, in to prepare her bath, she glanced at her watch and suddenly realized she didn't have enough time. Abandoning the idea, she instead splashed her face with cold water and instantly felt revitalized. Pouring a few drops of Christian Dior moisturizer on her hand, she dotted it on her cheeks, using her palms to smooth it from the wings of her nose outward and upward to the rest of her face. Then she turned on the fluorescent light above the vanity mirror and examined her face closely.

*Not bad*, she thought, *for a forty-two-year-old*! Although her features were somewhat plain, her complexion was what people usually described as peaches and cream. She had gotten married over a decade ago and had since lived an affluent life-style. Her good fortune enabled her to enjoy the luxuries of protecting her face from the sun, always including fruit and vegetables in her diet, and using the most expensive moisturizers twice a day. With such pampering, the only makeup she ever needed to use was a brilliant red glossy lipstick to set off her snow-white skin.

Her hair, however, had not fared as well. It had long since turned gray, but fortunately the use of hair color was common in Taiwan. She usually wore it dyed jet black, making her skin look even more pale. The stark contrast at times made people avert their eyes.

Even though she wasn't very old, she had put on quite a bit of weight. Stepping back two steps, she forced herself to look at her body. Her shoulders were broad and her breasts sagged. She had a heavy waistline and hips, a flabby stomach, and thick legs. She was so fat and flabby, she could hardly stand it. Two months ago, when she received Wenying's letter announcing her visit, she had decided to go on a diet. But there were just too many mahjongg games and social functions to attend. Her desire for beauty was not strong enough to resist the temptation of such delicacies as lichee fruit and eel rolls, shredded chicken with bean sprouts, crispy duck, and date-filled pastries. Besides, who else among her friends did not have a weight problem as they reached middle age? Wenying was probably no different. Otherwise, why was she always in a half-pose in all the pictures she had sent of herself? Wenyi gave her fat stomach a few gentle taps. Starting tomorrow, she would go on a diet. At the very least, she would not eat any more of those sesame dumplings after her mahjongg games at night.

After combing her hair, she put on a glossy rose-colored lipstick and went into the bedroom to change. She had bought her dress at a shop called Lolita's on Dezhi's birthday. At the time, she felt the padded shoulders were too thick, making her look like a Samurai—all she needed was a sword! However, Dezhi had insisted it was the style that year, and it made her look taller and thinner. The skirt was medium length with an elastic waist, and the blouse was worn out over the skirt, thus hiding the most protruding portion of her body, her stomach. Wearing her white shoes, she stood in front of the mirror, and although she could not be considered slim and pretty, she felt quite pleased with herself.

Satisfied, she looked at her jewelry and picked out three solid gold bracelets and a platinum ring with five small diamonds set in a heart shape. On her middle finger, she put on a ring with a large pearl and three little ones. She gazed admiringly at her right hand for a few moments and then, without thinking, stepped out of the room. Almost as soon as she had done so, she realized she had left the air conditioner on, and went back in to turn it off.

"Jinma," she ordered, "call Dezhi's office and tell Old Zhang to bring the car. When you're done, bring me a cup of coffee."

"Madam, are you going to pick up your sister now?" Jinma asked. "Isn't it still too early?"

Jinma had been working for her ever since she got married. She had a pleasant personality and was hardworking. Over the years, Dezhi had taught her how to cook Shanghai cuisine, but she still had not learned to speak Mandarin well.

"I want to leave early so I don't hit any traffic," she explained. Wenyi finished her coffee and had Jinma bring her white purse from her room. As she was about to leave, she reminded Jinma, "Please be sure my sister's room is straightened up. You can turn the air conditioner on at about six, but there's no need to turn it on any earlier."

"I know, I know," Jinma immediately replied.

The last time Wenyi had gone to the airport was to pick up her mother when she returned from the United States. Because of her connections at the airport, she had been allowed to go straight to the gate. Looking through the large glass window, she had been shocked by her mother's appearance as she slowly descended from the plane. She looked like she had shrunk! Although her back was not bent, she appeared much shorter than she had three years ago.

As soon as her mother stepped into the terminal, she had run up to her. Standing next to her, Wenyi had thought her mother resembled a wrinkled, shrunken dress, completely unlike her upright old self. She had taken the rectangular wooden box from her mother's hands, knowing that in it was the urn containing her father's ashes. At first her mother had hesitated, but then she let Wenyi take it from her. Wenyi had thought her mother would be in tears upon seeing her, but, instead, in a normal voice she had merely asked how Dezhi was doing, as if they had only been parted a few days. Seeing her mother so calm had made her feel better, and her own grief had instantly diminished. After all, it had already been over a year since her father had passed away.

Waking her from her reverie, Old Zhang announced that they were there and asked, "Would you like me to go in with you, Madam?"

"That won't be necessary," she replied, glancing at the huge clock in the airport. "Please pick us up in about forty-five minutes, okay?"

Waiting in two lines, the crowd craned their necks toward the door through which the passengers would exit. Although the air conditioning was on, she could smell sweat, garlic, and other unnameable odors. Standing at the end of the line, her body slightly tilted backwards, Wenyi took out her handkerchief and wiped the perspiration off her face. Trying to simultaneously cover her nose and fan herself at the same time, she caught a whiff of Clinique perfume on the handkerchief. *How thoughtful of Dezhi!*

"What an extraordinary blessing!" her mother often remarked. Although she would not openly admit it, secretly she knew that she was indeed very lucky. When it came to comparing herself with Wenying, she knew she was no match except for one thing, her good fortune.

Many years ago, Uncle Jiang, her father's colleague, came to visit them with the intention of matchmaking. He had Wenying in mind, but, at that time, Wenying had just passed the oral exam required to study abroad and was planning to go to the United States. All Wenying could think of then was her bright future in America. How could she possibly be interested in the son of a watch store owner?

After her sister left for America in flying colors, Wenyi worked for the Perfection Life Insurance Company for a couple of years. Solely to please her parents, she took the college entrance exam for the second time and barely made it into an agricultural college in Taizhong, a city in central Taiwan.

One day, she went to a local watch store to have her watch repaired and unexpectedly ran into the owner's son, Wang Dezhi. Their conversation was immediately dampened when he informed her that his father, Uncle Jiang, had passed away. Shortly afterwards, she left, and when she returned to pick up her watch, Dezhi invited her out for dinner. After that they started dating regularly. When she got married, her father's career was at its peak, so their wedding was a sumptuous one. The Wangs, who lived in Taizhong, rented the Air Force Officer's Club for the wedding ceremony and held a thirty-table banquet at the Deerfield Restaurant.

Wenying was unable to come to the wedding and sent five hundred dollars as a gift. Wenyi didn't mind at all, but Dezhi's mother complained to her mother, "What a pity! She has only one sister! No matter how busy she is, she should attend her sister's wedding. I know of many overseas students who come home often to visit their families. Why can't they come back for a visit? Considering she's married to a man with his doctorate, you'd certainly think that they could afford the airfare. Why don't you send her a telegram?"

Despite what Mrs. Wang believed, Wenying did not attend the wedding precisely because she could not afford the airfare. In her letter, she said that her child was too small to be left home, she could not take leave from work, the round-trip airfare was too expensive, and Jiaheng was unwilling to pay for it. Therefore, she could not come back and she hoped her family would forgive her. At the time, Wenyi was so caught up in the joyous, bustling wedding festivities that she barely missed the absence of her sister. It was not until later, when her friends and relatives asked her questions, or when they went through her three wedding albums and made comments on her sister's absence, that she began to feel disappointed. As her displeasure grew, she ceased writing to Wenying altogether.

The gate at the passenger's exit opened, and, all of a sudden, a commotion broke out in the crowd. Everyone stood on their toes and waved. Leaning forward to search for Wenying, she didn't see her sister pass right in front of her with a luggage cart. Hardly noticing her amongst the crowd, she kept looking in the other direction. After most of the passengers had left, she was really beginning to wonder where Wenying was when suddenly she caught sight of a woman standing alone in the waiting area. The woman's gray hair was cut very short, like a man's, and she wasn't wearing any makeup except translucent lip gloss. Her thin, slender eyebrows were dark, accenting her narrow face, but her eyes were very dull. There was a dark mole at the center of the diagonal line between the wing of her nose and the upper corner of her mouth. It was this mole, which had attracted many a suitor, that sparked Wenyi's recognition.

"Wenying!" she called out to her sister.

Wenying turned around, let go of the luggage cart, and stretched out her arms. In moments, they were holding each other in a tight embrace.

"Wenyi, I'm so glad to see you!" Wenying exclaimed. Feeling her sister's weight, she pulled away. "You've gained weight! You were so skinny when I left!"

Wenyi looked at her sister again. Now up close, she could see tiny wrinkles at the corners of Wenying's eyes, along the sides of her nose, and on her forehead. When she went to America, her skin was like porcelain, but now it was darker and dotted with freckles. Her short, page-boy hairstyle made her lean face appear longer than it really was. Wenying once had a full face and sparkling dark eyes. Just before boarding the plane to leave for America, those dark eyes had brimmed with glistening tears, making her look so lovely and vulnerable that their mother wept brokenheartedly.

Her charm was gone. When she left she was a ripe juicy peach, and now only the hard pit was left, wrinkled and angular. She was in good shape even though she had given birth to two children, but it still did not compare to the slender figure of her youth. Besides, Wenyi thought she looked sloppy wearing that oversized, light gray shirt and loose gray pants. She was completely different from the girl who used to wear such tight clothes she could hardly sit down to eat.

"Didn't Mother tell you? I don't do anything but eat all day! How could I not get fat? But, they say it's a good thing to gain a little weight as you start getting older. You look like you've aged, Wenying."

Like a patient unexpectedly stung by a needle, Wenying gave her sister a sidelong glance and let the remark pass with a smile. "Of course, it's been a few years since we've seen each other." She caressed her face with her hands, as if trying to smooth out her wrinkles. "I sat on that plane for hours and didn't sleep well. At my age, if I don't get a good night's sleep, it really shows."

A taxi drove up, soliciting their business. Wenying was about to wave it down when Wenyi stopped her, "I have a car. There it is, Old Zhang's coming right now."

As they rode on the freeway into the city, Wenying exclaimed repeatedly, "What's going on here? All I see are cars, where are all the people?"

"In the cars, of course. It's been years since you've been here, Taiwan has changed a lot," Wenyi replied.

"A lot! I guess it's a lot, I hardly recognize it! There are so many cars. It's not any different than American cities. All those high-rise buildings, they weren't here before!" Suddenly, she screamed and covered her eyes with her hands. "My God, how could that car cut in like that? He scared me to death!"

Sitting in the driver's seat, Old Zhang casually told her, "This is nothing, I've seen closer calls than that. You need four hands to drive in Taipei, or, sooner or later, you'll get into trouble. There are a lot of cars in America, aren't there? Do they drive like this?"

"Well, not like this, but I do think the taxis in New York City are pretty scary. Do you drive, Wenyi?"

Jovially, Old Zhang answered before Wenyi had a chance, "She's afraid to even sit in a car, much less drive the thing!"

Wenying turned toward Wenyi, "In America, if you can't drive, it's like not having legs. You just can't go anywhere."

"That's why I don't want to go there. I don't have the slightest desire to go to America. Frankly, I'm so used to life in Taiwan, I really don't feel like going anywhere else. Not like you . . ." Wenyi swallowed the last part of her sentence, thinking to herself instead, *you were born to live a hard life.* For some reason, seeing her sister so haggard lessened the resentment of all those years. She said softly, "I really don't understand Mother. Why does she prefer to live in America instead of Taiwan? I can't believe it's more comfortable living in a retirement home there than it is living here with us!"

Looking straight ahead, Wenying did not say a word. One of the biggest problems between them had always been their parent's living arrangements. Wenying was working in a library when her first child, Little Xin, was born. She and her husband, Jiaheng, had discussed bringing her mother to the United States to take care of their baby so she could keep her job. Jiaheng disagreed, complaining that if they invited her mother, her retired father would also come. He insisted their house was too small. The nursery had already taken up one room, so there was simply no extra room for two more people. Besides, he thought it was only right that a mother should raise her own child.

Before they got married they had agreed that her job at the library was only to be a temporary one; it supplemented his income and gave Wenying something to do. He had never taken her work seriously. Unable to persuade him otherwise, she ended up quitting her job to be a full-time mother.

However, raising Little Xin almost drove her crazy. She was so tense her milk dried up, and she had to switch to formula. Every day she mixed the formula and sterilized the bottles. The baby needed to be fed every four hours. It was first agreed that the feedings at two and six in the morning were Jiaheng's responsibility. But once he fell asleep, it was impossible to wake him. So she had to get up herself. Sometimes the starving baby would cry so much before Wenying could manage to get up that she inhaled too much air, and her stomach rejected the milk. Then she would cry even harder, and as much as Wenying tried to comfort her, she simply would not stop crying. Wenying was usually so exhausted by all this that she could hardly keep her eyes open.

Once the baby had been crying for a good half-hour when Wenying finally awoke. Jiaheng was either awake and refused to get up, or he was sound asleep, oblivious to the screaming baby. So she struggled out of bed, warmed the formula and changed the baby's diaper. She tried to feed the baby; but by that time the baby's face was already scarlet from crying and she would not drink anything. In a moment of panic and frustration, Wenying practically threw the baby back into the cradle, and then kicked it, sending the cradle to the other end of the room. It hit the wall with a bang, and the baby abruptly stopped crying. The silence of the night enshrouded the nursery. She stood still in shock. Suddenly, Jiaheng jumped out of bed. He rushed to the cradle and picked up the frightened baby. He looked at her, and his eyes were so cold it made her blood congeal.

"What kind of mother are you anyway?" he growled.

She wanted to retort, "If you were awake, why didn't you get up? Why don't you accept your responsibility as a father? Why can't you let me rest a little at night since I haven't even fully recovered yet?" However, over five years of marriage had taught her that no matter how many times she asked "why," he always had some answer that would satisfy himself, but rarely her.

Clenching her teeth, she picked up the bottle and took the baby from his arms. Wrapped in the glory of victory, he went back to bed. He had always misinterpreted her silence to be submission, and this eventually became one of the reasons their marriage fell apart.

Three years later, when she was about to give birth to Little Yi, she insisted that her parents come live with them. There was a reason she had waited three years before having a second child. She did not want to get pregnant again until she had worked for two years and saved up enough money for her parents' airfare.

Wenying looked at Wenyi and said, "On the way here, I stopped by Mother's place for a few days. Actually, it's really not bad there at all. San Francisco is nice and sunny, not as humid as Taiwan. It's good for Mother's arthritis. Plus, there are a hundred and fifty-six senior citizens living in her apartment building, and one third of them speak Chinese. Uncle and Auntie Wu live on the floor above Mother, and Aunt Zhu lives next door. Uncle Wu was an old friend of Father's, so I'm sure he'll take care of her. There are bus stops across the street, and Chinatown is only five stops away. It's really very convenient. I took them there for a Cantonese brunch, and the food was even more authentic than in New York City."

"But, what are our friends and relatives going to think of us? It seems like a disgrace to have two daughters, both with their own families, willing to dump their old mother in a retirement home!"

"Wenyi, it's understandable that you think that way because you live in Taiwan, but, in the United States, it's very common. Sometimes, it's inconvenient for parents to live with their children; they may not get along. It's easier for mothers and daughters, but sooner or later there are problems when a mother-in-law lives with her daughter-in-law. In many cases, it's the parents who ask to live in retirement homes where they can enjoy some peace and quiet."

"Was it Mother's idea to live in a retirement home?" Wenyi asked.

It was sunny outside, but all of a sudden Wenying felt cold. It must be the air conditioning. She grabbed the gray sweatshirt she had worn on the plane from her handbag and put it over her shoulders. Looking at the clothes Wenyi was wearing, Wenying could tell how well she was doing financially. Besides, Mother had told her many times that Wang Dezhi owned two jewelry stores in downtown Taipei and two others in Taizhong. He was planning to open another one located in the most expensive area in Taipei. Her mother had said, "When it comes to making money, nothing beats running a business of your own. Take Dezhi, for example, he doesn't have a Ph.D. or Dh.P., but he's a millionaire! Wenyi lives much more comfortably than you.

Next time you marry. . . ." Wenying had learned one thing after being married to Jiaheng for so many years, that icy glare, which instantly quieted her mother.

Surely Wenyi was not grumbling about the money she sent to the retirement home every month. So, what was the problem? Did she really care that much about what other people thought? Wenying had been through so much over the past couple years, trying to adjust to life as a single parent and learning to survive on her own. She didn't even have time to think about what she thought of herself, much less what others thought of her. It was enough for her that Mother was happy.

"I don't remember who's idea it was," Wenying replied. "I don't think anyone in particular brought it up. After my divorce, I needed to make some adjustments in my life. I found a job in New York and moved there with Mother. I worked in the city and lived in an apartment in Queens. My life-style was entirely different from before. Mother was cooped up in a small apartment all day, too frightened to even take a walk outside. She doesn't understand English, so she couldn't watch television, and there weren't any Chinese people nearby. Things got so bad that, at times, she only opened her mouth three times a day—just so she could eat. What kind of life was that?"

"Why didn't you send her back here? I still keep a room for her. You'll see it when we get to my place. The amenities are as good as those in American homes."

They hadn't noticed it, but the car had been parked in front of the apartment building for a few moments already. Old Zhang came and opened Wenying's door first. Wenyi instructed him, "Tell Jinma to come down here and carry up the luggage."

"Which floor do you live on? Don't you have an elevator?" Wenying asked in surprise. "Certainly we can carry it ourselves!"

"Of course there's an elevator! Come with me," Wenyi replied. "There's someone here to take care of your luggage, so don't worry, it won't get lost."

They ran into Old Zhang and Jinma at the entrance to the elevator. Jinma examined Wenying from head to toe and commented, "You two look a lot alike, but you're not as heavy as your sister!"

"Jinma, shut up!" Wenyi quipped. "Take these two suitcases upstairs. Old Zhang, are you going to pick up Dezhi now?"

"No, he said that he had to go somewhere and would take a cab home."

Displeased, Wenyi mumbled something to herself, and then said with a straight face, "Well, then, I guess you can go now."

"Will you be needing the car tonight Madam?"

She glanced at Wenying, who responded quickly, "I don't feel much like going out. That long flight exhausted me!"

"Go ahead, you can go home now, but don't forget to get here early tomorrow morning!"

Wenyi's rectangular living room was even larger than the living room in Wenying's first home in the suburbs of north Chicago. At one end was a huge round rosewood dining table, surrounded by ten high-backed chairs with carved wood designs and embroidered satin cushions. At the other end of the living room was a deep red imitation leather sofa. In front of the rectangular coffee table, on the parquet floor, was an oval imitation Tianjing rug, also red. Directly facing the sofa was a wall unit with a huge television, twice as big as Wenying's. At the end of the room were two glass sliding doors that led to a balcony, on which sat two pots, a cactus and a plantain. Wenyi had placed two red lanterns imprinted with black characters outside of each sliding door; one said "Happiness," the other, "Longevity."

Mentally, Wenying quickly refurnished the rooms in her own style. For the dining room, a Danish-style white sandalwood dining table and chairs with blue cotton cushions; for the living room, a white leather sofa, an oval glass-top coffee table, a black sheepskin rug, glass shelves facing the sofa containing a few small sculptures, a stereo in the cabinet under the shelves, and, finally, a print of the flaming "Red Poppy" by Georgia O'Keefe hanging above the sofa.

"Wenying, what do you think of the house, do you like it? The dining room set was custom-made by Happy Glory Art Company. It was very expensive! I think a living room should look plush, don't you?"

Jinma brought in the two suitcases and stood there, apparently waiting for Wenyi's next instructions.

"Jinma, take those to my sister's room. Do I have to tell you that? Wenying, would you like to freshen up or rest a little?"

"That sounds good to me, where's Little Chao?"

"Who knows? He never comes home before dark," Wenyi replied, as she led Wenying to her room. It was a good-sized room, furnished with a bed, dresser, a desk and chair, and a rattan rocking chair. It also had a balcony. "How does it look to you, Sis? Please stay here for a couple of days first. Then, if you really don't like it, you can stay at a hotel!"

"Come on, Wenyi, don't be overly sensitive! When I wrote asking you to book a hotel for me, I just didn't want to be a burden to you. With the weather this warm, I know it can be inconvenient to have a guest around. Since this is my vacation, I fully intend to spend some money, and if I don't stay here, it doesn't mean that I don't want to stay in your house." Wenying paused, "After living abroad for so many years, I must admit, I think a little like a foreigner myself these days. Don't you think so?"

Wenyi nodded, "You do, but still, we're sisters, and you're not a guest! If I put you in a hotel, what will people think of me? Besides, I assure you, this apartment is just as luxurious as those in the United States. Go ahead and rest for a while; the bathroom is right across the hall. I'll tell Jinma to prepare your bath."

Momentarily startled, Wenying hurriedly said, "There's no need to bother her, I can prepare my own bath. Actually all I need to do now is wash my face and lie down for a while, I'll wait until before I go to bed to take a bath."

Wenying's body was tired, yet her mind was restless. She washed her face and then laid down on the cool straw mat, covering her chest with a corner of the coverlet. She could hear voices through the half-open door and smell the aroma coming from the kitchen. She turned over and faced the wall.

Turning back some twenty years, she thought about the day before she left for America. She had been packing all day and visited over ten homes. Totally exhausted, her mother told her to go to bed. Lying there in bed, she had not at all felt like sleeping and could only smell the aroma from the kitchen where their servant, Wang-sao, was preparing a farewell feast for her. After a while, she heard Wenyi come in to tell her that it was time to eat. Her sister had already graduated from high school, and was waiting for the results of the college entrance exam she had just taken. After Wenying was in the United States, she learned that Wenyi did not pass. Back then, Wenyi was as skinny as a bamboo stick, one third the size she was now.

"Hey," Wenyi had called to her sister. "It's time for dinner, and everyone's waiting for you. Your sweetheart is here, too."

Lying with her face to the wall, Wenying tried to ignore her, but her chest heaved up and down. Angrily, she replied, "You know that I'm leaving tomorrow, why can't you speak to me a little nicer?"

Just two days before that Wenyi had told her tearfully, "Sis, I don't want you to leave. Who's going to help me with my homework? Dad's busy, and Mom doesn't care how I do at school. You're the only one who encourages me to study hard. If I fail the exam, Sis, tell me, what should I do? Now that you're leaving, who will help me?"

Suddenly, she woke up and turned around to see Wenyi standing at the door. "Did you fall asleep, Wenying? If you'd like to eat now, everyone's waiting to welcome you home!"

"Wenyi," Wenying said in exasperation, " I am on vacation. Why do you have to bother other people?"

"I didn't! I only invited Xiaofeng and his wife. We're all family."

Xiaofeng, their cousin, was their oldest uncle's son. He went to Japan after graduating from college, and, when he came back, he became a representative for Toyota. He had been doing very well ever since. His wife was the English secretary for the owner of Harmony Trading Company. They owned real estate in Taiwan and two six-unit apartments in the western half of the United States. Their two sons went to the American school in Taipei. Besides their work, they were always busy socializing. Xiaofeng's wife loved to play mahjongg. She and Wenyi ran into each other at the game table quite often, so Wenyi had discussed this dinner date with her on several occasions.

Xiaofeng was now bald, and he had also gained weight. At first glance, his face was like a fried peanut, elongated and shiny. His damp, soft hands were like warm, wet dough. Wenying had never met his wife, Yujiao. She was wearing a long, pleated scarlet skirt, with a black belt. A slender woman, she boasted a twenty-inch waistline, but her breasts were large in contrast. Wenyi later divulged that she had gone to Japan for plastic surgery. The heavy makeup she wore covered up her fine features, which moved with animation when she spoke. Watching her talk made Wenyi dizzy, as if she were still on the plane.

"Well, well, so this is Cousin Wenying! Xiaofeng says that when you were young, you were so popular that they nicknamed you 'Commander-in-Chief'! Did you just arrive? You must be exhausted! The last time I went to Los Angeles on a business trip, do you know what? I slept for a whole week before I got over jet lag! Didn't your children come with you?" While talking she examined Wenying from head to toe, looking at her gray hair and gray flat shoes.

"Would you slow down, Yujiao? Wenying hasn't even had a chance to say hello to her brother-in-law," Wenyi interrupted.

Reluctantly, Yujiao stepped aside with a smile. Dezhi had gained quite a bit of weight, with his protruding stomach catching most of the attention. Perhaps it was his weight, but he looked shorter than Wenying remembered. His hair was parted on the left, and combed all the way to the right to cover his bald spot. He was wearing a fine gray pin-stripe suit which fit him so well that she knew it had to have been tailor-made.

"Dezhi, how have you been? You've put on a little weight, but other than that, you're still the same."

"Wenying, welcome home! You look thinner, but you haven't changed much either!" Dezhi replied.

*What a difference!* He had almost cried out. Where had the Li Wenying, ripe like fresh litchis fruit, gone? All he saw was a thin, dry-lipped and dull-eyed middle-aged woman. Standing next to her under the light, his own wife, whom he had always thought was overweight, now looked much more attractive. He put his arm around Wenyi and said, "Did Jinma make your sister's favorite dishes?"

"Certainly! She made grilled yellow carp with scallions and stewed pork with tender bamboo shoots. Let's go sit down at the table. We're all family, let's not be so formal. Since today is Wenying's first day back, we'll just have a home-cooked meal. After she rests up a little, we'll have a real welcome home party."

Xiaofeng joined in, "Yes, you must allow me to be the host. We'll pick the date later. Hey, where are the three little rascals?"

Dezhi called out to Little Chao, their only son, who was fourteen, and Xiaofeng's two sons, Zhoguo who was seventeen, and Zhobang who was sixteen. All three of them were tall and good-looking. They came out of Little Chao's bedroom and greeted Wenying respectfully. Seating themselves at the table, the three teenagers busied themselves eating. Dezhi poured the aged Shao-xing rice wine, and Wenyi was occupied with telling Jinma what to serve and how to serve it. Xiaofeng and his wife told Wenying about their careers, children, and social life. And Wenying just sat there, eating, listening, and smiling leisurely. After two glasses of wine, her cheeks became rosy and her eyes sparkled; even her mole became luminous. Yujiao, who considered herself to be in her prime as well as happily married, suddenly noticed that Wenying, not much to look at a few minutes ago, now shone with a unique charm all her own. It was a charm she knew that neither she, Wenyi, nor any of her friends had!

Suddenly she interrupted Xiaofeng and asked, "Wenying, you're divorced, aren't you? How long has it been?"

"Jiao-Jiao!" Xiaofeng gently poked her naked arm with his chopsticks. "Wenying, never mind her. She's a blabbermouth after a couple of drinks!"

"That's all right, it's no secret," she assured Xiaofeng. Turning to Yujiao, she answered, "Yes, I am divorced; it's been two years now."

Since the subject didn't seem to be taboo to her, the others followed with their own questions. Chewing on a greasy sparerib, Xiaofeng asked, "I heard that under American divorce laws all property is equally divided between husband and wife. Is that right? And what about alimony: does it depend on the man's income?"

"Who has custody of your children?" Yujiao interjected.

"Well, we didn't have much property to begin with, mainly the house which we sold and then split the proceeds. The money I made all those years belonged to me, and his money belonged to him. I do get alimony, but since I've always worked, the amount is very small. If I remarry, I won't get any. Since the children are grown up now, it doesn't really matter who has custody. They take turns staying with me and their father."

Surprised at her own matter-of-fact tone, it seemed as if she were talking about someone else. She could never have been this calm a year ago. Perhaps it was because she was with her family and did not have to worry about being ridiculed or reproached. Turning to Dezhi, she exclaimed, "Dezhi, I really can't drink any more. I mean it, if I do I'll get drunk."

"What's there to worry about? You're at home!"

Wenyi interrupted him, "Don't push it, Dezhi. Look at her, her face is all red! Jinma, bring a bowl of rice porridge to Wenying."

"Let's finish the wine. Bottoms up! Wenying, welcome back, I hope you'll find a new partner soon."

"That's right, we'd love to attend your wedding," Yujiao chimed in. "Come, you three, join our toast to your Auntie's future."

Wenying leaned to one side as if someone had jolted her. She had not heard this kind of old-fashioned talk for a long time and found it harsh to her ears. However, seeing everyone waiting for her with their glasses held high, she picked hers up and emptied her glass. She drank so quickly that she choked, bringing tears to her eyes.

After dinner, the three boys went to Baskin Robbin's for ice cream while the adults remained in the living room chatting. Dezhi offered Wenying a cigarette; seeing it was a Winston, she took it. With one puff, the resolve that had helped her quit smoking for almost a year disappeared into thin air. At home, on the top shelf of the closet in her studio, was half a carton of Winston cigarettes. To purposely test her perseverance—no, to prove to herself—she refused to throw the carton away. Every time she opened the closet, she would stare at it, feeling proud of herself. It was most trying for her when, after work, she brought home fried rice or soup with noodles from a Chinese take-out restaurant. She couldn't wait to put the food in the microwave, boil some water to make tea, and finish her supper. Then she would want a cigarette desperately. Once she even had a package of cigarettes in her hand and was about to open it when she caught sight of Little Xin's graduation picture hanging on the wall above her canvases. She had asked Little Xin what she would like for her graduation present, and her daughter had replied, "Mom, if you quit smoking, that would be the best present of all!" Quickly, she threw the pack of cigarettes on the floor in despair, grinding her teeth, "I must owe her a debt from my previous life!" She went back to the kitchen, poured herself a glass of Irish Mist, and gradually calmed down. Later, she returned the cigarettes to the shelf and nodded slightly at the picture.

Actually, the truth was that she had given up her dreams of becoming a painter because of Little Xin and her younger brother, Little Yi. But during the two years after the divorce, if it hadn't been for their emotional support, she would not have had the desire to continue living. As for breaking the rules tonight, she thought, "Little Xin, please forgive your mother. Let her enjoy one of the few remaining sensual pleasures in her life, smoking, drinking. . . ."

"Cousin Wenying, do you play mahjongg? Last time I visited San Francisco, I played every day. But they still play with thirteen-tiles, which is no longer popular here. We play with sixteen tiles now, it's much faster, and you don't have to figure out all those complicated combinations. If you're interested, I'll set up a game for you," Yujiao offered.

"I don't play very often, it's too time-consuming," Wenying replied, savoring the good taste of her cigarette. To her, it tasted as gentle as spring rain at the end of April. When Dezhi offered her another one, she took it without hesitation.

"If you don't play mahjongg, what do you do with all your spare time, especially living there by yourself?" Yujiao asked.

"How do you know she's by herself?" Dezhi interjected with a shrug of his shoulders. He was about to snicker when Wenyi gave him a warning glare. Holding it back, he said, "There are many fun places to go in New York, and besides that there are a lot of Chinese people, too. I don't think you have to worry about her being bored."

When she first went to New York, she had also thought it was that way. However, after settling down, she realized that for a divorcee who was no longer young, had to work, and had no sizable assets, New York was more like a prison or simply a cruel joke. Going out for dinner alone—that she finally managed; going to art galleries during the day alone—she didn't mind at all; but, going to a singles bar or a theater alone—that she still could not bring herself to do. Not only was it awkward, but there was also the prime concern of safety. Once in a while, one of her friends would arrange a blind date for her; however, she refused to bring a date back to her apartment for sex. It wasn't that she did not have the need, but after all she was a Chinese woman raised in a traditional family.

So, during those two years, she spent most of her time in the tiny art studio she had set up in her apartment. She painted and painted, painting night scenes where the moon was never full. It was always waning or waxing, or it was a crescent moon hanging at the tips of tree branches, the cold moon behind the roof, the setting moon at daybreak, or a prying, timid moon. . . . Every time she finished a painting, she tore it up, and painted it again. She wanted so much to produce a painting of the moon that perfectly reflected her sense of helplessness, but she had yet to do it. Maybe after she went back, she would try again. With a cigarette in her hand, maybe she would finally be inspired.

Wenying's pensive mood affected everyone. Assuming that she was tired, they discussed the date for the dinner party with Wenyi and Dezhi, and then Xiaofeng and his family took their leave. Little Chao went to his room to do his math homework, anxiously demanding his father's assistance. By the time they finished, it was almost eleven. Dezhi came out and said, "I'm going to bed now, I have to go to Taizhong tomorrow. You two shouldn't stay up too late either, there'll be plenty of time to talk later."

Sitting with only the hum of the air conditioner in the background, the two sisters were left alone together. Wenyi turned it off and opened the sliding doors. Outside the air had cooled down. "Sis, why don't you go to bed, we can talk more tomorrow."

Wenying picked up the cigarette that Dezhi had purposely left for her, lit it and inhaled deeply a couple times. Why bother? This was her vacation, and she ought to relax. Looking at her sister, she said, "I'm not tired now, it's only noontime in New York, which is the best time of the day for me. Go on to bed, I'm going to sit here for a while."

"Then I'll keep you company. Usually at this time I'm still at the mahjongg table." Wenyi sat on the sofa chair facing the open sliding doors and put her feet on the coffee table. A comfortable breeze blew over her stomach. "Xiaofeng's wife is irritating. She likes to pry, so don't pay any attention to her."

Wenying smiled, giving Wenyi a start. Earlier, in the kitchen, Dezhi had whispered in her ear, "Your sister is old and skinny. She looks at least ten years older than you." Then he had squeezed her bottom. To hell with him! No wonder Wenying used to refuse to even look at him. He had some nerve bragging about how well he knew how to appreciate women! Of course, he was really only good at appreciating those dance hall girls and call girls, but when it came to Wenying, whose charm came from within, his naked eyes would never be capable of appreciating that.

"I didn't mind her at all. I knew she wasn't being malicious."

"Sis, since you don't mind, let me ask you something. Have you had any boyfriends the last couple years? Do you plan to marry again?"

"Are you just curious, like Yujiao, or are you genuinely concerned about my welfare?"

"I . . . of course I'm concerned."

She looked at Wenyi, put her cigarette out and brushed back her short hair with both hands. Wenyi noticed the blue veins on the back of her hands, and thought Wenying had most definitely lost her youthful beauty. Subconsciously she looked at her own soft, white hands, the result of never having to work in the kitchen or do housework.

"Wenyi, you really haven't changed a bit. Whenever you're lying, you always swallow a mouthful of saliva first. It's alright, though, but frankly, I don't have any plans. When I was first divorced, I felt good about being free. I was only responsible for myself. But, after a while, I began to realize how unbearable it is not having anyone to talk to about how I feel. I don't mind not having sex. During the last few years of my marriage, after I discovered that Jiaheng was cheating on me, I would not let him touch me. I went through those years alright, but now the most trying thing is the complete absence of intimacy. Especially on winter nights, how I wish to have someone to hold me as I sleep, to warm my body and my heart, to keep me safe. On nights like that, I really admire those Chinese widows of the past who remained chaste for years. How did they ever do it?"

She had smoked too much, and her mouth tasted bitter. She picked up the teacup, but set it down again. "Wenyi, do you have any soft drinks? This tea is too strong and will keep me awake. My biggest fear these days is not being able to sleep." When Wenyi returned with a Coca-Cola, she asked, "Do you have problems sleeping?"

Wenyi shook her head, "My problem is that I eat and sleep too much."

"It's good to put on some weight. Once you're over forty, you can keep your skin soft and moist and even look younger by putting on a little weight. Look at me, gray hair, dry skin, just like an old lady."

Suddenly, Wenyi was filled with pity and forgiveness, "Sis, your charm is still there, although at first you do look older than before. I think you should seriously consider finding someone for yourself. I wouldn't be able to survive for one day in a place like New York. Of all those Chinese men in New York City, isn't there one you like?"

Wenying sipped her cola. Feeling its coldness flow through her body, she looked at Wenyi and even her smile had a chill. "Where do I find someone I like? I don't know, unless I put an ad in the newspaper like those desperate women from mainland China looking for a husband. I can see it now: 'Middle-aged lady of fine looks and character, fluent in Chinese and English, good cook, willing to marry man of good background, under sixty, with skills and no bad habits, able to appreciate art. Those interested please call 381-9191.' Listen to me! You can imagine how many times I've recited it in my mind. I just haven't done it. To tell you the truth, in New York, or rather in the United States, there are millions of women like me who are looking for their Prince Charming!"

"Let me help you!" Wenyi exclaimed. "I'll arrange something, Sis, I'll arrange something."

"Wenyi, I only have two weeks. Let me tell you my plans first. After two days in Taipei, I'd like to take the Suhua Highway to see the eastern part of the island. When I was young, all I wanted to do was have fun. I didn't know how to appreciate the natural beauty of Taiwan. I'd also like to go back to Taizhong. If possible, I'd like to stay in the Emerald Pavilion at Sun Moon Lake one night." She paused for a moment, "Wenyi, I hope you'll have the time and energy to come with me. If not, I'll go by myself. I've traveled by myself a little over the last couple years. It's a different kind of fun, but it'll be much better if you come along. You could keep me company, and we'll be able to talk. You, Little Xin, Little Yi, and Mother are the people that are closest to me. I came back here for two reasons, Wenyi, to travel and to see you."

Wenyi was a good host and a good sister. Turning down her dinner engagements and mahjongg games, she went on the trip with Wenying. However, she was not an outdoor person by nature. She got carsick and could hardly walk. At the magnificent Toroko Pavilion and Tianxiang Resort, she could only walk a short distance before she had to sit down in the shade and wait for Wenying to return. When they were at Hualian, the moon was incredibly bright and the night air extraordinarily cool and clear. In spite of her fatigue, Wenying insisted on going to look at the moon in the mountains. They had hardly left the hotel when Wenyi began to cry about being cold and went back.

The next day, as they rode the bus down the treacherous, meandering Suhua Highway, with the Central Mountain Range on one side and the Pacific Ocean on the other, Wenying held her breath spellbound. She marvelled at the spectacular landscape and, at the same time, admired the composure of the driver. She recalled an early summer many years ago when she had traveled to Eastern Europe with Jiaheng.

They had stopped over in Dubrovnik, a city on the Dalmatian coast of Yugoslavia. It was a small, beige seaport that attracted many tourists and earned sizable revenues for the country. After enjoying the fine sea breeze and some local seafood, they rented a car the next day and drove the Budva on their way to St. Stephan, a small island south of Yugoslavia. Mainly a vacation resort for the very rich, there were only about a hundred households. During the winter, the town simply locked the gates and did not reopen them until the following spring.

The highway they had traveled on was very much like the Suhua Highway, situated on a precipitous cliff couched between the mountains and sea. Gripping the steering wheel tightly, she had fixed her eyes on the tortuous mountain path, when suddenly a swarm of dark clouds surged toward the sun. As they were about to cover it, leaving a thin thread of crimson light the color of fresh blood, Wenying felt a sense of impending tragedy, a beauty that was about to disappear. Thousands of feet below was the tossing Mediterranean Sea. Wenying imagined herself driving straight toward the borderline between the land of the living and the nether world. Both scared and bewitched, she almost lost control of the car. Jiaheng shouted, "Watch out! You're holding two lives in your hands!" It jolted her out of her reverie. The crimson light was gone, and she entered a dark tunnel.

"Wenyi, one year I went to Yugoslavia and saw. . ." She turned to see her sister covering her face with her hands. And then, as if she was afraid that wasn't enough to keep her safe, Wenyi buried her head in her chest. "What's the matter, Wenyi? Are you feeling all right?"

"I'm okay, I'm just scared! I don't want to look or I'll faint," she mumbled. "It's all your fault! You couldn't enjoy yourself at home and wanted to suffer like this. Feel my heart, is it still beating?"

Startled at first, Wenying grabbed Wenyi's shoulders and pulled her close to her. Patting her gently on the head, she said, "I forgot how much you've always disliked traveling. I remember when you were in elementary school, every time there was a field trip, you looked sad-faced and pretended you had a stomach ache. I really appreciate you coming with me this time, Wenyi."

The five-day trip brought Wenyi much suffering, but the two sisters did have many opportunities to talk. The older one talked and the younger one listened. The many knots that had existed over the years were finally untied. The bumpy life Wenying had led after she went abroad somehow balanced out the jealousy and resentment Wenyi had harbored for feeling inferior to her sister in both looks and intelligence. Besides, now she was the host and her sister the guest;

and, since the guest had to accommodate the host, Wenyi felt a sense of satisfaction.

After returning from their trip, the two rested for a couple days before Wenyi insisted that Wenying go out and buy some clothes. "I know people dress casually in America, but not here, and especially with you just coming from the United States. I don't care what kind of life you have there. When you're here, you should dress up a little and wear some makeup, too. As the saying goes, 'Buddha needs gilt, people need clothes.' Tomorrow, I'll take you to Lily's for a perm, a manicure, and massage, my treat. I guarantee you'll feel better. The day after tomorrow Xiaofeng and his wife are hosting a dinner party at Fuhua Restaurant. You'll definitely need to dress up for that."

"Why?" Wenying asked innocently.

"Well, there's no special reason, except maybe just to show Yujiao that you're not a country bumpkin."

"Did she call me a country bumpkin?"

"Well, she wasn't talking about you in particular, but she said that overseas Chinese are all cheapskates. Last time she went to New York to visit a friend, she wasn't taken to a theater or a restaurant. Her friend only took her to the Metropolitan Museum—two dollars admission— just to see some rocks hauled there from Egypt! Isn't that horrible? She was led here and there in the museum and all the while wearing high heels! Afterwards she couldn't walk for three days!"

The dinner party consisted of Wenyi, Dezhi, Wenying, the chief accountant for Toyota, Mr. Fan, his wife, and Mrs. Fan's cousin, Zhao Renzhi. They all sat with the hosts, Xiaofeng and Yujiao, at one table, filling it up. Wenying was conveniently seated next to Mr. Zhao. He appeared trim and gentle, but the eyes hiding behind his tortoise-shell glasses were bright and lively. With his hair dyed he looked about fifty. Only his neck, which sagged down between his closely shaven chin and starched shirt collar, revealed his true age. When the eight cold dishes were served, everyone toasted one another, took a few sips of wine, and ate a little. Following that were four warm dishes: steamed mushrooms, shredded lamb tripe, roasted pine nuts, and spicy frog legs. By that time, they were all in a relaxed and jovial mood. Yujiao, wearing a strapless black velvet cocktail dress with a red flower pinned to her bosom, ate very little, but in her usual fashion, talked a lot. On the contrary, Wenyi, dressed in a loose-fitting red blouse and skirt, talked very little but ate a lot. Xiaofeng and Dezhi exchanged toasts with each other, and Mr. and Mrs. Fan kept a low profile, handling themselves cautiously and properly. Zhao Renzhi played both the host and guest. He was offered toasts and food by the hosts, and at the same time thoughtfully attended to Wenying's needs. In between all that, he also managed to give Wenying a brief summary of his life.

He was retired, yet still an active entrepreneur, and had two children in the United States, both married but not quite established in their careers. Of course, he had visited them there. His daughter lived in the rainy city of Seattle, and his son lived in Chicago, a very windy place. Neither, he felt, was suitable for him. The saddest thing, he said, was walking alone in the wind or sitting bored in the rain. Unfortunately, his children both worked, and his grandchildren did not speak Chinese.

When the dessert, crispy date cake, was served, Xiaofeng pointed at it with his chopsticks, "This is the most popular dessert in this restaurant. Come, Renzhi, please give some to Cousin Wenying."

"You've been drinking and failed to notice that Renzhi has been taking care of our cousin all along! Here," Yujiao stood up, offering a piece of cake to them. "Sweet in the mouth, sweet in the heart!"

Even Wenyi felt she was going too far. She glared at her and was just about to open her mouth when Dezhi raised his glass and said, "Let's finish the wine and eat dessert."

He held the glass with both hands, nodding to Xiaofeng and Yujiao, "Thank you for the delicious food and fine wine. Please, stop by our house after dinner. We have some premium green tea and Brazilian coffee to offer you."

After dinner, Dezhi offered Wenying a cigarette. Zhao Renzhi quickly took out his silver-plated lighter and lit it for her. Then he took out a fat cigar for himself and lit it. Her father used to always smoke cigars, and from the time she was little, Wenying had loved the smell. As soon as Zhao Renzhi exhaled his first puff, she inhaled deeply. She recalled her college days when she used to accompany her father to cocktail parties and banquets in place of her mother. Youth was like a bolt of soft shiny silk. With her bright eyes and sparkling teeth, her shy smiles and dazzling beauty, she mingled with guests twice her age and was understandably the darling of the party.

Entranced by her memory, she smiled at Zhao Renzhi, "I just love the aroma of your cigar." The wine she had drunk flowed to her eyes, her voice and her smile, illuminating her sensual mole. Her charm radiated all about her, enveloping everyone at the table.

Dezhi stood up, walked behind her, and put his hand on her shoulder. His exposed bald spot gleamed under the light. He said in a drunken slur, "I remember, I remember you love the smell of cigars. Old Zhao, give me one, too!"

"Dezhi!" Wenyi's voice crackled in contrast to Wenying's soft, moist voice. "Didn't we just invite everyone to our place for a cup of tea? Why don't you wait until we get home?" Saying this, she stood up and nodded to Xiaofeng and Yujiao. "Thank you so much for your hospitality. We should all go to our house now."

Later, after everyone had left, the two sisters sat alone on the long sofa, each occupying a corner. The air conditioning was off; the electric fan stood facing them, slowly shaking its head. Wenyi had taken off her panty hose. With her bare feet on the coffee table, she let her full stomach stick out nonchalantly. On top of it she rested a wine glass filled with Coca-Cola. With one hand under her chin and one hand holding a cigarette, Wenying was curled up on the sofa with her legs bent under her. Such a pose revealed her tiny waist, making her look relaxed and lazy.

Wenyi glanced at her. "Sis, I gave you my word that I'll help you find a husband. There's no need to be so anxious. There are plenty of men like Zhao around. You can make friends with a few of them before you pick one. It was unnecessary to turn on all your charm for that old man so quickly."

Wenying was stunned. Her cigarette still in midair, she asked, "What charm have I turned on?"

"You know exactly what I'm talking about; it's typical of you. You have always tried to capture men who interest you. Only now, your age and position don't allow that. If you act too frivolously, you will only expose your anxiousness and invite ridicule. What's more, you could even scare them away."

Wenying listened carefully while she leisurely finished her cigarette. When it reached the end, she snubbed it out and sat up to face Wenyi. "You haven't ever forgiven me for being Father and Mother's favorite when we were young or for being more popular, have you?"

The tea was already cold, but she needed the cold liquid to clear up the dizziness induced by the wine she had consumed earlier. Once again the center of the party, she had drunk too much. Eagerly, she took two big gulps of the tea and said, "Turn on all my charm—that's what you think. When we were young, I was more attractive to men than you were. I was born that way and didn't have to use any tricks to capture the men I wanted. Some women have it and some don't. There's nothing you can do about it. But, look at me now." She opened her hands and put her legs down, trying to find the slippers with her feet, "There is no charm to display anymore."

She stood up and stretched. "You know, it seems funny to me that with your position, wealth, a meek husband, and," she looked at her younger sister pointedly and continued, "especially with your solid build, how can you possibly still feel so insecure?"

The glass on Wenyi's stomach heaved up and down noticeably. When Wenying was done speaking, she put the glass on the coffee table with a clank. Then she put her legs down and sat up defiantly, "Why should I feel insecure? I'm not the one who's divorced, or the one who's old and dry, and turning fifty!"

She deliberately avoided looking at her sister. Perhaps she dared not, perhaps she could not bear to look at her. But she went on, "Tonight, at the dinner table, you acted so desperately, everyone could see it. Let me give you some advice, Sis: don't get involved with a married man and don't underrate yourself. U.S. citizenship is worth more than ten young beauties here. Zhao Renzhi is sixty-three years old. All he dreams of is living in America. His children dislike him and would not apply for permanent residence for him, so he snoops around for one every chance he gets. I told you I know as many as five other men like him. I'll introduce all of them to you. You can take your pick; there's no need to act so frantic about it now!"

Wenying cackled, like roasted chestnuts cracking in the oven. "Let me give you some advice, too. First of all, don't worry that I'm interested in Dezhi. Twenty years ago I was not interested in him; I'm even less so now. Second, don't bother to introduce me to any man. I let you make the arrangement for Zhao purely because I appreciated your concern, at least what I interpreted as sisterly concern before tonight. I'm not boasting, but finding a man for the sake of marriage isn't the most difficult thing for me. Even though I look old and dry to you on the outside, I'm not old and dry within. Perhaps you can't see it, but others do." She slowed down intentionally, "Especially some men."

She finished the tea, leaving each tea leaf tightly stuck to the cup. She looked at them with pity for a few moments before she said sadly, "Don't worry about me. I'm going to be fifty, and I know how to take care of myself. I'm going to bed now."

She knew she was going to have a sleepless night, but it was better than facing a sister who would not fully trust her and could not understand her.

Wenying got up late the next day. She wasn't able to fall asleep until three or four o'clock in the morning, after she finally took a sleeping pill. She came to the dining room table with a heavy head.

Wenyi was there waiting for her. Seeing her come, Wenyi called Jinma to bring out the Yangzhou steamed dumplings she had bought for her and the rice porridge with green beans. Both were Wenying's favorites.

"I have no appetite. I didn't sleep well last night," Wenying said.

"Me neither, but try to eat something anyway. I've been waiting for you, and I'm getting hungry," her sister said.

Maybe she was not fully awake yet, but she could not remember Wenyi's voice ever sounding this gentle. Wenying reached out and patted her sister's plump shoulder with her hand, "You can afford to skip a meal or two, Wenyi! After I return to the States, I'll send you an exercise kit to help you trim your stomach." Wenyi was her younger sister. She had to forgive her no matter what.

"I was going to ask you if you could stay a few days longer? Zhao Renzhi called and invited us to go to his villa at Yangming Mountain the day after tomorrow."

"I don't think so, Wenyi. I only have two weeks vacation."

"Sis, now that you're here, please just stay a few more days. Besides, Zhao Renzhi . . ."

"I know. He's already got my address and phone number in New York."

"Oh, so you . . ." Wenyi looked at her sister with surprise.

"Let's eat, my appetite is back. We can talk afterwards."


### Note

1. "Two Sisters" ("Jiemei yin") was translated by Hsin-sheng C. Kao and Michelle Yeh with the permission of the author and publisher, and is published here in English for the first time. This translation is based on the story's original in the collection entitled *Xiangjian huan* (Taipei: Huangguan chubanshe, 1989), pp. 13–46.

# Yu Lihua's Blueprint for the Development of a New Poetics: Chinese Literature Overseas

## Hsin-sheng C. Kao

### Yu Lihua's Three Literary Explorations

Over the last three decades, the production of overseas Chinese literature has flourished. This literary phenomenon has proceeded with notable consistency, a consistency ignited by many writers' acute longing for their homeland and the irresolvable sense of existential marginality experienced when living in foreign lands. The articulated struggle between the old and new land and the conceptualized suffering of exclusion characterize a new poetics, overseas Chinese literature. Like other Chinese literary genres, overseas Chinese literature contains fully developed plots and well-rounded Chinese characters, yet the settings and conflicts within which the characters exist are largely removed from their home soil.

Among writers of this category, Yu Lihua has been recognized as a leading spokesperson for Chinese intellectuals in the United States, and her works are considered precursors to the Chinese literary movement overseas. Author of fifteen works, including novels and short stories, Yu's writing is widely read on both sides of the Pacific Ocean, and she is generally recognized as the founder of elite intellectual Chinese exile literature. She writes honestly and compassionately about a world of cultural fusion and clashes and the identity crises and assimilation processes that occur living in the United States or other foreign lands. By offering diverse and innovative approaches to these concepts of internal exile, her texts leave a memorable imprint on the mind of the reader.

Yu Lihua's attempt to give meaning and justification to her emigré characters' existence in a new country through an examination of values common to both cultures puts her in company with such writers as Henry James, Joseph Conrad, Vladimir Nabokov, Heinrich Boell, Eduardo Galeano, Saul Bellow, and Isaac B. Singer.[1] Under her pen, the old society or the old China becomes equivalent to the old self, which is associated with one's cultural heritage, parental lineage, and historical continuity. The new society, America, is equated to the world of reason, opportunity, and progress. This, in turn, is forcefully connected with one's adopted identity, career, and self-worth. Caught between the old and the new, an understandably infinite set of conflicts arise, leading to confusion over one's own traditions and culture and feelings of estrangement from both environments.

Referring to these realistic conflicts, Yu Lihua once remarked in a 1983 literary interview in Singapore that her novels only breathe freely when they have their roots in reality. For years, she has advocated the need to grapple with the extent to which reality encompasses the utmost details of life.[2] A variety of observations and influences, some of them highly autobiographical, have served as the framework for the themes and artistry of her creative works. As Vivian L. Hsu says, Yu Lihua "was one of the first Chinese students from Taiwan to come to the United States. In some ways, Yu Li-hua's [Yu Lihua's] life experience in the United States is typical of many student-intellectual emigrés from Taiwan."[3] Born in Shanghai in 1931, Yu Lihua lived in both mainland China and Taiwan before she came to America in 1953. Over three decades of living in the United States have indeed provided her with a perspective on the nature of different realities and conditions that exist for overseas Chinese in America. Yu Lihua candidly admitted to Yan Huo that she knows more about Chinese people in America than about Chinese in China or Taiwan.[4] As a novelist, this has given her the incentive to explore and expose the issues of human frailty, and the anxiety of separation, displacement, and nostalgia toward one's homeland. With her acute sense of reality, Yu is adept at translating these disjointed and lost feelings into an examination of the discrepancies between the promise and fulfillment of the American Dream, and of life itself.

In the United States, a number of works with Chinese backgrounds or themes have been written and published in English. Among them are early Asian-American writer, K. Y. Lee, who wrote *The Flower Drum Song;* Maxine Hong Kingston and her award-winning book, *The Woman Warrior;* and, more recently, Amy Tan's two bestsellers, *The Joy Luck Club* and *The Kitchen God's Wife.*[5] In terms of their subject matter, some writers have resorted to sensational distortion and dramatic stereotypes,[6] and others have attempted to reflect the existing bicultural situation in the United States and the accompanying unresolved tensions between inclusion and exclusion, assimilation and rejection.

Yu Lihua, however, stands apart from these writers. The difference lies not only in her writing in the Chinese language instead of English, but also in her continuous effort to create Chinese literature, in Chinese, and to publish in Chinese journals and newspapers in China, Taiwan, and abroad.[7] Her writings assure her a place in the mainstream of contemporary Chinese literature. Categorically speaking, the common plight of her Chinese characters in America is that they must undergo and survive a rash of purgatorial sufferings before coming to terms with their status as an overseas Chinese. Like Dante's Virgil, each character must acknowledge his or her self-identity problems and confront the immense issues of either transcending or submitting to these problems.

The thematic emphases of Yu's writing can be categorized into three stages. The first and the earliest stage of her writing, mainly in the sixties and early seventies, centers on the thematic concept of the "rootless generation" (*meiyougen de yidai*). The second stage is a transitional one and mostly focuses on female personae as protagonists. It revolves around the continual process of "searching for roots and selfhood" (*xungen he xunziwo*) and "identity confusion" (*rentong de mihuo*). Lastly, the phase since the late eighties examines different levels of problems associated with the perennial themes of "returning" or "homecoming" (*huanxiang*), and "awakening" (*juexing*). To Yu Lihua, all three of these themes have complex implications, yet they complement one another by presenting the fictional text from various angles. This complex web is skillfully spun by the author's method of story development, with each strand weaving itself into others as a necessary step toward the eventual thematic conclusion.

First Writing Stage:
Themes of Rootlessness and Satirical Implications

Perhaps the best way to delve into Yu Lihua's creative world is to observe how she handles these themes in the novel *Again the Palm Trees, Again the Palm Trees* (*Youjian zonglu, youjian zonglu*, 1967).[8] This work is highly representative of the student-intellectual emigré and exile theme, and won her national recognition for the third time in ten years when she was awarded the prestigious Jiaxing Award for best novel in Taiwan in 1967. Her first award, the Samuel Goldwyn Creative Writing Award in 1957, was for her English story "Sorrow at the End of the

Yangtze River,"[9] and she received widespread acclaim for her tragic historical saga, *Recollections of Qing River* (*Menghui qinghe*), published in 1963. It was her catch phrase, the "rootless generation" (*meiyougen de yidai*), in *Again the Palm Trees, Again the Palm Trees* that made her a "trendsetter" in the world of literary overseas writing during the sixties and early seventies.

Mou Tianlei, the protagonist in *Again the Palm Trees, Again the Palm Trees*, is the quintessential overseas Chinese intellectual of that time. In him, Yu fully conveys the hope and disillusionment of his generation of overseas exiles. Yu's fascination and truthfulness to detail flows directly to Mou's characteristics: uprooted from his own traditional culture, symbolized by the majestic image of the "palm tree," and doubly alienated from his new life in America, he desperately reaches out to others, trying to overcome his unbearable sense of loneliness and disconnection with self, society, and country. However, the story develops with an ironic twist. As the novel unfolds, Mou Tianlei, after ten years of studying and teaching in America, returns to Taiwan in the hope of rejuvenating his "Chineseness." To his disappointment, *homecoming* becomes a satirical term that does not soothe him, but rather intensifies his isolation and loneliness. The dialectical polarities posed by the differences between East and West, memory and reality, and fantasy and actuality dismiss his conscious attempts to regain his old beliefs and happiness. That Mou Tianlei "cannot go home again" is aptly commented on by writer-critic Pai Hsien-yung (Bai Xianyong) in "The Wandering Chinese: The Theme of Exile in Taiwan Fiction": "Even Taiwan, supposedly the only bulwark of Confucian tradition, cannot offer him protection for his cultural vulnerability."[10]

The feeling of "cultural vulnerability" was indeed shared by an entire generation of young Chinese that were drifting without any definite direction to guide them in their striving, goals, or fulfillment. *Again the Palm Trees, Again the Palm Trees* provides us with a valuable conceptual framework for looking at society during the sixties. These societal crises are mirrored through Mou Tianlei's oscillation between optimism and pessimism during the periods before and after his return to Taiwan, as well as his involvement with other characters. Both cultural and personal dimensions are integrated into the social commentary contained within the text, as Mou Tianlei summarizes to his younger sister, Mou Tianmei:

> Once, Gertrude Stein told Hemingway that they were the "Lost Generation." In our case, for our generation, it probably should

be called the "Rootless Generation." Indeed, your guess is right. I will go back to the States, but not for our parents' sake . . . nor for Yishan's [his fiancee's]. . . . It is for my own sake that I will return to the States. . . . Though I have no roots there, I am already used to it, reconciled to it. I am used to the nostalgic feelings that tainted my life there, and at the same time, I now realize that I'm very at ease with the lifestyle there. The most important thing is that I create hope for happiness—hoping to return to Taiwan every few years. If one has a hope like that, one could imagine all kinds of happiness springing from that hope. For instance, like we are now, the happiness of sitting opposite you, telling you my true feelings. (pp. 176–77)

What makes this statement poignant is Yu's concern with the traditionally strained Chinese pattern of communication and with those, like Mou Tianlei, who must bear it. However, the last hope of bridging this gap—Mou Tianlei's hope to stay in Taiwan temporarily to teach and begin a literary journal of substance with his former mentor and teacher, Qiu Shangfeng—vanishes quickly, as unexpectedly as the car accident that abruptly takes Professor Qiu's life.

Thus Mou Tianlei does not pursue his hopes. He has been created by Yu Lihua as a model, portraying the character striving for the most complete self-consciousness possible. However, if he had stayed in Taiwan to continue Qiu's unfulfilled dreams, then the novel might have become a novel of consciousness. As observed by Pai Hsien-yung, also a writer of Chinese exile literature, the consciously thoughtful Mou Tianlei is doomed as surely as those other Chinese intellectuals who are incapable of completing their commitment:

Mou T'ien-lei [Mou Tianlei] is a Rootless Man because, cut off and unfulfilled, he has been transplanted from his motherland before his cultural heritage could come to full personal fruition. . . . The wandering Chinese has become a spiritual exile: Taiwan and the motherland are incommensurable. He has to move on. Like Ulysses, he sets out on a journey across the ocean, but it is an endless journey, dark and without hope. The Rootless Man, therefore, is destined to become a perpetual wanderer.[11]

It does not do justice to reduce this enormously complex novel to a mere emigré student theme. Yet it is crucial to single out this thematic emphasis in order to explore Yu Lihua's intention to encompass the unsuccessful interface between one's past and present, hopes and dreams, and Eastern and Western culture, a common phenomenon of that period.[12] Yu Lihua's dilemma as a writer, though, is that she can retell neither each emigré student's experience of flight and internal alienation, nor the clashes between dreams and reality. She must create Mou Tianlei's story relevant to that milieu, yet form her own story. She must construct a framework that is simultaneously convincing on a realistic level and objective enough to give her story its expansive substance, if she is to communicate the mind-set and existential dilemma common to an important segment of her generation, as she did in this story.

In connection with this "rootless generation" theme, one of Yu's most successful narrative techniques is her antithetical symbolism, namely, her use of palm tree imagery. This particular image evokes deep-rootedness, solidity, overpowering majesty, and the ability to stoically endure the pounding of big or small storms. Yu Lihua purposely selects this image to mock the weakness of the "rootless generation." As the story develops, the palm trees appear erect at four different crucial stages: they satirize the story's tempo; they extend to Mou Tianlei's nonverbalized self-perceptions; they define the story's thematic significance; and, lastly, they constitute the fundamental component of the mocking underlying structure.

Mou first sees the palm trees on the way to his home on Renai Road in Taipei. Their gigantic trunks remind him of his lost youthful dreams, now only hardening his irretrievable sense of loss and lamentation over his past (p. 54). The second time Mou sees the palm trees is during a visit to his alma mater, National Taiwan University. He associates the palm trees with his titanic college ambition to "tower" the world, stand out in the crowd, and make a name for himself. Yet, in the same place, ten years later, he sees in himself nothing but the illusions of his high aspirations (p. 225).

His third encounter with the palm trees is in Tainan, his childhood home, also Yu's childhood home. Mou sees the warm sunlight shining softly on the trunk of a palm tree, giving him a soothing and dependable feeling of security (pp. 273–74). Finally, he sees the palm trees again at his alma mater, after Qiu's death. Stricken by grief, he purposelessly rambles and meanders there, and suddenly comes to the realization that his beloved mentor embodied the essence of the palm trees: majestic, huge, towering, with a sense of mission, armed with positive thinking and strength, and deeply rooted in Chinese culture and tradition (p. 372). This time, the palm tree imagery is an eye-opener for Mou, hopefully constituting a motivating force for continuing his journey of life.

The satirical nature of the theme is marked by Yu's use of the palm tree's resilience, and her stress of this resilience progresses as the imagery appears repeatedly. The palm trees' resilience also serves as the multiple selective omniscience characterizing the protagonist's internal points of view, which in the end metaphorically redeem him by forcing him to reexamine his negative attitudes toward life.[13]

While discussing modern fiction, William James wrote, in *A Pluralistic Universe:* "In the end, nothing less than the whole of everything can be the truth of anything at all." Yu Lihua has dedicated herself to capturing this truth of wholeness. She understands these overseas Chinese scars of survival, the honors and burdens of their "Chineseness," and their inward quest toward some ineffable region of self-worth. These factors continuously affect their personalities in innumerable ways; it is her mission to be their spokesperson, documenting their nuances, vulnerabilities, and complexities. Thus her short story collections, *Autumn Again* (*Yeshi qiutian*, 1964), *Homecoming* (*Gui*, 1966), and *Stars on a Snowy Night* (*Xuedishang de xingxing*, 1966), all touch upon these themes; her lengthy novels, *The Change* (*Bian*, 1965) and *The Task* (*Kaoyan*, 1974), reveal with intensity and forcefulness a detailed account of the spiritual essence of the era in which they lived.

Yu Lihua leaves the reader little doubt that she has always been stronger as an analyst of the theme of rootlessness than as a theorist. A representative novel written during this period, *The Task*,[14] exemplifies her ability to depict the painful tests and pressures that this rootless generation has endured, including career, marriage, and love crises—all taken to *task*—threatened, indicted, and denounced. The return to these particular themes not only coincides with Yu's specific concentration on the professional aspects of her rootless characters, but it also comes at a time when she is probing ever more deeply into one of the phenomenons of modern life, alienation.

The malaise of alienation, according to Yu, is caused by the invisible traditional burden carried by all overseas Chinese intellectuals: "Nothing is as noble as pursuing knowledge" (*Wanban jie xiapin, weiyou dushu gau*). Thus, the first and most urgent thing that a dutiful Chinese person must do is plunge into school, hopefully earning a doctorate to glorify his or her parents and ancestors. Unfortunately, attempts at reaching these goals remain ineffective so long as the individual remains ignorant of the nature of the new world in which one must live. Subtle job discrimination and racial inequality are two of the most common problems seen everywhere.

In comparison with Mou Tianlei, the protagonist Zhong Leping in *The Task* seems to be well-adjusted to American life in the beginning.

He attends a first-rate university, where he obtains his doctorate in physics, and is hired immediately as an assistant professor by a prestigious university. A content and dedicated Chinese-American intellectual who cherishes the values of quality work and family life, he gradually becomes dismayed to find that the visible reality of his skin color and subtle discrimination in the academic field have made the goal of assimilation into the American "melting pot" seem unrealistic and unattainable. The results are heartbreaking dismissals from one university to another and finally the unjust and humiliating treatment he receives during his tenure application. When his departmental chairperson, Arnold, coldly tells him that his tenure appeal was denied, Zhong "felt so chilled, as if he were being doused with icy water from the top of his neck down his spine" (p. 71). This hardworking, conscientious professor is so shocked that he cannot help but ask himself: "How could academicians act so unjustly?" (p. 103). Again, he thought of Arnold's face:

> He still did not understand why Arnold treated him like a scapegoat. Was it jealousy? But, their research specialties were completely different. Could it be that he had offended Arnold? There was no personal contact between them at all. Or, was it because of racial discrimination? (pp. 169–70)

Rage and frustration finally force Zhong to hire a Jewish lawyer to appeal his case. Zhong wins the nasty battle, and the reader feels relieved that at last the protagonist can retain his job and restore his family harmony. Unfortunately, the obsessive, vindictive, and vengeful Arnold makes no attempt to hide his antagonism against Zhong, which finally results in Zhong transferring to another, insignificant university. At the end of the novel, Zhong finds himself alone, without his wife, professional aspirations, or zest for life, in a land which he once believed to be a pluralistic, integrated "melting pot."

Yu Lihua aligns Zhong's alienation with the racial movement in America during the sixties.[15] In its keen observation of ongoing social and political changes, Yu's *The Task* emerges as a justification for the need for racial assertiveness. When readers are left to examine Zhong's life, his inner struggles, and the violation of his pride by prevailing racial prejudices, Yu's novel ceases to remain a reflective and self-conscious work. Instead, it reveals a profoundly ironic and adversarial view of the dual process of equality, be it academic, social, or political. Zhong never really challenges his peers or mocks the tenure process, and he is completely unaware of the nature of the educational hierarchy in which he is supposed to function. His experience reveals the hidden sinister forces of racial discrimination, and conveys an authentic feel of the blunt experience suffered by people living in foreign lands, including Yu's rootless Chinese intellectuals.

Transitional Stage:
Yu's Female Personae and the Search for Self-Identity

The descriptions of Mou Tianlei and Zhong Leping's rootlessness become, in the fictional context, a metaphor for Yu's all-inclusive creative process, embracing denial, powerlessness, dismay, and resignation. These negative connotations of the American Dream push her characters toward the abyss of sorrow and darkness. Another striking approach that best captures this lonely journey is Yu's portrayal of her female characters, from Zhichun of "Zhichun's Decision" to Fu Ruman of *The Fu Family*. The fragility of life is skillfully compressed by Yu into the faces of many Chinese women, whether they are students, housewives, mistresses, young children, or old maids. Their tearful faces and withered souls are a real and collective testimony of the bits and pieces of the existential search for their own identities and sense of recognition. Individually, during this lonely pilgrimage, some find shelter in compromise, some are exploited and paralyzed in a fast-moving society of progress and wealth, some abort their struggles by their own timidity, and some are defeated by the iron hand of reality. It is only a few chosen ones that bravely transform the agony of entrapment into self-assertive transcendence and admiringly confront the totality of life itself.

Yu's female characters are more complex and vulnerable than their male counterparts in terms of fictional intensity. Likewise, they are more concerned with "selfhood" than with "roots." Since their lives are entwined with their male partners, their tasks of finding self-identity are at least three times as difficult: first, because of their "invisible role" as a housewife or mother; second, because of their timidity and traditional stance of silence and conformity; and, third, because of their delayed awareness of self-assertion. Yu aptly describes her own early disillusionment in America: "From a girl holding a dream above her head, . . . to one with the dream in her hands, . . . and finally to one stepping on the dream under her feet. . . ." [16]

Though Yu speaks symbolically and regretfully of the insubstantial, wasteful years of her prime using these three graphically descending nouns, *head*, *hands*, and *feet*, the essence of this quote remains more concrete and specific than any words she has written. In Yu, as well as in her struggling female characters, these words best capture the reality of the search for self-identity and the power of disillusionment. Li Wenlu, the female protagonist of *The Change*, is the thematic embodiment of the mirage of happiness, the ambiguity of identity, and the banality of a spiritually impoverished life, wandering aimlessly in the Promised Kingdom, the United States.

In dealing with these recurring themes, Yu Lihua's two early novellas, "Autumn Again" ("Yeshi qiutian") and "Once upon a Springtime" ("You yige chuntian"),[17] both published in 1963, demonstrate a sensitive revelation not only in terms of the plot, but also in the many emotional and psychological undercurrents that surface.[18] In fact, a closer reading of these symbolic titles reveals that "spring" and "autumn" denote that the existence of each season is but a transitory phenomenon. Yu's heroines, like the cyclic change of seasons, are subject to change and transitoriness, change beyond their understanding. Their lives, like those of Li Wenlu or Wu Siyu, are emphatically meaningless. Yet it should be noted that Yu never uses her stories to insult humanity, nor does she overemphasize human degradation and hopelessness. Despite her detachment in the conclusion of "Autumn Again," she refrains from becoming so naturalistically impersonal that she fails to distinguish humanity's place in the order of things. Yu leaves nothing to fate or blind necessity; everything is always the result of free will and choice. With the absence of religious overtones, Yu's world belongs to men and women, and they must pay for their blunders as well as the good things. Thus, in "Once upon a Springtime," it is not the original sin, but the cardinal sin, prompted by emotional alienation and sexual desire, that becomes the pit into which her protagonist Tan Yunmei falls and from which she must extricate herself. The following are Tan Yunmei's departing words with her young lover, Lu Yu, who works as her children's Chinese tutor. This scene occurs after her son was blinded in a car accident:

I'll never forget the happiness you have given me. Yet, I also want you to remember that once you had a perfect spring, a spring with a lonely middle-aged woman, don't remember anything else. Now, I'm a middle-aged woman who has a son that will never be able to see another spring. I'm determined to sacrifice myself for him. I know from now on, I'll be lonely. Yet, in the midst of loneliness, I'll recollect those happy hours with you. . . . We have to depart, this is necessity. . . . (p. 208)

Equating "spring" with happiness, Yu's "Once upon a Springtime" is but another variation of an overseas Chinese woman's quest for happiness and meaning, and her discovery of the truth of its illusory nature. As we learn from the above passage, Yunmei's search leads her from an emotional attempt to define "happiness" to an objective realization to define "self." Surrounded by her immediate family and blind son, Tan Yunmei at last comes to the conclusion that self-alienation and loneliness in a "foreign land" is not particular, but universal. Her human dignity can be redeemed upon the realization that endurance and perseverance can help her live out her life fully. Furthermore, she realizes that she should not attach herself to the illusion of "love-as-spring." Instead, she should equate herself with the dull and bleak seasons of autumn and winter. Thus, in this painful process of recognition, Tan Yunmei submits herself to the finality of life.

Tan Yunmei and Li Wenlu's essential journeys from the first stage of innocent acceptance, to growing dissatisfaction with marriage and emptiness, and their final grasp at finding their self-identity are the thematic essences which Yu attempts to illuminate. She is recognized by literary critics as the pioneering founder of the philosophy that the search for selfhood begins with high hopes yet inevitably leads to a period of disillusionment before fruition.[19] Not only her married heroines have to pay heavy dues for their marriages, but her single ones must pay as well. In their quest for love, they must drag themselves through the baptism of pretension, self-suppression, and compromise. This is satirically revealed by her choice of story titles, such as "The Waiting" ("Deng"), "Her Choice" ("Tade xuanze"), "The Exchange" ("Jiaohuan"), "Shifted Love" ("Yiqing"), "Goodbye David" ("Zaijian Dawei"), "Zhichun's Decision" ("Zhichun de xuanze"), and *The Fu Family (Fujia de ernumen)*.

"The goal to self-realization," as critic Ye Roxin has described, "is based on a paradoxical fusion of discovering one's own vulnerability and accepting suffering as an honest, engaging act of life itself. The higher the realization, the deeper the suffering."[20] Out of all her works, including the latest one, *The Joy of Reunion (Xiangjian huan, 1989)*,[21] not one of her major heroines can find a reality in herself sufficient to house her soul, and the agony over this terrible conflict between awareness and suffering leads to the character's success in the process of self-discovery.

In her short story "The Waiting",[22] the heroine is an intelligent, charming overseas Chinese student, a "soul in exile." Fan Ben, her steady boyfriend for ten years before coming to the United States, cannot join her because of lack of money. Yu's heroine-narrator states:

He definitely couldn't leave Taiwan this summer. He decided to give it up and asked me not to wait for him. Why didn't he suggest my going back instead? If I returned, we could get married, and both of us could work, which would be sufficient enough to support a family. . . . These two years in the States have been quite harsh indeed. . . . I have come to a kingdom deserted even by God, and attended a school without a single Chinese soul. (p. 94)

She does not go back. Instead, she buries her pride and marries a lustful, rich Jewish widower, Amberson, who is old enough to be her father. Soon her comfortable life is reduced to an empty existence full of frivolous social engagements and superficial personal contacts she uses in an effort to numb herself. Thinking of her mother and Fan Ben, the two most precious people in her life, she sends a thousand dollars to her mother and twelve hundred to Fan. She writes to her mother:

I told him why I had to get married, and I also mentioned that although I "sold" my body for a few thousand dollars, he does not have to "sell" himself in exchange for this twelve hundred dollars. If he comes to the States he will be totally free. My sacrifice, of course, was intended for our future union. Yet, if he refuses to marry me, I could understandably not blame him, because people have different attitudes toward the concept of "love." . . . (pp. 99–100)

Even so, she still dreams of their future reunion. She waits, and two weeks later she receives a letter from her mother:

Dear child, my age is not suitable for me to come to the States to live. It is too late for me to learn a new language and change old habits . . . . However, I am relieved that you have found some-one to settle down with. . . . But, isn't he too old for you? Does he understand you? . . . I threw a small reception here for you. I invited a few relatives and some of your old friends. Fan Ben came, too. He got drunk and shouted that you married your husband for money; he's a rich man, isn't he? I believe you're not so ignorant, but Fan wasn't happy, and I don't blame him. I'm returning the check to you. Dear child, I'm working now. . . . I don't feel safe keeping so much money at home. (pp. 102–3)

Mother's letter shocks her, but Fan Ben's letter is much more painful. It contains nothing except the check she sent him. In the beginning she waits, yet in the end she cannot persuade her mother or Fan to come. Instead, she loses ten years of genuine love as well as her mother's trust. The things she yearns for will never happen. Now she is faced with a new unwanted life, as her doctor informs her that she is expecting.

As the details of our heroine's fate show, Yu is able to objectively show twisted and deformed hope through the direct presence of day-to-day reality. Thus the illusory "waiting" for her beloved mother and boyfriend becomes a synonym for "waiting" for the impossible, which is consistent with Yu's use and modification of the trappings of the American Dream and the loss of self-dignity. According to Yu, because of the protagonist's failure to confront herself honestly in the face of external reality, existence implies suffering. At the end of this story, through these two responses, the reader is aware that the heroine's marriage is in no way justified by her intentions. Instead, it becomes a powerful irony, thwarting and isolating her from seeking future freedom and ideals. However, for Yu, this irony is not the irony of cynical pessimism. On one hand, it reveals the enfolding and inevitable shadow of daily reality; on the other, it exhibits the darker side of man's strength and fortitude for survival. "The Waiting" leads Yu's heroine to an awareness of, and a compromise with, the indifferent and callous totality of life. Be it in the East or West, this totality will always be associated with the unnameable limitations and inabilities of her characters.

Another overseas Chinese woman writer, Nie Hualing, writes about Yu Lihua in the preface for Yu's *Homecoming*:

> Yu Lihua is constantly changing and improving. Each time we meet, she always talks about the books she has read and the new perspectives she has developed. She not only has an enthusiasm for life and abstract ideas, but also has the capacity to absorb anything. Therefore, she always projects herself as an intelligent, refreshing, and lively person. (p. 7)

Nie's statement is a most poignant one. Indeed, Yu's zealousness and observations of reality and ideas extend her thematic contents from the early pessimistic tone, reflecting historical changes and its effects, to an increasingly strident tone as she reorients her writing in a more sociopolitical direction. Politics not only provide Yu with an avenue for change, but they also influence her to write in a more concrete and

humanly specific way than she does in her earlier works. During the
seventies, she demonstrated her capability to keep abreast of the times
through this evolution in her writing. At the very least, she created a
fresh framework of analysis through which cultural and personal
dimensions such as rootlessness and the conflicts between the old
and the new could be integrated into new directions: the search for
the self, identity issues, and political consciousness. As Yu discusses
with Yan Huo:

> Personally, I feel overseas Chinese literature, the literature of the
> rootless generation, started in the fifties and extended fruitfully
> into the decade of the sixties, ending in the early seventies. Since
> 1972, world politics have changed drastically. China and the
> United States have established diplomatic ties, challenging many
> overseas Chinese to confront identity issues and to identify with
> their "politically" recognized China. Now, those wandering Chi-
> nese of yesteryear can return to their own country and devote
> themselves to their homeland. Those who cannot readjust to their
> native soil can always come back to the States again and embark
> upon a life with new perspectives and feelings.[23]

When *New Chinese Women (Xin Zhongguo de nuxing,* 1977) and *The
Fu Family (Fujia de ernumen,* 1978)[24] were published, a significant
change was noted in her portrayal of characters since her 1975 visit to
China. Through them she was anxious to disassociate herself from her
previous pessimistic summarizations. She describes her new attitude
in the preface of *The Fu Family:* "Currently, I, myself, am a happy
person who not only carries an old burden, but also has acquired a new
attitude (p. v)." Here, Yu confesses that the characters of the previous
stage were burdened by their ancestral heritage and blotted out by
culture shock in the United States. However, her recent characters,
especially the female ones, now undergo experiences of self-examina-
tion and realization. In this new state of diplomatic normalization,
many of the old fears, such as deportation and denial of legal residency
status, have been shoved to the back burner, allowing the emergence
of alternative options for Yu's heroines in the critical framework of her
new stories.

The first representative work, *New Chinese Women,* contains seven
short stories. In terms of the overall theme, these stories constitute
three visible and/or invisible realms, and each realm is separated by
Yu's methods of intrinsic typification: the first is the lamentation over
the sufferings of the "old" Chinese society; the second is the excitement

and anticipation of the "new" Chinese society; and the last is the attraction to the American Dream or materialism and eventual disillusionment. By means of these multiple perceptions, almost any given action of her novel can be interpreted on distinct levels of antitheses, producing the effect of simultaneity or concomitance on multiple planes. This particular method resembles Aldous Huxley's *Point Counter Point* technique; Yu achieves her effect by the sudden juxtaposition of various moods and points of view dictated by multiple layers of perception. The following are two such examples:

> It reminded me of a filthy rich friend of mine. His father was once an important Guomindang official in China. Before the Liberation, in 1949, he armed himself with an insurmountable stash of money and valuables and moved his entire family to the States, where they lived off interest like rich idlers. . . . Doesn't he know that these fanciful things in his paradise-like condo are the blood, sweat, and tears of poor Chinese people of the past? (p. 40)

> I have lived so many years in the States, especially in the city. Metropolitan life is meaningless, like back tires endlessly chasing after the front tires. Life is a perpetual rotation from one square box to another: home, car, office, and TV screen, all square boxes. With regard to the countryside, I haven't seen any vast land like China's for years. I don't even know what a cottonfield looks like. (p. 25)

This countertone, in essence, constitutes the characters' underlying disappointment in the failure of their own high aspirations and hopes for both sides of the Pacific, and these unresolved concerns can only be dissolved later in Yu's writings of the eighties.

When *The Fu Family* was published in 1978, Yu Lihua discussed her thematic intentions:

> I am concerned about their [characters'] internal development. I am writing from different levels of the intellectuals' points of view on the scale of individualization that occurs during their journey from the mainland to Taiwan, and then to the States. I am also writing from the perspective of the native Chinese' consciousness in search of identification with the motherland and their own identity. (p. 52)

Thus Yu creates her characters in conceptual terms but articulates them in precise words; they embody her thematic visions and intent. The story centers on five overseas Chinese, all children of the Fu family, and the grand family reunion in Taiwan which includes an elaborate celebration of their father's birthday. As the story unfolds, each of them recalls his or her life in the United States, and leads the reader through a journey into the realm of thought and ideas that manifest themselves in each character's current living situation. Yu explains in her preface that each family member is a slice of life, representing this era's reality:

> [Fu] Ruman, who has lost her purpose to live; [Fu] Rujie, who has lost his job and will to fight; [Fu] Rujun, who has achieved self-actualization through persistence and perseverance; [Fu] Ruhao, who broke away from learned molds and has bid a fundamental transformation in the realm of rich business; and, then there is an unknown yet hopeful sibling, [Fu] Ruyu. . . .

The five Fu children are the authentic embodiment of overseas students who seek to formulate a new worldview, to renovate their cultural order so as to become an integral part of it, or opt toward self-oblivion. Collectively, their multiple perceptions offer Yu diverse and innovative approaches to the concept of internal as well as external exile. In each of them, Yu hints at a drift or estrangement with their native culture, represented by their authoritative father. At the end of the story, it is ironic that Fu Senior collapses from a stroke in the midst of the celebrations, effectively symbolizing the collapse of cultural retention. Yu's story thus expands to confront the ultimate moral and cultural challenges. The shocking nature of the Fu children's anxiousness over the family fortune instead of their father's health implies a pessimistic skepticism about "returning to one's roots," *huigui*, as evidenced in "Coming and Going" ("Guiqu laixi"): "When I was awakened by the early warm sunshine, I realized that I am but a traveler. Taipei is not my home anymore, though time and time again, I have come back for her and left because of her. . . . I am so disappointed . . . it is no longer the same, and even more difficult to recognize any likeness in her at all anymore" (p. 12).

The criticism and allegorization of these changes are distinct. Even if nostalgically Yu exhibits images of disappointment in her characters' attempts at grasping Chinese nativism, she soon discovers, as we have discovered in the Fu saga, that cultural isolation is not self-imposed, but greatly enhanced by an era that, essentially and tragically, is indifferent and unconcerned. Thus cultural background becomes a cross to bear for as long as one tries to carry it in a self-centered, individualistic manner. The alternative solution for Yu, as well as for her characters, is awakening and transcendence, as we find in her latest writings.

### The Latest Literary Stage: Returning and Awakening

In her latest works, Yu Lihua's thematic concerns shift from the portrayal of the limited and incomplete to more reflective preoccupations with constructive reconciliation and recognition. She conveys this reconciliation in the epilogue of *The Joy of Reunion*:

> This is a turbulent era: grand reunions, enormous sorrow and happiness, fulfillment, and despair. . . . Yet, how much happiness, fulfillment, and despair. . . . I am afraid not much, perhaps even none. . . . Yet, each event has two-sided implications: the joyless side of sorrow and happiness, separation and reunion, and the joyful side of sorrow and happiness, separation and reunion. (p. 290)

In the views expressed above, it is clear that a tolerant and coexistent concept of polarity or dualism is acceptable to Yu. Though themes of rootlessness and a host of other manifestations of alienation in her previous works are a large part of overseas Chinese life, the aspirations and goals might be attainable if her characters properly understood these two aspects of reality. If they united their insights concerning the differences and energies of aspiration, they would achieve a balanced level of existence, neither grossly overexaggerating human differences nor ignorantly underestimating tolerance. Be it culture, gender, or the freedom of choice, the fusion of these aspects is the only remedy for freeing oneself from the conflicts produced by the extreme polarities. In "Two Sisters" ("Jiemei yin") and "Mothers and Daughters" ("Munu qing"), both in *The Joy of Reunion* anthology, Yu guides us into this polarized agony through the torment of her heroines, as first seen in "Two Sisters." She then raises them toward redemption, where differences are accepted and reconciled, as evidenced in "Mothers and Daughters."

Yu's themes are subtly interwoven throughout "Two Sisters,"[25] which focuses on the interplay and profusion of different traditions. It renders significance to her work while at the same time providing a comparison of the dichotomies embedded in the collective layers of the overseas Chinese psyche. The plot is a simple and familiar one: an elder sister's brief visit to her home country, Taiwan, after twenty years' absence overseas. The implied meaning of homecoming reveals the emergent values and changes of Yu's time. The narrative presents the story with a minimum of descriptive detail and little introspective analysis expressing the author's point of view; however, it is filled with abundant dialogue, unmannered spontaneity, and numerous situational confrontations. Deliberately isolating the two sisters, Wenying the eldest and Wenyi the youngest, Yu condenses the setting into a microcosm furnishing an immediacy of emotional variables and exposing her characters' naked selves.

As the story unfolds, the younger sister is seen as the conscious embodiment of materialism in Taiwan after twenty years of economic growth. The intrusion of foreign values and the glamorization of the superficial is revealed through Yu's description of Wenyi's makeup:

> Pouring a few drops of Christian Dior moisturizer on her hand, she dotted it on her cheeks, using her palms to smooth it from the wings of her nose outward and upward to the rest of her face. Then she turned on the fluorescent light above the vanity mirror and examined her face closely.

> *Not bad,* she thought, *for a forty-two-year-old!* Although her features were somewhat plain, her complexion was what people usually described as peaches and cream. She had gotten married over a decade ago and had since lived an affluent life-style. Her good fortune enabled her to enjoy the luxuries of protecting her face from the sun, always including fruit and vegetables in her diet, and using the most expensive moisturizers twice a day. With such pampering, the only makeup she ever needed to use was a brilliant red glossy lipstick to set off her snow-white skin. (p. 14)

Although Wenyi is presented in a less than flattering light, her older sister, Wenying, embodies the values of transvaluation and the estrangement of modern Chinese intellectuals and artists. The effect of twenty years' life overseas on Wenying is seen through Wenyi:

> The gate at the passenger's exit opened, and, all of a sudden, a commotion broke out in the crowd. Everyone stood on their toes and waved. Leaning forward to search for Wenying, she didn't see her sister pass right in front of her with a luggage cart. Hardly noticing her amongst the crowd, she kept looking in the other direction. After most of the passengers had left, she was really

beginning to wonder where Wenying was when suddenly she caught sight of a woman standing alone in the waiting area. The woman's gray hair was cut very short, like a man's, and she wasn't wearing any makeup except translucent lip gloss. Her thin, slender eyebrows were dark, accenting her narrow face, but her eyes were very dull. (p. 18)

Instead of giving Wenying a "false" image to comply with the general expectations of glamor, Yu creates a seasoned, mature, middle-aged woman who is unique and unpretentious in her own way. It is in this subtle contrast that the adjective *two* in "Two Sisters" serves not as a mathematical number but rather as a dichotomized metaphor introducing the thematic message by comparing the two different worlds represented by the two protagonists. Ironically, Yu's comparison implies that those who pride themselves the most on being the keepers of Chinese culture, such as the Taiwanese residents Wenyi, her husband Dezhi, and their well-to-do relatives, are the ones least able to cherish or preserve it. Instead, it is these wandering souls, like Wenying, with their enthusiastic thirst for their roots and home, who will be able to strike a just balance between their heritage and themselves. As sarcastically stated by Wenying: "Even though I look old and dry to you on the outside, I'm not old and dry within. Perhaps you can't see it, but others do" (p. 45).

It is undeniable that Yu's attitude toward "returning home" is not a zealous affirmation, but rather a critical assessment. It is an attitude directly related to the dialectic of being-for-oneself or being-for-others. The impossibility of Wenying ever pressuring herself to conform to the unwholesome and false values embodied by Wenyi's vain clothes, placid decor, and snobbish attitudes is the ontological starting point for Yu's discussion of the composite image of a complete Chinese person, be it related to identity, roots, or heritage. It is in this sense that a seemingly perfect union of two sisters could not succeed in achieving harmony.

The failure to achieve harmony between the two sisters is presented primarily through broad use of the techniques of contrast and comparison. For instance, the seasoned Wenying is first seen through a comparison between her previous self and her changed condition under the impact of the passage of time. Then she is seen through a contrast between her new self and her changed and worldly younger sister Wenyi (p. 42).

In most instances, Yu does not inform her reader of the inner workings of these characters' thoughts. She merely presents the multi-faceted elements of materialism and allows the reader to put them together themselves. However, according to Yu, external reality is the projection of inner consciousness, and thus materialism in this story reflects the prevailing mentality among many well-to-do Taiwanese. During her 1987 visit to Taiwan, Yu witnessed this harmful impact on the Taiwanese people. For Wenying, modern advancements such as air conditioning do not soothe her search and purpose for homecoming; they only freeze her to the point of total despair. It is despair brought about by her inability to enjoy products of modernity, her inability to escape from her longing for past warm memories, and above all, her own realization of the perpetual loss of her beloved heritage. Thus the very heart of the matter is the implication that homecoming is but a paradise lost. It is in this sense that Wenying and Wenyi are created as tools to magnify the opposite roles intensified by the passage of time and cultural displacement. Introspectively, their "happy reunion" proves to be nothing but a sarcastic revelation and comment on what has gone wrong with prosperity.

If the number *two* is understood as the two extremities denoting the concepts of materialism and traditionalism in "Two Sisters," then the letter *s* in "Mothers and Daughters" signifies the enduring values of pluralism and the transcendence to a healthier attitude of all-inclusiveness. Similarly, the plot revolves around the reunion of two sisters after thirty years' separation by man-made barriers and politics, and the timeless quality of their mother's and younger sister's foster mother's love. Within this complex frame, Yu renders a vibrant and connected personal and collective account of Chinese history over the past thirty years. Many of Yu's works deal with the themes of alienation and disillusionment as exemplified by the division of China into two separate parts, or by the Pacific Ocean into two distinctive cultures. However, the portrayal of these differences interests her primarily as it affects her characters and their abortive attempts to bridge these divisions. In her latest works, Yu is no longer preoccupied with individuals and the milieu surrounding them. Instead, she attempts to cross over man-made boundaries in order to reach a redeeming, coexisting solution. It is in this sense that the novella "Mothers and Daughters" represents a higher level of understanding and a more gratifying solution for drifting Chinese souls: transcending the boundaries of difference and misunderstanding.

In the story, Shaowen, the major character, teaches college in America and lives contentedly with her widowed mother, choosing to be single. As the story unfolds, we find the determined and headstrong Shaowen just back from her successful visit to China to find her lost younger sister Shaozhen, who was left to her foster mother in mainland China at a tender age. Now the latter, at the age of forty-two, is a mother of six children and an exemplary low-rank worker in a musical instrument factory. She is a living testimony to the social changes and struggles of recent Chinese turmoil, an embodiment of sheer hardship. The imprint of past history is vividly revealed through Yu's description of Shaozhen:

> She was struck with sudden grief. Poor Shaozhen had been abandoned by her parents for half a lifetime and struggled through years of hard labor. Little Wang told her in Beijing that Shaozhen, like a typical peasant, was married at sixteen due to poverty. This was followed by the difficult birth and rearing of six children. She didn't have much of an education, let alone any traveling experience, like Shaowen had. Each line etched on Shaozhen's face was symbolic of a laborious and impoverished life. (p. 35)

Yet, by way of contrast, this external roughness reveals the inner qualities of Shaozhen's striking personality: warm, tender, forgiving, and loving. Shaowen states:

> She did not have many years of schooling and the people around her had a similar background, so her speech and gestures seemed a little dull, or I guess you could say unsophisticated. But, her attitude was different, it's hard for me to explain. After being with her for a few days, I felt that she was much more honest and pure than either Shaoyu or I. And, the more she seemed this way, the guiltier it made me feel. (p. 69)

This internal and external relativism concerning Shaozhen introduces a fundamental principle that is akin to Yu's attitude toward overcoming and transcending superficial differences. Though there is no denial that economic hardship and political differences have a tremendous impact on people, it is only in the souls of Shaozhen's generation and the revelation of spiritual values that the old traditions prevail. The following is a passage Yu uses to indicate that human guilt and misunderstanding can be erased through the original goodness of human nature. The characters begin to think of themselves no longer as separate entities dwelling apart in divided political or economic realms, but rather as concerned members of the same family, harmoniously swept along by the tide of their destinies:

Silently, Shaozhen got up. It was cold. She put on her mother's jacket and went into her room. Luckily, the moonlight was coming directly through the windows, so there was no need to turn on the light. Shaozhen reached for her clothes and was about to leave when she saw that part of the lavender blanket had slipped off to the ground. She quickly put her clothes down, bent over to pick up the blanket, and tucked it around Mother's neck. As her hands touched the pillow, they paused. The pillow was wet. Suddenly, Mother extended her arm, grabbed her shoulder and said, "Shaozhen, I'm sorry! I know in my heart that I love you, I just couldn't say it out loud."

Shaozhen threw herself in front of mother's bed, half kneeling down, her head resting on the blanket under mother's neck. Her tears poured down like a waterfall.

A hand patted her gray hair. She curled her body in the stillness. She wouldn't dare; she couldn't; she wouldn't. It wasn't her foster-mother's hand. The hand was softer and weaker than foster mother's.

It was Mother's hand. Her real mother's hand. (p. 138)

It is this extended loving hand that not only symbolically joins the engulfed misunderstandings and differences but also strongly bridges the dichotomized polarity of Yu's heroines. The final reconciliation reveals Yu's attempt to eradicate these differences accumulated over years of harsh sociopolitical reality. To Yu, the Chinese cultural heritage is the sum total of intellectual and humanistic achievements, and can be varied and adapted from time to time and place to place. In this sense, these four protagonists embody the realistic totality of the past thirty years. This is especially unique in view of Yu's earlier works, in which polarities are revealed but rarely reconciled. Thus it is instantly striking to find, in this latest novella, four symbolic areas of synthesis rather than antithesis.

First, Shaowen is explicitly created to represent the overseas Chinese "Ulysses," searching and attempting to find her lost home and roots. Her sister, Shaozhen, the embodiment of Chinese chastity as symbolized by her name, *zhen*, is the source of hope and inspiration for all Chinese at home or abroad. Second, their birth mother and foster mother, who have provided life and nourishment for the two sisters, are the essence and spirit of Chinese culture. Third, Shaowen and

Shaozhen also symbolize the inner and outer reality of Chinese people in their many manifestations. The two mothers are symbolical tools used to erase tensions or resentment created by geographical displacement and political divisions. Finally, they were all created to expand the definition and significance of harmony and coexistence. Thus, each of them synthesizes the polarities of life which correspond to the cultural totality they symbolize.

## Conclusion

In the article "Divided Nation, Undivided Land: On the Nativism of Chinese Overseas Writers" ("Guopo shanhe zai: Haiwai zhojia de bentuxing"), Zhang Cuo discusses Chinese overseas literature as part of authentic Chinese literature. Referring to some writers residing in the States, Zhang states:

> Their writings are definitely not English literature, nor American literature. Overseas Chinese in foreign lands declare they have no home, but that their home spreads out with them as they go and includes every inch of their wandering. They declare they have no country, but under their divided nation remains the undivided land.[26]

The common sentiment, shared by almost every critic, is that overseas Chinese writers embark on their own personal quests through their writing, displaying a soulful yearning for their homeland. In them, we find a conscientious choice to write not only in the name of art, but also with a sense of mission that is courageous and morally responsible.[27]

It is in this sense that Yu Lihua's works have their historical and literary significance. The literary stages we have discussed reflect the development of overseas Chinese literature during the past four decades. From the thematic emphasis on rootlessness, to the search for self-identity, to the concept of homecoming, Yu Lihua's novels reveal three overall stages in the development of her creative vision. The first stage, of which *Again the Palm Trees, Again the Palm Trees* is representative, understandably adheres most closely to the theme of rootlessness. Yu's emphasis centers around the various shapes and colors that provide the "drifting" qualities of her characters. They feel as though they are cut off from the world of the familiar and normal, and their very existence in a pluralistic society ironically threatens their ideals, beliefs, and ways of life. These drifting qualities intensify their isolation, which in turn forces them to gradually withdraw from involvement or community, finally sinking into the consolation of solitude.

The second stage, with its emphasis on female protagonists, as in *The Fu Family*, is revealed through variations of the conditions seen in *Again the Palm Trees, Again the Palm Trees*. Yu has shifted from the previous stage of "helplessness" to a stage of "hopelessness" and cultural confrontations. The years of struggling and adjusting to a new life in the land of opportunity appear to dull Yu's characters' zest for the American Dream. They are tired of the struggle and seldom develop a healthy awareness and appreciation of the world around them. Likewise, the notions of polarity between East and West, homeland and the exiled realm, as well as the broader view of reality and illusion, seem to retard or even abort their potential to embrace and affirm different aspects of life in this pluralistic society. Female characters, such as Tan Yunmei and the Fu sisters, are thus created to satirize the positive feelings of union, home, and hope through Yu's descriptions of the pathetic compromises they make concerning marriage, money, and their careers. Some of their actions even sink themselves deeper into trouble, such as Li Wenlu's descent into a hell-like home environment, serving as highlighted sarcasm against those overseas intellectuals whose original purpose of coming to the United States was symbolically considered an upward progression away from their past. The disillusionment from this second point eventually leads to a heightened sense of confrontation. Their desperate clinging to the old and recollections of the past further intensify the reciprocally hostile polar opposites where every aspect of life is denied and there is a dichotomy between dream and reality, past and present, and East and West.

The latest stage in Yu's writing is expressed through a more introspective subtlety, engaged in the attempt to reconcile this polarity antithesis. In "Mothers and Daughters," Yu illustrates that both poles are equally endearing, and that through the laws of humanity one can overcome prejudice, allowing harmonious coexistence. At this stage, there are neither negative feelings nor obsession with rootlessness. Instead, the awareness of rootlessness becomes a positive force, transforming man's soul into a more affirming strength, seeking inclusiveness as the ultimate goal, as Shaowen, Shaozhen, their mother, and the latter's foster mother symbolize.

Yu Lihua's fiction truly reflects the reality of life for overseas Chinese intellectuals. Though it is difficult to measure the full impact of the cultural and existential reality of her fictional material, few writers dealing with the same themes are able to achieve the same depth and complexity in their writing. This analysis has indicated how her themes of alienation emerge directly from her own personal encounter with reality and how these feelings dictate the main thread of her story development. Yu's diligent and skillful thematic progression is an affirming and upward movement from rootlessness to reconciliation and from alienation to a full-fledged, well-rounded Chinese person whose all-embracing ideal of humanity makes nationality of secondary significance.

## Notes

1. To explore concepts and rhetorics of exile in Western literature, including various origins, periods, and themes, see Maria-Ines Lagos-Pope, ed., *Exile in Literature* (London: Associated University Presses, 1988); Michael Seidel, *Exile and the Narrative Imagination* (New Haven, Conn.: Yale University Press, 1986); Sam B. Girgus, *The New Covenant: Jewish Writers and the American Idea* (Chapel Hill: University of North Carolina Press, 1984); Andrew Gurr, *Writers in Exile* (Atlantic Highlands, N.J.: Humanities Press, 1981); Grace Farrell Lee, *From Exile to Redemption: The Fiction of Isaac Bashevis Singer* (Carbondale, Ill.: Southern Illinois University Press, 1987); and Jean DeJean and Nancy K. Miller, eds., *Displacements* (Baltimore, Md.: Johns Hopkins University Press, 1991).

2. See Yan Huo, "Yu Lihua yu liuxuesheng wenxue" ("Yu Lihua and Overseas Chinese Literature"), in *Haiwai huaren zuojia lüeying* (*Brief Sketches of Chinese Writers Overseas*) Hong Kong: Joint Publishing Co., 1984), pp. 32–53.

3. Vivian L. Hsu, ed., *Born of the Same Roots: Stories of Modern Women* (Bloomington: Indiana University Press, 1981), p. 183.

4. Yan Huo, p. 42.

5. See also Frank Chin's *Donald Duk* and two newcomers in the literary arena, Gish Jen's *Typical American*, and Gus Lee's *China Boy*. For further information, see "Chinese-American Writers" in *Shijie ribao*, weekly supplement, special issue (July 7, 1991): 1–2, 4–6.

6. Amy Ling comments on these representations since the 1960s: "The stereotypes continue to serve as blinders for dominant Americans and to stand as barriers to the fullest acceptance and development of Asian-American women." See Amy Ling, *Between Worlds: Women Writers of Chinese Ancestry* (New York: Pergamon Press, 1990), p. 12.

7. See Chen Ruoxi's "Bentu yu xintu" ("Homeland and New Land") in "Dongxifeng," *Zhongbao* (December 17, 1985); and Zhang Cuo's "Guopo shanhe zai: Haiwai zuojia de bentuxing" ("Divided Nation, Undivided Land: On Overseas Chinese Writers' Nativism"), *Lianhe wenxue 7*, no. 3 (January 1991): 24–28.

8. Taipei: Huangguan, 425 pages. First edition, 1967; tenth edition, 1980. Reprints include Fujian: Fujian renmin, 1982; and Beijing: Youyi, 1984. The movie right was purchased by producer Li Hanxiang in 1968.

9. "Sorrow at the End of the Yangtze River, " written in English. It was published in *UCLA Review* (March 1957): 1–13.

10. See Pai Hsien-yung, "The Wandering Chinese: The Theme of Exile in Taiwan Fiction," *Iowa Review 7*, nos. 2–3 (Spring–Summer 1976): 205–12.

11. Ibid., pp. 208–9.

12. See further analysis of this novel by Yin Di, "*Youjian zonglu, youjian zonglu*" ("On *Again the Palm Trees, Again the Palm Trees*"), in *Yin Di kan xiaoshuo* (Taipei: Dajiang, 1970), pp. 177–84; and Ouyang Yinzhi, "Guowang de xinyi: Boxi meiyougen di yiqun" ("Emperor's New Clothes: Analysis of the Rootless Generation"), *Nanbeibao yuekan*, no. 95 (April 16, 1978): 53–58.

13. See detailed analysis of this novel by Xia Zhiqing (C. T. Hsia), "Ping Yu Lihua de *Youjian zonglu, youjian zonglu*" ("Analysis of Yu Lihua's *Again the Palm Trees, Again the Palm Trees*"), which has been included as the novel's preface, pp. 7–24. Xia praises Yu's skill in creating vivid and impressionistic descriptions, and at the same time giving each one emotive and realistic touches.

14. *Kaoyan* (Taipei: Dadi); first edition, 1974; second edition, 1975. Reprint, Beijing: Renmin wenxue, 1982.

15. See Zhong Meiyin, "Xiaotan Yu Lihua de *Kaoyan*" ("Brief Discussion of Yu Lihua's *The Task*"), *Zhongguo shibao* (April 13, 1975); and Ding Ling, "Yu Lihua" ("On Yu Lihua"), *Tianjing shibao* (February 1983).

16. Preface in *Homecoming (Gui)* (Taipei: Wenxing, 1966), p. 9.

17. Both stories are collected in *Autumn Again (Yeshi Qiutian)* (Taipei: Wenxing, 1964), pp. 9–159 and pp. 161–209.

18. For discussion of these and other stories, see the article by An Ran, "Ping *Yeshi qiutian*" ("On *Autumn Again*"), in *Gongjiaobao* (October 24, 1969).

19. In regard to these salient characteristics of her philosophy, see Feng Zusheng, "Xiaotan Yu Lihua de tansuo" ("On Yu Lihua's Search"), *Zhongshan daxue xuebao*, no. 1 (1981): 32–41. Also see Chen Ruiwen, "Yu Lihua de changpian xiaoshuo: *Bian* zhong de renwu ji zhufubing" ("Yu Lihua's Novel: Discussion of Characterizations and Female Problems in *The Change*"), *Zhongwai wenxue*, no. 12 (May 1974): 30–42.

20. For details, see Ye Ruxin, "Yu Lihua de daolu" ("The Literary Path of Yu Lihua"), in *Taiwan zuojia xuanji* (Taipei: Zhongliu, 1966), pp. 115–27.

21. Taipei: Huangguan, 1989, 289 pages.

22. "The Waiting" ("Deng"), collected in *Stars on a Snowy Night* (Taipei: Huangguan, 1966), pp. 102–26.

23. Yan Huo, pp. 43–44.

24. *New Chinese Women (Xin Zhongguo de nuxing)* (Hong Kong: Qishi niandai, 1977); and *The Fu Family (Fujia de ernumen)* (Hong Kong: Tiandi, 1978).

25. For the original, see *Xiangjian huan (The Joy of Reunion)* (Taipei: Huangguan, 1989), pp. 13–46. The English version of "Two Sisters," included in this collection, is translated by Michelle Yeh and myself. Page numbers refer to the original.

26. Zhang Cuo, p. 27.

27. Ibid., pp. 24–28.

Nie Hualing

聂华苓

# Nie Hualing

Nie Hualing (b. 1925) was born in the Hubei Province in central China to a traditional family caught up in the revolutionary changes that were sweeping the country. Her grandfather's career as a scholar-official was cut short by Dr. Sun Yat-sen's revolution in 1911. Her father, an army officer in the Nationalist government, was killed by the Communists. During the Sino-Japanese War, she went to Chongqing as a refugee student, attending middle school and then college. Shortly after graduating from the Western Languages Department of National Central University in 1948, she and her family fled to Taiwan, where she began her literary career.

During her fifteen years in Taiwan, Nie Hualing established herself as a short story writer and as literary editor of the prestigious and reform-minded magazine *The Free China Fortnightly* (*Ziyou zhongguo*). The stories she published during the fifties were among the few serious works being produced at a time when the literary scene was dominated by anti-Communist propaganda. Eschewing politics, she sought to portray the mainlanders who were caught between their struggle to make a living in Taiwan and their longing for the homeland they had left behind. Her association with *The Free China Fortnightly* was both salutary and unfortunate.* It brought her into contact with the best intellectual minds on the island; it also brought her face to face with the Guomindang secret police. When the government finally closed down the outspoken magazine and imprisoned its publisher Lei Zhen, Nie was put under police surveillance.

In 1964, Nie came to America at the invitation of the Writer's Workshop at the University of Iowa. She was actively involved with the school's International Writing Program, serving first as associate director and, for the past ten years, as director. As co-founders of this unique program established to foster international understanding, she and her late husband, Paul Engle, were nominated for the Nobel Peace Prize. She retired from the program two years ago in order to devote more time to writing. She now serves as the foundation president for *Today* literary magazine.

During her tenure at Iowa, Nie played a triple role as editor, literary critic, and creative writer. She and her husband edited translations and literary works by various authors from around the world. She wrote a study of Shen Congwen [Shen Ts'ung-wen], a well-known Chinese writer active during the 1920s and 30s, and edited the two-volume *Literature of the Hundred Flowers*. This work was the first attempt to introduce to English readers the literature produced in the People's

Republic of China during the short-lived "Hundred Flowers Movement" of 1956. The annual gathering of Chinese writers in Iowa, which she started in 1979, is also the first such event to bring together writers from mainland China, Taiwan, and overseas Chinese communities.

Nie has written four novels or novellas and eight volumes of short story collections, prose, and essays. Because of her bilingual talents, she has accumulated an impressive reputation as a translator from Chinese to English and vice versa. She is also credited with at least seven volumes of translated literary and critical works.

## Note

* From an account of the *Free China Fortnightly* incident, see Nie Hauling's essay "Yi Lei Zhen" ("Remembering Lei Zhen"), in *Aihehua zaji: Sanshi nian hou (Notes from Iowa: After Thirty Years)* (Hong Kong: Joint Publishing Co., 1983), pp. 326-344.

# Many Things to Tell, but Hard to Tell[1]

## Nie Hualing

Red, pink and white roses bloomed wildly in the garden, adding a touch of color to the small stone house. Lotus saw the roses as she left the house at dawn. She knew that Mary had watered and fertilized them to keep them blooming. She didn't dare pick a single blossom.

Birds twittered in the maple woods. Father was back there where the birds were calling. Lotus headed in that direction.

She saw the water tower and the red frame house. Large fields of corn, soybeans, and clover stretched out over the horizon—patches of light and dark green. White farm houses, round gray silos, old windmills, white sheep, and brown cows—that was Iowa.

Thin mist enveloped the hills. A light rain was falling. The Wapsi River flowed at the bottom of the hill. Lotus could not see it hidden by the woods on the hillside. But she could hear the water flowing. Where was it flowing? She didn't know. The waters of the Yangzi River flowed into the Eastern Sea, she knew that. Her childhood had been left on that river.

Lotus made her way around the mansion. The daisies along the path were in full bloom. She made a large bouquet and headed toward the birds calling in the maple woods. Her father had probably picked these same daisies and had walked along the same path. A small cardinal, a blue bird, an oriole flew among the trees, a rabbit hopped along the path, right in front of her, not the least afraid. This was a new experience for Lotus. If people feared other people, birds would also fear people. People could capture them, beat them, strangle them, crush them. She shook her head. She couldn't even escape from the bird, which her mother had loved and Lotus had crushed with her own feet in the Cultural Revolution. Even birds in Stone City were so free, not afraid. If it weren't for Grandma—

Lotus looked up. There was Grandma, back to her, standing in the graveyard and staring at Bill's grave. In her hands was a bouquet of pink roses. Lotus wanted to turn and flee. Grandma turned around.

The two of them froze, one in the maple woods with a bouquet of roses in hand, the other outside the maple woods with a bouquet of daisies. The little rabbit darted happily on the ground between them, its little eyes shining. But the two of them didn't move. Mary vaguely shook her head. Perhaps she could not believe that Lotus, that Chinese girl, stood before her, or she didn't approve of that Chinese girl coming to visit her son's grave.

"Grandma," Lotus finally said. "I'm sorry. But I didn't know you were here."

"You ought to know." Mary pointed the roses at Lotus. "My son is here. I've been coming here every weekend since he was brought back here. The old man didn't know about it before, either."

"Why?"

"Why? So he wouldn't be sad. I wanted to protect him. He used to be busy with the farm. Now he's had a stroke. As long as he's alive, I won't die. As long as I'm alive, he won't die." Mary paused, pointing at the cemetery. "This is my place. Other people don't come here. Just me. Why have you come?"

"I want to see Father."

Mary walked slowly toward Lotus, looking her straight in the eye. "You came to meet Billy. You came here last night. I know. There was a bouquet of daisies on the grave."

"No, no." Lotus shook her head. "I came to see Father, not Billy."

"You never saw him. Can you have feelings for him?"

"Yes, very deep feelings."

"I don't believe it. You've never mentioned your mother, and she's still alive. But you've come all the way to Stone City to find your dead—all right, your father. What are you up to?"

"Nothing. Very simple. I've come to my father's place to see my grandpa and grandma. If you don't like me, I can move now. But if you say I'm not William Brown's daughter, I won't leave."

"All right, I agree you are his daughter."

Lotus stared at her, trying to figure out if Mary meant what she said. Mary stared back at her without any expression.

"Grandma, you hate me. Why?"

"I hate Chinese."

"Why?"

"They killed my son."

"Mother said he was wounded by mistake, died in the student movement during the Chinese Civil War."

"It was a plot! A plot!" Mary shouted, agitated. "Chinese hate Americans. They call us paper tigers, imperialists, capitalists."

Paper tigers, imperialists, capitalists—these words were all too familiar. Lotus had yelled them herself during the early days of the Cultural Revolution. But how was she to explain the evolution of Chinese history to this American grandma in Stone City?

"Grandma, that happened a long time ago. It's different now."

"But too late! My son is dead. Do you know how young he was when he died? Do you know how much he meant to me? Do you know what has kept me going all these years? Do you know how lonely two old people can get? Do you know how old people feel when there's no one to help? How they can just die and stink and no one cares?"

Lotus moved closer, wanting to comfort her, but not knowing what to say. She only reached in her pocket and took out a handkerchief to hand her.

Mary shook her head. "I don't use other people's handkerchiefs." Tears flowed down her wrinkled cheeks.

"Grandma, I can't explain things about me, my mother and China in a few words. Please give me a little time."

"I haven't got much time left. All I want is to have a few more days of peace before I die. I don't need any excitement to get me all riled up."

"If I bother you, I'll move out now," Lotus said calmly.

"The old man wouldn't stand for it. It might kill him."

"Oh, what do you want me to do?"

"I don't know. I just don't know." Mary walked over to Bill's grave and laid the pink roses down next to the gravestone. She then turned around and walked away, her back bent, coughing.

A fine rain began to fall.

Lotus stared as she went away. She wanted to go and help her, but she was afraid Mary would get upset again. Lotus went over and laid the bouquet of daisies on the other side of the grave. She looked again at the inscription:

William Brown (1920–1949) Died in China

"Is Lotus a Communist, Pa?"

"Whatever Party she belongs to, she's still my granddaughter."

Lotus overhead her grandparents speaking when she pushed the door open returning from the cemetery. She wiped her shoes on the doormat, said "good morning" toward the two old folks in the room, and started up the stairs. They were sitting at the small round table in the kitchen, drinking coffee.

"Lotus," Old Brown called to her, "come on in. Have a cup of coffee and talk with me."

Lotus poured a cup of coffee from the coffeepot on the stove and sat down beside the small round table.

"You've been out for a walk, haven't you?" Old Brown asked.

Lotus nervously nodded and stole a glance at Mary. Her face showed no emotion.

Old Brown looked out the window. Lotus followed his glance, mechanically copying his reaction. They could see the light and dark green of corn and soybeans. The blurred outlines of two or three white sheep and brown cows were barely visible in the misty rain, but the color of the fields was distinct and fresh, with the sheen of the water. The chirping of the birds seemed even clearer, filtered through the rain.

"Lotus, do you like your father's old home?"

Lotus gave an embarrassed nod, and glanced again at Mary. She was still stone-faced. Stone City was really true to its name: cold and hard.

"When your father was little, Stone City was really something," he said. "Life revolved around the general store out by the Wapsi River. It was the train station as well as the post office. At that time there were only some twenty families living in Stone City. They'd go down there every day to pick up their mail and buy things in the store. I ran the store, was postmaster and stationmaster all at the same time." He laughed. "Lotus, I'm an old soldier. In the First World War, I was decorated for bravery, and visited places all over Europe. But you know, I still like being the owner of that small store best. I did everything. The train would come every afternoon right at 5:55. I'd be out on the platform waiting for the mail sack. Bill would ride the pony down from the mansion to watch the train running and blowing its whistle. He never got tired of seeing it come. I had a cousin who lived in Greeley, Iowa. She raised chickens, made the best fried chicken—so crisp and delicious. She'd give a box to the conductor of the train. As soon as the train arrived, he'd hand me the fried chicken."

"I loved to sit around and talk." Mary couldn't help joining in the conversation when it dealt with the good old days. "The store sold candy, cigars, cigarettes, Coke, ice cream. People coming in for their mail would always buy a little something and sit down a while. They'd gossip about their neighbors doing this or that—there was nothing in Stone City I didn't know about."

"And everyone else knew all about what was going on in your family, too," Old Brown said.

"Well, there wasn't anything in our family that other folks could gossip about. The four of us were happy and worked hard. But, in the fifties, the post office closed. In the sixties, the store closed. From then on Stone City was dead to the world—no more postmark of its own. Now, Stone City's become contaminated with all these outsiders."

Lotus froze. She, too, was an outsider and moreover, was a foreigner. When she was in China, she had also been a "foreigner."

"Lotus," Old Brown said. "I've wanted to ask you this ever since you came. When did your mother and father meet? How did they meet? Why didn't they come back to the States together? There are two big cardboard boxes up in Bill's room with letters, journals, clippings, and pictures from his years in Chongqing and Nanjing. I've looked them all over. But there isn't much about your mother. Every once in a while there would be a sentence or two about a Chinese girl in his diary, but it didn't look like the two of them were in love. After he died, the Communists took over Nanjing immediately. The American Embassy shipped his ashes back home. That was it. Nobody came forward and said 'I'm Bill Brown's wife.' Why not? Why didn't she?"

"I don't understand either," Mary interjected. "We didn't have the faintest idea he had gotten married in China."

"I don't know very much about them," Lotus replied.

"Your mother never told you?"

"At first he, excuse me, she couldn't talk about it. Later, there wasn't any time to tell me."

"Of course she didn't talk about it," Mary said. "Americans were paper tigers—imperialists."

Lotus bit her lips.

"America is the best country in the world! I'm proud of my country."

"I'm proud of China!" Lotus replied, not knowing how she could utter these words. When she was in China, she hadn't felt proud of China. She had only felt disillusioned and lost.

"Lotus, the problems of the older generation, the problems between China and America, don't concern you," Old Brown said. "You're Bill's daughter. You're one of the Brown family. Stone City is your home."

How many years had Lotus been waiting to hear those words. "One of the Brown family." "Stone City is your home." But now she realized that she'd still be a "foreigner" in Stone City.

"Grandpa, I don't have a home. I'm used to it." She stood up. "Do you want any more coffee?"

"No, thanks," Old Brown said. "Lotus, if you have any problems, just let me know."

"All right, Grandpa. But, I don't have any."

Lotus went upstairs and headed straight for Bill's room. She noticed that the Bible which her mother had wanted her to bring along had been added to the things on the desk. She recalled the footsteps she had heard outside the door the first night she came. She now was certain that it had been Mary taking the Bible into Bill's room.

When Lotus went to visit Bill's grave she had invaded Mary's territory. Coming into "Bill's room" now was trespassing on Mary, too. It was a never-ending war, but the object they fought for had vanished thirty-three years ago.

Lotus stood nervously in Bill's room. When there was some noise from downstairs, she tiptoed to the door and listened. No one came. When she was in the room she felt as if she were living with her father. The closet floor and shelves were piled high with his books, scrolls, journals, photo albums, and newspaper clippings. There were also two large cardboard boxes on the closet floor. On one was written "Chongqing (1943–1945)—Bill." On the other, "Nanjing (1947–1949)—Bill." Lotus opened the two boxes—the Chongqing box was full of letters, journals, notebooks, and pictures, but the Nanjing box held only several photographs and a few letters. Two boxes of China's wars—the war against Japan and the later Civil War. She had come from thousands of miles away to find the Chinese cities here in Stone City—the cities where her father had once lived. She picked up a notebook out of the Chongqing box. Inside were miscellaneous jottings and short journals. She started to read it, standing by the closet.

Chongqing is cold, damp and overcast. No sun in half a year. But mountains, rivers, and city are beautiful. The steep mountain-side, the dense fog, the crisp tinkling of bells, bamboo torches suddenly lit up in the fog—a man comes riding a horse out of the mist. The bells still jangling on the horse.

Black-clothed policemen, crippled beggars. Stinking kerosene lamps. Rats race down the streets. How I miss the Brown Mansion and that green, green valley.

Today is my birthday—August 18—but no hickory nut cake from Mom. Making hickory nut cake is a great Brown family tradition. Nancy and I would shinny up the tree and toss nuts down into the basket underneath the tree. We each had our own basket.

We'd compete with each other to see who could pick the most nuts. Mom, Nancy and I would gather around the kitchen table and hull the nuts by hand. Our fingers would turn brown from hulling. Father would smell the hickory nut cake baking in the oven before he opened the door. "Hickory nut cake—smells delicious!" he'd shout as he came in. I love all of them.

China's war against Japan isn't just a war to fight the Japanese. It's a time of self-awakening for the Chinese, a turning point in Chinese history.

I was downtown late one night. Drafted soldiers were carrying backpacks, holding paper umbrellas, wearing straw sandals. They looked straight ahead. The guard carried bayonets.

There are two types of Americans in Chongqing (my beloved countrymen, it wasn't until I was abroad that I realized how important you are to me). One type is disillusioned because they came to look for "old" China. The other type admires the strength and perseverance of the Chinese in their struggle to survive. I belong to the second type.

The Chinese aren't a people who fear death. They celebrate death. They happily go about preparing red coffins and colorful shrouds for themselves. The funeral procession for the dead is a happy affair—beating drums, blowing horns, even the Western trombones playing "The Merry Widow." The Chinese are really inscrutable. But Iowans also celebrate death—they eat a lot of food after a funeral.

The Chinese language is music. The Chinese express their feelings by the tones of the language, not by facial expressions, just the opposite of Americans. They also express themselves when they eat: Moaning, sighing, exclaiming in joy or surprise— Oh! Oh! Oh! They cry, their voice rising and falling, like the groan of lovemaking. When we eat we don't express anything. We sit straight in our chairs, knives and forks, one in each hand. It's so dull.

Chinese women are spring breezes, or silk, or satin, projecting a calm, radiant happiness to others. I don't know how to behave with them. I'd rather have a vivacious, cheerful, outgoing Iowa girl—Lucy, how are you doing? Is the windmill still there? We used to climb that windmill when we were little, watching it turn in the wind. It would turn so slowly. When the windmill was about to switch directions, I'd yell at you: "Lucy, hurry! Go to the other side!" Mom would stand under the windmill yelling, "Bill, hurry up! Come down. You could get killed up there!" We'd already be on the other side when the windmill changed direction. We'd laugh.

Chinese music is part of everyday life. The shouts of the coolies, the singing of the riverboat pullers, the cries of hawkers on the streets. The Chinese even make music when begging: beating two pieces of bamboo and singing about poverty, hunger, death, war and etc. Often there will be a crowd of people in the street encircling two people singing. It sounds to me like an opera. But people in the crowd say they're having a quarrel.

It's a great challenge to come to Chongqing. China is at the other end of the earth. It is true. Europe is closer to America. When I first arrived I was quite unhappy, but got used to the life here after a while. Perhaps because I met a lot of young Chinese. I teach English in the Training Program for Chinese Interpreters who will work with Americans. Some Chinese professors also teach in the Training Program in addition to their regular duties at their universities. They are very poor. Some professors carve chops, sell clothing or set up roadside stands to sell goods in order to earn a little extra money to raise their families. Young people feel very depressed and wonder where China is going. Left? Right? The Chinese youth are China's conscience. Everybody in China fears civil war.

Chiang K'ai-shek came to our program to preside over the graduation ceremony. He called the roll one by one. He delivered a speech, encouraging young people to propagate Chinese traditional moral values in order to ensure victory in the Sino-Japanese war, and to make China strong. When he finished his speech, the whole student body and faculty rose to their feet waving their arms and shouting "Long live Chairman Chiang." But we Americans couldn't make ourselves join in with them.

Tushan, close to Chongqing, was lost to Japanese. Peace talks between the Nationalists and Communists have broken off. Everyone is scared. Many young people have joined the army. Students in the Training Program have increased all of a sudden. Too much emphasis on political ideology for the students. There ought to be more emphasis on strengthening their English ability.

Professor Li from National Central University also teaches in the Training Program. He has a doctorate from Yale. A perfect gentleman, proud, dignified. Of the Chinese intellectuals, I admire him most. He overworked himself, died suddenly of a heart attack. Jin Yan took me to the memorial service in his honor.

Lotus was surprised to find her stepfather's name appearing in her father's diary. So her two fathers had known each other in Chongqing during the Sino-Japanese War. She turned to the next page, looking for her mother's name, Fenglian.

If you want to understand China, the best way is to have tea in tea houses. Chinese students love to go to tea houses. But it's a first for me. They can sit there for hours on bamboo chairs, drinking piping hot tea in covered tea cups. Jin Yan took me to a small tea house situated along the Jialing River. Slogans posted on the wall read: "Obey the Supreme Commander Chiang!" "Don't discuss political affairs." Jin Yan's girlfriend, Liu Fenglian, was also there. An innocent young girl.

Her mother's name finally appeared. Lotus's heart began to thump, as if she were probing into her parents' secrets. She quickly leafed through the next several pages trying to find another mention of her mother.

In April I was transferred to Operational Service of Supply in Xian to work as a liaison officer. We transport war material and cooperate with guerrilla forces and the local Chinese. We have set up an intelligence network there to deal with Japanese forces. The Burma Road from Kunming has been cut off. Every drop of gasoline and ammunition has to be airlifted from India over the Himalayas to China. I came over the Hump to China. There was engine trouble, we almost went down. I hope to live long enough to return to Stone City.

China is in great need of American assistance. But the Chinese seem to be suspicious of Americans transporting war materials to China, especially the Chinese in the deep interior of the country. They haven't had much contact with foreigners. You can't really blame them. For the past hundred years, China has suffered from foreign imperialism and many large cities became concessions, divided up by foreign powers. It would be like a friend taking over the Brown Mansion and inviting his friends to take over the water tower, the small stone house, the fields. But the Brown family would be forced out to live in the slums. If that happened, we would also want to throw out the foreigners.

The Chinese are a great people—even the mentally retarded love their country. There are many moving stories. But there are brave Americans here as well, like my friend Franklin. He stayed all by himself in a broken-down temple on a mountain and directed one squadron after another of B-29 bombers in their fight against a division of mounted Japanese soldiers.

Nationalists, Communists, Japanese—they fight with one another. We cooperate with both the Nationalist guerrillas and the Communist guerrillas. We have only one goal: to defeat our common enemy, Japan. Nationalism is most important to the Chinese right now. The youth have a sense of mission: to make a free and independent China after the war. Even the children fear civil war. The Nationalists attack all the political dissidents. Terrorism and oppression may drive intellectuals, especially the young, to the left.

Lotus hurriedly skimmed the text, looking only for her mother's name, Fenglian. She had almost finished the notebook without coming across *Fenglian*.

The airplane had engine trouble, but I got out of it with my life. My parachute happened to land in a village. The peasants are especially friendly to Americans who have landed there. The Chinese peasant is very much like the Iowa farmer—hardworking, sincere. The one fortunate thing to come out of this misfortune has been my opportunity to have close and daily contact with the Chinese people. So many stories about their heroic deeds—I'd have to write a book about them. When we came back alive, our colleagues had a big celebration. They thought we had died.

Lotus continued to skim through the diary. So her father had been "sent down to the peasants' village," too. Father and daughter would have had a lot to talk about. Through her father's eyes, the Sino-Japanese War was more real to her now. It was a pity that he had not written about his experiences in the peasants' village in more detail. Suddenly *Fenglian* appeared on the following page.

I left for Chongqing as soon as I got back to Xian. I saw Jin Yan and Fenglian again. It seemed like years since I last saw them. I feel as if I've been living in China for a century. I was happy to see both of them again. Jin Yan said little, looked abstract, as if something weighted heavily on his mind. Probably he was lovesick. Fenglian is a darling, innocent girl. She hadn't the slightest interest in politics, but Jin Yan worries over the future of his country and his people. They could well represent the two types of youth in Chongqing. I like both of them very much. We three have become good friends. We went for a walk in the park. I told them about my adventures in the northern Shanxi villages. Fenglian kept asking, "And then, what happened?" It seems Chinese girls are even more innocent than those in Iowa.

We chatted as we walked. Suddenly firecrackers went off on all sides of us and the sky was filled with colorful fireworks. The Japanese had surrendered.

We screamed and shouted happily with the Chinese on the streets, then took a ride in a horse carriage along the Jialing River. We had a wonderful time.

I can return home now. I wish I could get on a plane at this moment and fly back to Stone City.

Lotus opened up the cardboard box labeled "Nanjing," but found only letters and postcards which Bill had written to his parents along with several snapshots. One of the pictures was of Bill and an American woman with her full, sensuously curled lips. There was no picture of Fenglian. Nothing about Fenglian in the whole Nanjing box.

What an empty romance. Her mother had been deceived. In 1967 her mother was attacked by the Red Guards. Lotus found her kneeling on the school playground, her head bowed, a large placard hanging from her neck which read, "Slave kneeling to serve American imperialists!"

As Lotus was taken to the school playground by the Red Guards, her mother did not show any surprise when she caught sight of her. She looked as if she had expected her daughter would be taken from Beijing to Chongqing in order to expose the crimes of the mother. One of the Red Guards was randomly cutting one strand after another of Fenglian's dishevelled hair. The clipped hair scattered over her gray clothing. Her face was gray as her clothing. The leader of the Red Guards wore a hat cocked to one side and clenched a knife in his teeth, his hands resting on his hips. A red arm band was wrapped around his left upper arm. When he spoke he took the knife out of his mouth and brandished it at Fenglian:

"Go on reciting the *Quotations from Chairman Mao.*"

"The counterrevolutionaries will never fall down if you don't beat them. They are like a pile of garbage. If the broom doesn't appear, it will never disappear by itself."

"Wrong! The counterrevolutionaries will never fall down if you don't beat them. *It is like sweeping the ground.* If the broom doesn't appear, *the dust* will never disappear by itself. Repeat it."

"The counterrevolutionaries will never fall down if you don't beat them. It is like sweeping the ground. If the broom doesn't appear, the dust will never disappear by itself."

"Are you a slave serving American imperialists?"

Silence.

"Are you a slave serving American imperialists?"

Silence.

The leader brandished the knife and shoved his face close to hers and glared. "Are you a slave serving American imperialists?"

"Yes."

"Sing 'The Barking of the Black Gang.'"

"I don't know how to sing."

Lotus almost blurted out, "Mother! You *do* know how to sing!"

"We'll teach you," the Red Guards' leader said. "I'm an ox, a devil, a ghost, a snake! Sing it out! Repeat each line I sing!"

"I'm an ox, a devil, a ghost, a snake."

"I've committed crimes."

"I've committed crimes."

"I've committed crimes."

"I've committed crimes."

"I must be watched by the people."

"I must be watched by the people."

"Because I'm an enemy of the people."

"Because I'm an enemy of the people."

"I must confess."

"I must confess."

"If I don't confess."

"If I don't confess."

"Cut my body into pieces."

"Cut my body into pieces."

"Now—confess your crimes! Liu Fenglian! Liu! Feng! Lian! They mean willow, lotus, breeze. A capitalist name! If you confess, we'll let you off easily. If you refuse, we will be very harsh. Confess now. What was your relationship with the American secret agent, William Brown?"

Lotus stared at her mother in horror.

She looked at Lotus, then lowered her head: "Husband and wife."

Lotus had never known that her mother had been married to an American imperialist. Her mother had never told her. Even her grandmother had kept this from her. She had been deceived for seventeen years. She was seventeen back in 1967.

"Adulterers! You were adulterers!" The leader screamed.

"No, no! We were married in the hospital room before he died. Two doctors were our witnesses."

Lotus heaved a sigh of relief. The American secret agent was dead.

"You were married in an imperialistic way. We don't recognize that kind of marriage. The marriage was illegal. You were adulterers. You were helping him gather intelligence on the Civil War."

"I was not! He was not gathering intelligence! He loved the Chinese. When he came to China the first time, he came to fight the common enemy of China and America—the Japanese. He came back to China during the War of Liberation. He wanted to speak out for the Chinese youth. He wanted to report on the Chinese student movement and inform the whole world about it."

"In 1944 he went into guerrilla territory to gather intelligence."

"No, No! He went there to work with guerrilla troops. His helicopter had engine trouble. He parachuted out into a village in northern Shanxi. It was during the time of the United Front, when the Nationalists, Communists, and Americans were working together against the Japanese."

"Die-hard reactionaries." All the Red Guards on the playground began to chant Mao's sayings. "They are die-hard reactionaries today. They will be die-hard reactionaries tomorrow. They can't stay that way forever. Die-hards are hard but will die. They'll change into a pile of stinking dog shit condemned by all people."

"Die-hard," the Red Guards' leader said, brandishing the knife at Fenglian. "We have materials on you in our hands. What you've said contradicts them. Who is this to you?" He pointed at Lotus.

"My daughter."

"This daughter of yours," he turned his head and looked at Lotus. "She is the bastard of you and William Brown."

"Mother," Lotus broke into tears and fell to the ground. "Is it true? Is it true?"

"Lotus," Fenglian also began to cry, "Your father and I were very serious about each other. We were married."

"The Party has made a thorough investigation of your background. We've got it all right here." The leader spoke up again. "Don't deny it. You committed adultery with the American secret agent. After he died you married Jin Yan to cover your crime—to cover up this bastard!"

"No! No! I can't take it!" Lotus jumped from the ground and dashed toward the exit. Where would she go? Jump into the river? Jump off a building?

Several Red Guards grabbed Lotus. "Revolution is not a dinner party," all the Red Guards began to chant Mao's sayings. "Revolution is not like writing, or painting, or embroidering. It can't be that refined, gentle, or restrained. Revolution is violence—violence that one class takes in overthrowing another class."

Her hair in disarray and her clothing ripped, Lotus ran back to face her mother. She spit in her face. "I'm not your daughter! My name is not Jin, or Liu! I don't want your name! You're a counter-revolutionary! A running dog of American imperialists!"

"American imperialists are paper tigers that can be crushed by one blow!" The Red Guards again took up the chant.

Lotus ran into Fenglian's room as the Red Guards were ransacking it. Lotus grabbed a small yellow parakeet out of its cage in the corner of the room. It called out "Lotus, Lotus!" She threw it on the floor, stomped on it over and over again until it stopped calling her name. It would never call her name again. She gathered up her mother's records, threw them out onto the playground and stomped on them until they broke into pieces. The Red Guards found Fenglian's photographs and books: *A Tale of Two Cities, Tess of the D'Urbervilles, Gone with the Wind, The Complete Works of Shakespeare, Anthology of Three Hundred Tang Poems, The Scholars, Anthology of Classical Prose,* and *Dream of the Red Chamber.* They threw them all out onto the playground. Lotus lit a match and set them on fire. Fenglian sprawled out on the ground, close to the fire. The flames were coming to her, but she didn't move. She stared blankly into the flames, her face expressionless, her eyes dry.

## Notes

1. This excerpt, from an unpublished translation of the novel *Far Away, A River,* is included here with Nie Hualing's kind permission. It is translated by Jane Parish Yang and edited by the author herself. The Chinese title for the novel is *Qianshan wai, shui changliu* (Hong Kong: Joint Publishing Co., 1985).

# The Themes of Exile and Identity Crisis in Nie Hualing's Fiction

## Shiao-ling Yu

Nie Hualing belongs to a generation of Chinese intellectuals uprooted time and again by the political upheavals of twentieth-century China. When the Sino-Japanese War broke out in 1937, they fled from the occupied areas as student refugees to Chongqing, the wartime capital of China, and to other areas inland. When the Communists took over the mainland, they followed the Nationalist government to Taiwan. From Taiwan they came to America as foreign students and stayed on to pursue careers. America was the last stop on their long journey; there was nowhere else to go. In this land of immigrants, they were finally secure. But, at the same time, they became "double exiles," both physically and spiritually separated from their homeland. Culturally speaking, America was even more alien to them than Taiwan.

Given the common experience of these people, it is not surprising that C. T. Hsia finds a sense of desperation in post-1949 fiction written by Chinese writers in Taiwan and America.[1] Nie Hualing's writing is no exception. For Nie, this sense of desperation is compounded by "a fear of politics." The death of her father, a victim of the political rivalry between the Nationalists and Communists, struck fear in her heart at the age of eleven.[2] When she began to write short stories in the fifties, exiles from the mainland afforded her a natural subject. In her preface to *Taiwan Stories (Taiwan yishi)*, she wrote: "The characters in these stories are urban, middle-class people who drifted from the mainland to Taiwan. They are all people without roots; they all suffer from homesickness and hope to return one day. I lived among them ... and felt the same kind of homesickness, the same kind of emptiness and despair."[3]

The story "The Several Blessings of Wang Danian" ("Wang Danian de jijian xishi") exemplifies her treatment of these exiles. It is a comic, ironic depiction of the hero's foolhardy plan to get rich and, at the same time, a symbolic representation of Taiwan's pathetic political situation. On a realistic level, the author provides abundant descriptive details allowing us to see and smell the inside of a schoolteacher's home: chairs with wire-bound legs, a bookcase made of wooden crates, cooking fumes, and cigarette smoke mingled with odors from the baby's unwashed diapers. Yet this pigsty of a house is Wang Danian's "blessing" number one. He, his wife, and their two children had lived in a single room before being awarded this house for meritorious service.

The central irony of this story is reserved for the unveiling of Wang's plan to breed fish. As he sits on his rickety rattan chair, he confides to his old friend and former classmate, whom he nicknames the Sage, how they can buy twenty thousand fish fry at seven cents a piece and net two hundred thousand dollars[4] by selling them as grown fish. The Sage is impressed and agrees to quit his job to join in the venture. In contrast to the credulous Sage, Wang's wife is merciless in puncturing her husband's pipe dream, reminding him of his many past "confidential plans": "Wasn't the prep school confidential? Wasn't the chain of correspondence courses confidential? Wasn't the plan for a farm confidential? Perhaps this time you'd better advertise."[5]

Wang Danian's dream of getting rich is reminiscent of a story written by mainland Chinese writer Deng Tuo about a peasant who dreams of building a fortune from a single egg. When he tells his wife that he plans to get himself a concubine when he becomes rich, she promptly smashes his egg.[6] Deng Tuo's parable was meant to satirize Mao Zedong's grandiose Great Leap Forward; Nie Hualing's story, too, is a political satire. Viewed in this light, the realistic details take on symbolic meanings. Danian's odor-filled room with its tightly shut windows represents Taiwan with its suffocating intellectual atmosphere and isolation. His schedule, which calls for doing fifty push-ups morning and night and reading Richard Nixon's speeches, is an ironic reminder of the gap between his and Taiwan's announced intentions and actual deeds. Danian, we are told, is too lazy to keep his schedule taped securely to the wall and is unable to follow the English lessons on the radio without the help of an English-Chinese dictionary. His unrealistic plan of breeding fish symbolizes Taiwan's equally unrealistic avowal to recover the mainland. Constrained by reality, Taiwan's highly trained American-equipped armed forces can only display their prowess in military parades. Likewise, Danian's favorite pastime is to "review his troops"—watching his son goosestep before him wearing a G.I. cap and chewing gum. Taiwan's helpless condition is finally brought home when Danian's creaking rattan chair collapses under him.

Nie Hualing's successful use of symbolism endows this story with much greater meaning than just a vivid portrayal of the life of Taipei's "little people." A comparison of this story and another version of the same story, entitled "Dinner" ("Wancan"), shows the author's attention to the technique of storytelling. "Dinner" has the same setting, characters, and story line as "The Several Blessings of Wang Danian"; it describes two old friends reminiscing about their college days and discussing, among other things, how to make a little money. In "Several Blessings," Nie cuts out most of the dinner table banter and concentrates on the plan to breed fish. She also chooses her details carefully, each representing some aspect of life in Taiwan. The different results achieved in these two stories demonstrate that it is not so much the story itself but how it is told that determines the final outcome. Whereas "Dinner" serves up a "slice of life," "The Several Blessings of Wang Danian" succeeds as both realistic and symbolic writing.

Ye Weilian singles out this technique of blending the realistic and symbolic as an important characteristic of Nie Hualing's fiction. He points out that in Nie's more successful works, she endeavors to capture the psychological truth of her characters as it is revealed at specific moments through specific actions, "but avoids overt symbolism or explanations as much as possible."[7] This is true in "The Several Blessings of Wang Danian." Although the hero's actions and the condition of his apartment have symbolic significance, they are also convincingly realistic. Readers become aware of the author's symbolic intentions only when they are well into the story, or after they have finished reading it. The description of Wang Danian's rickety rattan chair is a good example of this delayed revelation. The chair appears in the very first paragraph of the story, and it blends in very well with the other makeshift furniture. Toward the end of the story, after Danian has deliberated on his fish-breeding plan, he tips backward in a moment of elation and the chair collapses under him. At this instant, the truth about Danian's plan and Taiwan's precarious situation is revealed, but the effect is achieved without obvious symbolism or explanation. The absence of blatant didacticism makes this story different from Deng Tuo's political satire, which was obviously designed to drive a message home. Unlike Deng Tuo's Aesopian fable, Nie Hualing's story is also a compassionate study of her fellow exiles. Like the characters in Bai Xianyong's *Taipei People (Taipei ren)*, Nie's exiles lead more diminished lives in Taiwan than they did on the mainland. For them, their losses are irretrievable. "We can never get those good years back,"[8] as the Sage points out. Reminiscing about the past, therefore, becomes a way to assuage the pain they suffer in the present. In Danian's mind, for example, his wife, Wenqin, is still the pretty young coed who strolls down lovers' lane between two rows of willow, her face "as bright as the moon on a night when the sky is clear." "Now, crow's feet had frayed her eyes,"[9] and she has lost her youthful figure after giving birth to two children and becoming pregnant with a third. The Sage was once very active in his student days, when he was also a budding poet, but is now ground down by the dull routines of a small provincial school. He "has a vacant facial expression, a monotonous voice, and a smile that apologized to everyone all day long."[10] Wang Danian, too, is forced to count his "blessings" in order to forget his frustrations. While gently poking fun at his folly, the author also shows compassion for him.

In the "Lottery Ticket" ("Aiguo jiangquan"), we meet another group of expatriates who live in the same crowded government housing as Wang Danian. Like him, they hope for a miracle that will change their lives—winning the two-hundred-thousand-dollar lottery prize. Their wishful thinking, as one would expect, is not realized. After a mock-serious ceremony of signing a contract among themselves and an anxious vigil for the drawing of the prize, they end up holding a ticket that fails to win even the smallest prize of ten dollars. The torn ticket becomes a symbol of their lives, torn between the mainland and Taiwan: "The old pine tree on the ticket has only half of its trunk and bare branches left, and the other half with its gnarled roots has disappeared."[11]

Besides their rootlessness, the characters in this story also suffer from an acute sense of being confined and having nowhere to go. One of them takes "long-distance walks" in his three-*tatami*-size room, perhaps an ironic comparison to the famous Long March of the Red Army.[12] He describes his daily exercise in this way: "I walk very slowly, one step at a time. When I run into the wall, I turn back and continue walking, one step at a time. Run into the wall again, turn back, walk one step at a time. Run into the wall, turn back."[13] Yet another person quips that his only recreation is procreating children. He has already sired four children, and his wife is pregnant again. To these stranded people, the hope of returning to the mainland becomes more remote with each passing day, as faint as the name tags on their suitcases and as hollow as Taiwan's official slogan counterattacking the Chinese Communists. Yet they desperately cling to this impossible hope:

"Do you think we can go back to the mainland?"

"Sure!"

"Sure? How do we get back?"

"We'll fight back."

"Who will do the fighting?" Mrs. Ku cocks her head, half smiling.

"You fight, he fights, I fight. The Army, Navy, and Air Force fight."

"All right, you go fight. Old Ku and Old Wan go fight."

Mrs. Ku bursts out laughing, "I'll just stay here and wait. Wait, wait, and wait."[14]

To highlight Taiwan's isolation, the author has her characters act out a comic dialogue between a father and son who have just landed on a certain Taiping island. The son remarks, "Once you get on this island, you'll never get off."[15] It becomes immediately clear that this stranded pair is none other than Chiang K'ai-shek [Jiang Jieshi] and his heir apparent, Chiang Ching-kuo [Jiang Jingguo], who continue their dynastic rule on the island while pretending to be democratic. The father tells the son, "When we become democratic, we will be even more democratic than America."[16] As a political satire, this comic dialogue suffers from being too transparent. Unlike "The Several Blessings of Wang Danian," which achieves unity between the realistic and symbolic, the father and son episode in this story is an intrusion into an otherwise smooth narrative.

The exiles' sense of loss, while largely due to the political situation of the country, is also a deeply personal one. The story "Shanshan, Where Are You?" ("Shanshan, nizai nar?") looks at this personal loss, which is brought on not by wars and revolutions but by the fickleness of fate. The hero takes a bus to visit his old sweetheart whom he has not seen for fifteen years. When he reaches his destination, he discovers that the loudmouthed woman passenger on the bus is the Shanshan of his dreams. The author skillfully contrasts the passengers' boring conversations with the inner world of the hero's memory. The Shanshan he remembers is a shy young girl who covers her mouth when she smiles, a little gamine who swings on the branches and stuffs oranges into her mouth during their raid on an orange orchard, and the graceful young lady whom he saw for the last time in Chongqing after V-J Day. Now, all of these beautiful images have been erased by time. In their place is the fat and vulgar woman who boasts of her accomplishments in playing mahjongg and producing children. The dream of his youth, which she symbolized, is shattered by the hard reality of the present.

For Nie Hualing, the war years, despite all the hardship and suffering, were also golden years. She and her characters look back to this period nostalgically. In "A Little White Flower" ("Yiduo xiaobai-hua"), Nie again contrasts the youthful dreams of the past with the lackluster present. Two old classmates meet in Taiwan after a separa-tion of sixteen years; one is a mother of five, the other, a spinster schoolteacher. The former, who was nicknamed "Little Swallow" in her student days and who used to read love letters with a flashlight under her quilt, now performs the monotonous routines of a house-wife. The latter, once a mischievous tomboy who stole the principal's chicken, is now a stern principal herself. Her profession seems to have transformed her into a woman of ice and steel. Her room, even in the hot summer days of southern Taiwan, is like a block of ice. She wears a steel-gray dress and severely cropped hair. "Her whole person is like an unlubricated machine, every joint is rusty."[17] Only the memory of their girlhood warms their hearts. As they hum their favorite song, "When We Were Young," a song that appears often in Nie's stories, they are transported to a scene from their youth, sitting under a big tree by the Jialing River and dreaming young girls' dreams.

The author also felt the need to return to the place of her youth, a small town called Sandouping, where she lived during the war years. At that time, she longed to go away to see the big, wide world. Looking back, she wrote: "After all these years, my longing has turned the other way—back toward Sandouping. I long to return there and relive my life."[18] This longing prompted her to write the story of Sandouping in her first novel, The Lost Golden Bell (Shiqu de jinlingzi). In the preface, she states: "In my memory, I again returned to that place and lived amongst those people. I could even smell its peculiar odors—a mixture of the smells of gun powder, mildew, blood, sunlight, and dry grass."[19]

The novel begins with an evocation of these memories, recounted by the heroine, Lingzi, as she arrives at Sandouping and surveys her surroundings. The reader is immediately drawn into the sights and smells of this bustling river town. Tea houses, noodle stands, small eateries, and shops selling tow ropes line the river embankment. Bales of cotton and gray army uniforms are loaded and unloaded onto wooden boats of various sizes. An assortment of people—a wounded soldier with one arm in a sling, a boat captain in a starched white cotton shirt and trousers, a porter carrying two buckets of water on a shoulder-pole, the owner of a cotton yarn shop with a pipe in his mouth—are climbing up and down the muddy steps that lead from the water's edge to the town above. There are also the familiar smells of blood and mud baking in the sunlight.

Her novel is also about a young girl's coming of age, the eighteen-year-old Lingzi. Responding to the question of whether she, herself, is the heroine, Nie has said: "No, I am not. I created her. However, I am her, because I, too, was once as young as she."[20] The original source of this novel was a story Nie Hualing's mother told her about their Sandouping neighbors in which a young widow fell in love with a married man. However, before their plan to elope materialized, the man was executed for trafficking opium.[21] When Nie wrote the novel, she was not content to simply tell a love story. Instead, she made Lingzi the central character, and her involvement in the relationship between Aunt Qiao, the widow, and the unmarried Uncle Yinzhi evolves into a story about her journey toward psychological and emotional maturity. From her first awakening to love to her discovery that the object of her affection loves someone else, Lingzi goes through an agonizing process of finding her goals in life.

The title, *The Lost Golden Bell*, symbolizes this "solemn and painful process." The golden bell is an insect that resembles a cricket. It appears very early in the novel, and its melodious chirping fills Lingzi with a feeling of enchantment and mystery:

Suddenly I heard a sound—intermittent, low but clear. I don't know where it comes from. Like a golden thread, coil after coil, it circles the field, it circles my heart. The more it circles, the longer and brighter it becomes. I can almost see a fine strand of golden light. There is something in this sound. Perhaps it is happiness, but I hear sorrow. No, it is not sorrow either—not the kind of sorrow ordinarily associated with old age, sickness, and death; it is something different. As long as there is life, it exists. It is very deep, very thin, very light. You can feel it, can even hear it, but cannot catch it. It makes me feel depressed. I've never heard anything so moving.[22]

The golden bell stands for a kind of longing felt by Lingzi. The object of her quest could be love, but is much more; it includes all the things or experiences she wishes to have in life. However, these wishes are as elusive as the sound of this insect. The inspiration for choosing the golden bell as a symbol came from Katherine Mansfield's story "The Canary." The Chinese word for canary is *golden-thread bird*. Nie Hualing has said that she often feels a kind of loneliness that is part of life itself, a kind of feeling very much like that which Mansfield describes when she hears the canary's sweet song.[23]

In her novel, Nie skillfully integrates this symbol into her plot. As pointed out by one critic, the golden bell appears nine times, each time signaling a turning point in the development of the heroine.[24] Lingzi first hears the chirping of the golden bell upon her return home to Three-Star Village from Chongqing, where she attends school. Her strong emotional response marks the beginning of her quest. She immediately wants to catch the insect, but the sedan-chair bearer's remark is very suggestive: "You can't catch a golden bell so easily, Miss!"[25]

Later, she makes another unsuccessful attempt at catching this elusive creature in the mountains with her playmate Yaya, a girl who is similar to her in age, temperament, and the desire to find her way in life. Then she receives a golden bell as a gift from Uncle Yinzhi, a distant relative destined to play a crucial role in her growing up. This uncle is a doctor on leave from Chongqing. His education and maturity set him apart from the boys Lingzi knows. She is attracted to him because she desires the advice and counsel of a father figure, especially since her own father is dead and also because she is eighteen and just awakening to the attraction of the opposite sex. Her love fantasy, however, is shattered when she discovers that her favorite uncle is secretly in love with the pretty Aunt Qiao, and he even asks her to be their messenger. Disappointment and jealousy prompt her to expose their illicit affair. The devastating consequences of her action—Aunt Qiao is sent away by her in-laws, and Uncle Yinzhi is arrested on trumped-up charges—coincide with the disappearance of her golden bell. As a result of these events, she achieves a certain recognition of herself and the complexities of life. Her good friend Yaya also learns a lesson about life when her elopement with an army officer ends in failure and she returns home. The two girls reminisce about the time they looked for the golden bell in the mountains. Even though Lingzi has lost her golden bell, the process of her search has propelled her on the road to self-discovery.

In contrast to the golden bell, the author makes use of another symbol, the cuckoo. In Chinese literature, the cuckoo symbolizes unrequited love. One legend tells the story of Wangdi, King of Shu, who committed adultery with the wife of a government minister. Afterwards, he fled into exile in shame and became a cuckoo. Tang dynasty poet Li Shangyin (?812–858) used this allusion to sing of undying passion in his celebrated poem "The Patterned Lute" ("Jin se"): "Wangdi's spring passion cries in the cuckoo's song."[26] A cuckoo's cry also signifies the passing of spring and, by implication, the passing of one's youth. It is said that cuckoos cry until their mouths shed drops of blood. In this novel, the cuckoo is associated with the ill-fated young widow, Aunt Qiao. Her first appearance is accompanied by a cuckoo's cry:

All of a sudden I [Lingzi] heard a cuckoo cry, very far away yet very clear. Where is it? Perhaps in some ghostly virgin forest, there is this lone cuckoo with its grayish-brown body, black beak, black-striped belly, and long black tail. It perches on a gnarled old tree, crying its heart out in a sad song. Aunt Qiao sits by the bed, looking very attentive and contented. She is massaging her mother-in-law's skinny leg with the monotonous and rhythmic pounding of her fist. Monotonous and rhythmic, in this old funeral hearse, in this gloomy evening—this is her life![27]

However, beneath Aunt Qiao's contented appearance burns a young woman's passion. She makes a desperate attempt to break away from the "funeral hearse" by committing adultery. Although Nie Hua-ling's novel does not end as tragically as the story her mother told her—Uncle Yinzhi is not executed, and Aunt Qiao does not become a nun—the future that faces this widow is equally as gloomy. The price she pays for her indiscretion is her spiritual death. She tells Lingzi that the scandal has wakened her from her dream:

When I wake up, I find myself still in the dark room, frightened, cold, and alone. But when you realize that you were born into this dark room and that there is no way you can run away, I don't want to run away anymore. I saw how the monks were locked up in the temples—they were locked behind several gates and every gate had several locks. Now my attainment has surpassed that of the monk. There is no need for gates and locks. I won't run away anymore.[28]

As the Chinese proverb says, "There is no greater sorrow than the death of one's heart." The cuckoo, with its heartrending cry, is a fitting metaphor for this young widow whose heart has died and is resigned to her life in the "funeral hearse."

In contrast to the golden bell, which symbolizes youth, the cuckoo with its more subdued colors of gray and black represents maturity. This meaning becomes clear when Lingzi expresses her desire to search for her cuckoo after she loses her golden bell. The two symbols denote different stages of her growing up: "The golden bell and cuckoo have no meaning in themselves; the meaning lies in the process of the quest."[29]

At the end of the novel, when Lingzi leaves Sandouping with her mother and Yaya, she sums up her experience in this way:

> When I left Three-Star Village, I knew I would never go back. Life's journey is made up of many stages; after you go through one stage, you will never go through it again. Just like my golden bell, after it is lost, it will not come back again. I want to jump on that big boat and float to the other side of the mountain, float to where the sun rises. There I can perhaps find my cuckoo with its grayish-brown body, black beak, black-striped belly, and long black tail.[30]

The appearance of these two symbols at the juncture when Lingzi is embarking on a new life signifies both the conclusion of her old search and the beginning of a new one. The phrases "the other side of the mountain" and "where the sun rises" are also rich in symbolic meaning. They represent the aspirations of our questing heroine.

Besides symbolism, another characteristic of this novel is its lyrical prose. Many passages in this book read like poetry, such as the following description:

> Upon waking up, I almost did not know where I was. A sudden burst of birds' singing, like exploding sparks, rained down on the mountains. The small square window was pasted on the mud wall like a paper cutting. A few sturdy branches were glued to the glittering blue paper, but they were not glued on securely. The leaves still dangled.[31]

Ye Weilian cites this paragraph as an example of Nie Hualing's use of "epiphany," which James Joyce discusses in his fragment *Stephen Hero*. Joyce adapted this term to signify a sense of sudden radiance and revelation while observing a commonplace object. An equivalent of this in Chinese literature can be found in poems such as Wang Wei's nature poetry, in which nature is allowed to speak for itself without any interference by the poet.[32]

The passage quoted above also fuses external scenery with inner feelings. Lingzi's feelings of uncertainty and anxiety are revealed through her surroundings. The window that resembles a paper cutting, the glued-on branches, the dangling leaves, and the sky that looks like a piece of glittering blue paper all suggest a very fragile and insubstantial world. This world keeps with the heroine's state of mind as she is about to begin her quest and faces an unknown future. Her statement "I almost did not know where I was" not only describes her momentary loss of bearing upon waking up, but also implies that she does not know her way in life. Nie Hualing's description of Grandaunt Zhuang's sickbed may also be regarded as an example of "epiphany." The haunting image of the "funeral hearse," the bed, symbolizes the fate of this old woman, the fate of her daughter-in-law, Aunt Qiao, and the fate of the whole moribund traditional Chinese society.

Although the author carefully selects her symbols and images, she is less successful with her characters. The characterization of Lingzi is a case in point. As noted by Ye Weilian and novelist Xu Yu, Lingzi appears much too mature for her age. Her many analyses of her own psychological state and that of the other characters are beyond the capability of an eighteen-year-old. In her eagerness to show the changes that have taken place in Lingzi, Nie has filled her book with analysis and lectures.

Another fact she ignores are the mores of Chinese society at that time. In a small town in the forties, it was very unlikely that a young girl could have the kind of romantic relationship with an uncle that Lingzi has. Ye Weilian further points out that when the tragic love affair between Uncle Yinzhi and Aunt Qiao is about to reach a climax, the author has Lingzi perform a "compensatory action" by braving a snowstorm to deliver a letter from Uncle Yinzhi to Aunt Qiao. This episode weakens the tragic tone of the novel. The author brings her story to a hasty conclusion without describing the psychological and emotional reactions of the two unfortunate lovers to the sudden turn of events.[33] Despite these shortcomings, Nie Hualing's successful use of symbolism and her evocative language makes *The Lost Golden Bell* a milestone of her Taiwan period.

Coming to America has broadened Nie Hualing's writing, giving her a new perspective on the Chinese experience. Her novel *Two Women of China: Mulberry and Peach (Sangqing yu Taohong)* is one of her most ambitious explorations of the theme of exile. It is, as she modestly puts it, "an unambitious writer's ambitious undertaking."[34] It tells of one woman's psychological transformation and final breakdown against the backdrop of the great upheavals of modern China. Mulberry and Peach, the two personalities locked within the heroine, also symbolize a divided country and divided people.

Nie tells the story in the form of diaries and letters, linking the past and the present. The four parts of the book are made up of diaries kept by Mulberry at different periods in her life and letters written by Peach during her flight across America. These four parts resemble four acts in a play, each showing a different stage of the heroine's transformation. The four stages of her life also represent turning points in the history of her country. The first portion is set in 1945 during the final days of the War of Resistance against Japan; the second section takes place in Beijing on the eve of the Communist takeover; the third part occurs in Taiwan, after the country has split in two; and the final episode is set in America, where the heroine's personality split is complete.

The use of diaries in the novel is appropriate for its subject, Mulberry/Peach. It affords an excellent vehicle for the character to reveal her psychological and emotional state in all its intimacies. Peach's letters, which preface Mulberry's diaries in each section, serve to highlight the conflict between the two personalities. By placing the heroine's personal history in the larger context of the history of the country, the author succeeds in integrating the individual's fate with the nation's destiny.

The heroine begins as Mulberry, a teenage girl in inland China, and ends as Peach, a middle-aged woman in search of refuge in America. The theme of exile is set forth in the very beginning of the novel by a boatful of refugees traveling up the Yangzi Gorges, fleeing the Japanese. The passengers on board, the old, young, educated, and unlettered, represent a cross section of Chinese society. The Old Man from Beijing has been fleeing the Japanese for eight years. Sixteen-year-old Mulberry is running away from home. Her eighteen-year-old friend, Lao Shi, does not even have a home. She tells the others: "My address is the air raid shelter in Chongqing."[35] Her father had suffocated in a shelter along with more than ten thousand people during a Japanese air raid. The Refugee Student, whose mother was killed during the Japanese bombing of Nanjing, plans to go to Chongqing to enlist in the army. The Peach-flower Woman, a peasant woman in her twenties, is going to Sichuan to look for her husband, but does not know his address. All of these characters have been rendered homeless by the war. As the Old Man observes: "In this war, all our roots have been yanked out of the ground."[36]

The intertwined fate of the characters and their country is further illustrated by a series of images of them being stranded. The reader witnesses the first such scene when the refugees' boat capsizes and is grounded on the rocks. Their efforts to get help from the tow-line pullers and the passing ships are to no avail. Their predicament symbolizes the situation of the country. China, despite its long and glorious history, is now utterly helpless. The Old Man remarks: "We're stranded in the midst of history! . . . All around us are landmarks left by the great heroes and geniuses of China!"[37] Historical relics also become ironic reminders of the current situation. For example, the Eight-fold Array, a labyrinth of stones designed by the legendary Zhuge Liang of the Three Kingdoms period, reminds the old gentleman of the present divided state of China: the Nationalist government in Chongqing, the Communist government in Yan'an, and the Japanese puppet government in Nanjing. Faced with this personal and national crisis, the Old Man, who represents tradition, seeks answers from history. He summons the spirits of two famous historical figures, the great Tang poet, Du Fu (712–70), and the aforementioned Zhuge Liang, to divine their fortunes by the ancient method of "sand writing." This method of divination is done by placing a T-shaped frame in a box of sand with two people holding the ends of the frame. The spirit of some dead person is then summoned, and the frame writes words all by itself, revealing people's fortunes. The Refugee Student, who represents the progressive younger generation, scoffs at such superstition. He states: "This is not the time to become intoxicated by our thousands of years of history! We want to get out of here alive."[38]

Mulberry is stranded for the second time in the besieged city of Beijing, where she has gone to live with her fiance's family, the Shen's. In this section, the author again uses symbolism to represent China at a critical juncture of its history, through the creation of the memorable Aunt Shen, Mulberry's mother-in-law. She represents China's traditional order in its dying throes. Paralyzed and bedridden, the old lady confesses to her son, Jiagang, and Mulberry the sins she committed during her lifetime. She had murdered her husband's concubine after the latter gave birth to a son. She had also deliberately raised her own son, Jiagang, to become a pampered weakling so she could have control over him. Now, nearing death, she murmurs unconsciously: "The Wall of Nine Dragons is falling down. The Wall of Nine Dragons is falling down."[39] This wall is a monument from China's imperial past; its imagined crumbling by the dying woman signals the end of an era. The end finally comes when Aunt Shen breathes her last breath and the People's Liberation Army enters Beijing.

Nie Hualing continues to use the symbolic mode to describe Mulberry and her newly wedded husband's long trek out of the Communist-controlled areas. The tumbledown temple in no-man's land symbolizes the desolation of the country, where the old has been destroyed and the new not yet built. In this old temple with faded gold characters, "the Buddha with a thousand arms lies on its back on the mud floor. The child in the Goddess of Mercy's arms is headless. Only the Laughing Buddha is intact, still laughing."[40] The Laughing Buddha seems to be laughing at the hapless refugees who huddle under the eaves of his temple in search of safety. Their fear and anxiety are captured in "palm talk," a means by which Mulberry and her husband communicate by writing characters on each other's palms. The following exchange is an example of the taut, tension-filled dialogue the author uses in parts of her novel:

> AFRAID
> SLEEP, DON'T BE AFRAID
> FIRST, SAFETY
> SAFETY
> WHERE[41]

Mulberry is stranded a third time in an attic in Taipei, where she and her husband have gone into hiding because he is wanted by the police for embezzlement. This four-*tatami*-size attic above a storage shed, filled with dust and cobwebs and infested with rats, symbolizes Taiwan and its isolated condition. Here, Mulberry's psychological split begins. She leads a double life by hiding in the attic during the day and sneaking out at night. Her husband also becomes a divided person, dividing his time between sleeping and reading his two piles of old newspaper clippings. One pile, with its advertisements of cures for impotence and its rumors about vampires eating people, represents Taiwan. The other pile, showing scenes of old Beijing, represents the China he left behind.

To depict life in the attic, the author implements a kind of "shorthand" language, the "palm talk" referred to earlier and the writing of Chinese characters with matchsticks. These two "shorthands" become the standard form of communication in the attic and an ironic comment on the freedom of speech in Taiwan. Mulberry's daughter is very fond of the matchstick game, but the words she writes are loaded with pain and violence, words such as "kill, escape, crime, police, wound, dream, insane, and death."[42] She also draws a comic strip called *The Adventure of Little Dot* to express her desire to go outside to play. The outside world is represented by a very different set of words, such as "grass, leaves, stones, vines, jasmine flowers, moon, stars, clouds, bugs, and fireflies."[43] This fragmented language of the attic corresponds with the fragmented lives of the characters.

Nie Hualing also introduces a touch of surrealism in her description of life in the attic. Jiagang is shown repairing the clock at the beginning of his confinement. Two years and many repair attempts later, the clock still points to thirteen minutes past twelve. The stopped clock symbolizes complete separation from the outside world; even time has stood still. By implication, Taiwan's isolation is complete. Or, as Mulberry tells her daughter: "The earth is a huge attic. The huge attic is divided into millions of little attics just like ours."[44]

Leaving her attic in Taipei, Mulberry comes to America, where she is stranded in a different way. Living in an alien country with an alien culture, she is now considered an illegal alien and wanted by the immigration service. The chase across America, as noted by Bai Xian-yong, is very much like the experiences of K in Kafka's *The Trial*.[45] Indeed, her entire existence resembles a Kafkaesque nightmare in which her past traumas are juxtaposed to her current flight. She is continuously haunted by the ubiquitous man in dark glasses, the immigration agent, and by scenes of horror from her past, such as the Nanjing Massacre and the bombing of Chongqing. Her hallucination, after being interrogated by the immigration agent, is typical of her many nightmares. In this particular scene, she is running on top of the stone wall in Nanjing and being chased by many men in dark glasses. She sees members of her family, her father, mother, brother, and husband, among the heaps of corpses lying beside the wall. She sees herself dead, too. Her identity turns into a number, her alien registration number.

After this interrogation, Mulberry loses her memory. In Mulberry's place, Peach emerges and proudly announces to the world: "I am not Mulberry. Mulberry is dead."[46] To show the contrast between the two personalities, Nie Hualing draws on the symbolic meaning of these two names. As Mulberry herself explains, she was named after the holy tree in China. Mulberry leaves fed the silkworms that produced silk for China.[47] Mulberry has also been associated with Chinese womanhood from the earliest days. Luo Zu, wife of the legendary Yellow Emperor, was credited with discovering silkworms, and after this discovery, picking mulberry leaves and raising silkworms was a principal occupation of Chinese women. Descriptions of these activities abound in Chinese poetry. One poem, the Han dynasty ballad entitled "Mulberry by the Path" ("Moshang sang"), easily comes to mind. It is about a beautiful mulberry-picking girl named Luo Fu who refuses the advances of a government official.[48] The beauty and virtue embodied in this "mulberry maiden" represents the epitome of Chinese womanhood.

The peach is also associated with feminine beauty in Chinese tradition. The following poem is taken from the *Book of Poetry (Shijing)*:

> The Peach tree is young and elegant;
> Brilliant are its flowers.

This young lady is going to her future home,
And will order well her chamber and house.

The Peach tree is young and elegant;
Abundant will be its fruit.
This young lady is going to her future home,
And will order well for her chamber and house.[49]

The young peach tree represents the bride in the first flush of
youth, its brilliant flowers and abundant fruit symbolizing her beauty
and fertility. In the novel, the Peach-flower Woman personifies this
life-giving sensuality, her ample breasts providing sustenance for her
baby and the Chinese nation. Peach also partakes of this life force, as
can be seen from her connection with the Chinese creation myth. She
tells the immigration agent that she was born when the Goddess Nuwa
created the universe. However, in her present fallen state, her feminin-
ity is manifested solely as sexual appetite. Her fall from grace can be
documented through her sexual degeneration. As an innocent sixteen-
year-old virgin, she is raped by the Refugee Student aboard the
stranded boat. This violation of her body is followed by the breaking
of her jade griffin, a family heirloom and a symbol of her purity. Later,
she loses half of her griffin to the Refugee Student in a gambling game
and leaves the other half in Beijing. Her marriage to Shen Jiagang in the
besieged city of Beijing is a hastily arranged affair devoid of conjugal
tenderness. The only words he says to her on their wedding night are
"Mulberry, you're not a virgin!"[50]
   During the period of hiding in the Taipei attic, Mulberry's fears
are often expressed in sexual terms. She imagines that the rats on
the roof are gnawing her breasts, nipples, and vagina. Frustrations
growing out of her long confinement drive her to seek sexual relief
by having an affair with Mr. Cai, an old friend of her father and
owner of the attic. Years later, this affair becomes the subject of an
investigation by the immigration office. An agent questions Peach
about the matter:

"When did you start to have sexual intercourse with Mr. Cai?"
"I can't recall the exact date. I only remember it was after we left
the funeral home."
"You mean after you saw his wife's body was put in the coffin?"
"That's right."
"So, that's how it was. How many times did you have intercourse
with Mr. Cai?"

"I don't remember. That happened ten years ago."
"How often did you have intercourse?"
"I'm not sure."
"How long did each act of intercourse last?"
"I don't know. I went to sleep after intercourse. I didn't look at my watch."[51]

Peach's matter-of-fact answer shows that she has now turned into a woman with no sense of shame. She feels absolutely no moral scruples about her actions and is willing to be picked up by any man as she hitchhikes across America. While the submerged Mulberry feels guilty about the life of promiscuity Peach plunges her into, Peach is blithely happy about her sexual escapades, including bearing an illegitimate child. To have an abortion or not to have an abortion becomes a point of contention between the two personalities, and it is Peach who wins. By the end of the novel, Peach's transformation is complete. Not only has she has cut herself off from traditional Chinese values, but she is no longer bound by any ethical standards. As an amoral person, she becomes permanently exiled from human society.

However, Peach is not alone in her exile; her fellow Chinese emigrés all suffer from varying degrees of alienation. Professor Zhang Yibo is another "split" person. He longs for Chinese things, but he has to live in America. He wants Peach, but refuses to divorce his American wife even though their marriage exists in name only. His wife describes their relationship as one between "the upstairs Chinese" and "the underground American." She and her American lover live in the basement. Zhang also behaves hypocritically. He wants Peach to have an abortion so he may protect his "dignity" before his students.

Jerry and Danhong are another mismatched Chinese couple. As a second-generation American, Jerry is indifferent to Chinese problems and thus spares himself the pain that afflicts the other immigrants. However, his tranquility is achieved at the expense of turning himself into a machine: his face is the color of steel, his living room has black walls, and he prefers to interact with machines because he believes they create order. He even believes that, in the near future, babies will be created by machines. Living with this frigid husband, Danhong is forced to find affection in her Pekingese dog, which she calls "Little Pekingese" and treats like her baby.

The most positive character among these overseas Chinese is Deng, a student in his thirties, who tries to create meaning in his life by forming a Chinese action committee. However, his "action" is shown in an ironic light when he and Mulberry listen to a recorded action committee speech after they run out of gas in a ghost town. Immediately after this tape, they play a recording of hogs being butchered in a packing house. "Here is concrete action,"[52] Deng remarks self-mockingly. He represents the typical vacillating Chinese person who cannot decide on a course of action. "Go back to Taiwan? I couldn't stand it! Go back to the mainland? I can't do that either. Stay here? I am nobody!"[53] His dilemma, and that of countless other Chinese immigrants, is summed up by Peach in her reply to the immigration official's question of where she would go if deported: "I don't know." Cut off from their native country and culture, and unable to find a new identity in their adopted country, these Chinese exiles are truly a "lost generation."

However, tragic as these Chinese are, they are not the only "lost" people; rootlessness is a global phenomenon. The lumberjack with whom Peach shares an abandoned water tower near Des Moines is a Polish Jew and a survivor of Auschwitz. He tells her: "This is the age of the foreigner. People drift around everywhere."[54] Even native-born Americans become drifters. In her flight across America, Peach meets many Vietnam War protesters who also live a life on the run because of their political beliefs. The shared feeling of these social outcasts is captured in the lyrics of a Beatles song, which Peach hears in a roadside cafe:

> He's a real nowhere man,
> Sitting in his Nowhere Land
> Making all his nowhere plans for nobody.[55]

In this story about one woman's personal dissolution, the author has allegorized the fate of a divided China and shed light on the human condition in modern times. She achieves this through her manipulation of symbols. She has created a convincingly realistic world of the schizophrenic, which, by a series of projections, becomes representative of the condition of the whole nation. The juxtaposition of Peach's flight across America with the American astronauts landing on the moon is also richly symbolic. It reminds us that although man has conquered an alien planet, he has also become an alien on his own planet. When Peach is driven out of the water tower, she writes a message on a wooden plaque. Imitating what was written on the plaque the astronauts left on the moon, this plaque stands as an epitaph for all the displaced people in the world.

A WOMAN WHO CAME FROM AN UNKNOWN PLANET
ONCE LIVED IN THE WATER TOWER
FEBRUARY 22, 1970–MARCH 21, 1970
I CAME IN PEACE FOR ALL MANKIND.

Peach
March 21, 1970[56]

In her latest novel, *Far Away, A River (Qianshan wai, shui changliu),* Nie Hualing continues to explore the question of exile and identity crisis. Lotus, the thirty-two-year-old daughter of an American father and a Chinese mother, comes to Stone City, Iowa, her late father's hometown, to find her roots after becoming a disillusioned "revolutionary" in China. Her search for identity, like Mulberry's loss of hers, is set against the background of the turbulent history of modern China.

As in *Mulberry and Peach,* the author makes extensive use of the epistolary form to link the past and the present. The novel is divided into three sections. The first section describes Lotus's arrival in Iowa, the cultural shock and alienation she feels, and her disappointment at her grandmother's cold reception of her. The second part consists entirely of letters Lotus's mother writes to her, recounting her love story with her late American husband, Bill Brown, during the eventful years of 1944 to 1949 in China. Lotus writes comments on the margins of these letters, revealing her own emotional and psychological growth. The final section again moves the reader to Iowa. By now, Lotus is no longer the angry, bitter, and lost young woman she once was. The three-month spiritual journey she makes enables her to find her place in life.

The river in the title stands as a symbol of Lotus's odyssey across time and space. This meaning can be seen in the song Lotus's American cousin and would-be lover, Billy, dedicates to her:

> Somewhere a river is flowing, flowing,
> And that's where I'll be going, going.
> Where is that river, where?
> How do I find my way there?
> Is it far, far away,
> Or wherever I stay?
> And where in the world am I?
> Over the ground and under the sky?
> Are these *my* hands, is this *my* face?
> Where is my own place?
> Someone please tell me. Must I go alone?

Must I go alone? Alone?
Somewhere a river is flowing,
flowing,
flowing.[57]

It is in a small teahouse by the Jialing River that Lotus's mother
Fenglian first meets her future husband. From then on, the river figures
prominently in their coming to know each other. One evening, in a
Chongqing park facing the river, Bill tells Fenglian and her Chinese
boyfriend, Jin Yan, about his experience of being parachuted behind
enemy lines and rescued by the peasants in a Shanxi village. It was an
event which made a deep impression on him and influenced his future
course of action. During a memorable ride along the river on the
historical occasion of the Japanese surrender, Fenglian tells Bill intimate details about her family. In addition to having two wives, her
father also had a male opera singer as his lover. Bill responds with the
song "Slow Boat to China." They also discover that they are both
"children of the river." Fenglian grew up by the Yangzi River, a river
rich in history and legends; Bill spent his entire youth on the Wapsi
River in Iowa. Now, almost four decades later, their daughter comes to
the Wapsi in search of the father she never knew. Yet, while she is in her
father's country, her thoughts travel to her mother's country and the
Jialing River: "Over there the Jialing River is also flowing. Right now I
am thinking about the river where my two fathers and mother spent a
happy time together, where the Chinese fishermen struggle to make a
living, and countless Chinese people climb the riverside steps daily."[58]
    Whereas the Wapsi has its parallel in the Jialing River, Stone City,
Iowa, has a Chinese counterpart, too. Nanjing, capital of the Nationalist Chinese government after World War II, was called Stone City in
ancient times. It is here that Bill and Fenglian meet again after the war
and are married in 1949. It is also here that Bill is fatally wounded while
reporting on a student demonstration. The final phase of the Chinese
Civil War was played out in Nanjing, with its fall marking the end of
an era in modern Chinese history.
    Stone City, Iowa, also had a more prosperous past. It was once
a boomtown because of its rich limestone deposits. The Brown family
was one of the three prominent families to open up Stone City's
quarries. Now the quarries have long been closed, and the city has
become a virtual ghost town with only a handful of inhabitants
remaining. Among them are Lotus's grandparents. But this ghost
town was where Bill Brown grew up and where his ashes were
buried. His life was divided between two Stone Cities; one in China,

one in America. Hence, Lotus's search for her family tree must begin here: "This is my goal for coming to Stone City. When I know who my parents are, I will have found my own roots. I was just a floating duckweed before."[59]

An important technique Nie Hualing uses in this novel is the method of contrast. This method is well suited to her subject: Lotus's search for identity, which is a process of bridging two cultures and two historical periods. Like places, the characters also come in pairs. Lotus and her mother are a contrasting pair who have much in common yet are worlds apart. The author uses the word *lotus* for both of her heroines' names, and the title of the English translation of this book is *Lotus*. The mother's name, Liu Fenglian, means "willow, breeze, lotus." Mother and daughter also have similar experiences in love. Fenglian falls in love with an American young man by the banks of a romantic river and in a famous old city in China; Lotus will retrace her mother's steps in America. The daughter's story is a continuation of the mother's, but in a different setting and time.

However, despite the similarity in the pattern of their lives, Lotus and her mother are total strangers. Raised by her maternal grandmother in Beijing while her mother stayed in Chongqing, Lotus knew nothing about her American father. She thought her stepfather, Jin Yan, was her real father. When she learns the truth during the Cultural Revolution, she hates her mother for marrying this "American secret agent" and making her the bastard child of an "American imperialist." She joins the Red Guards in attacking her mother. The resulting alienation from her mother is one reason she desires to learn more about her dead father, to whom she feels closer.

Bill and Billy are another similar but contrasting pair. Billy is the son of Bill's sister Nancy. He is named in memory of his uncle and resembles him physically: blond hair, soft blue eyes, and the characteristic pugnose of the Brown family. They are both attracted to Chinese women, a fact which infuriates Grandma Mary. She warns Billy shortly after Lotus's arrival: "Three generations of the Brown family males have fallen in love with Chinese women. Even this old man here! Billy, you're hooked, too!"[60] Billy and Lotus are attracted to each other because they are both lonely. For Lotus, Billy is the only person she feels close to in the cold "Stone City"; his likeness to her father satisfies her longing for the father she has never seen. In turn, Lotus gives Billy a sense of security and inner peace after his many casual relationships with other women. He has grown fond of the Chinese woman's deeply caring but undemonstrative way of loving. "Now I understand why Uncle Bill fell in love with your mother," he tells Lotus.[61]

Uncle and nephew also follow similar paths in their political actions. As a young man during World War II, Bill answered the call to defend his country by going to China to fight the common enemy of China and America, Japan. His wartime experiences changed his life. He gave up his chance of marrying his childhood sweetheart, Lucy, and of settling down in Stone City after the war ended. Instead, he went back to China to report on the Chinese Civil War, especially the student movement. He identified with the young Chinese intellectuals and became deeply involved in their activities. The Chinese student movement in the late forties has its counterpart in the American anti-Vietnam War movement during the sixties. In both cases, the young people attempted to translate their beliefs into political actions. Billy belongs to the antiwar generation in America; he escapes military service by going to Canada. He tells Lotus that he will never wear a military uniform. In the eyes of Old Brown and Mary, Billy does not measure up to Bill. Bill is a war hero; Billy is a draft dodger. But, in their different ways, they both represent the ideals of their respective generations.

Lotus's two boyfriends, one Chinese, one American, and her mother's two boyfriends, also one Chinese and one American, form still another set of contrasts. Fenglian's Chinese boyfriend, Jin Yan, was her classmate in college, and it is he who introduces her to Bill just before he goes to the Yan'an headquarters of the Chinese Communists. In contrast to Bill's spontaneous and easy manner, Jin is reserved and serious. Although he cares about Fenglian deeply, he has never expressed his love openly. He plays the role of an elder brother and protector. He marries Fenglian after Bill dies because he wants her baby to have a father with a Chinese name for protection under the Communist regime. Like Bill, Jin is a political activist. During the war, he, along with many other young people of his generation, volunteers for military service. He then goes to Yan'an, believing that the Communist party is the hope of China's future. Trust in the party prompts him to criticize its policies, and he becomes a victim of the Anti-Rightist Campaign of 1957. After waiting twenty-four years for his return, Fenglian learns that he has died in a labor camp. Compared with him, Bill Brown is more fortunate. Bill, at least, has the satisfaction of dying for a cause he believes in; Jin is persecuted to death by his own party.

Billy and Dr. Lin play the same roles in Lotus's life that Bill and Jin Yan did in her mother's. Billy is two years younger than Lotus. His open and direct way of showing affection makes this girl from Mao's China uncomfortable. However, his openness is also a welcome relief after the tangled human relationships she has been through in China. She feels carefree and happy when she is with him, but lack of a common cultural background also creates a gap between them. Dr. Lin is a middle-aged Chinese-American. Like Professor Zhang Yibo in *Mulberry and Peach*, he is homesick for China and Chinese things. His marriage to his American wife is falling apart from a lack of mutual understanding. After his wife moves out, Lotus moves in as a housekeeper for him. The appearance of a pretty young woman from China at this difficult time in his life eases his loneliness. He develops a complex mixture of emotions toward Lotus: as father, elder brother, protector, and special friend. A heart specialist, he cures Lotus's "heart illness."

As with Mulberry, Lotus's traumatic experiences include sexual abuse. When she is sent to a village during the Cultural Revolution, she is raped by three "black shadows" over a period of time. One of these "shadows" turns out to be the young man she had loved but rejected because he had been admitted as a Communist party member while she had not. She was deemed to have a "bad family background." The rape by her rejected lover is a poignant episode, characteristic of human relationships at the time. As Lotus put it, "Zhu Li and I were not equal in politics, but equal in bed."[62] She finally confides her "shameful past" to Dr. Lin. He tells her about the erotic sculptures in the temples in India and tries to convince her that sexuality is not ugly, but is the life force of the universe. This opinion is similarly expressed in *Mulberry and Peach*. For Mulberry, her rape at the same age of sixteen marks the beginning of her sexual degeneration. In the case of Lotus, Dr. Lin's timely advice restores her self-esteem and her capacity to love and be loved.

Like Mulberry, Lotus also has an identity problem. She is half-Chinese and half-American, but is unable to identify with either country. She first becomes aware of her special condition when she is taunted as a "half-breed" by a group of schoolchildren. After that, she thinks of herself as deformed, somehow not quite normal, but unable to understand in what way she is abnormal. During the Cultural Revolution, the humiliation she suffers as the bastard of an "American Secret Agent" makes her lose hope in China. Now, in America, the hostile reception she receives from Grandma Mary makes her feel like an outsider in her father's hometown. While reading about her father's experiences in China in the letters her mother wrote to her, Lotus cannot help but envy her father's good fortune in being accepted by the Chinese: "I am an outsider in Stone City. I want to get in, but cannot."[63]

This sense of not knowing where she belongs is shared by another character in the novel, Dr. Lin's nine-year-old daughter, Lily. Her father wants to raise her as a Chinese; her mother wants to raise her as an American. When her parents separate, she is pulled both ways. Lotus feels a special empathy with the unhappy girl. She tells Dr. Lin that both she and Lily are "abnormal," because they are neither Chinese nor American.

One of the most moving episodes in the novel is when Lotus tries to prove to her American grandparents that she is indeed the Brown family's Chinese granddaughter. The only tangible proof she can offer to support her claim is a Bible left by her late father. It was with this Bible that Bill Brown married Liu Fenglian shortly before he died in a hospital in Nanjing, with two Chinese doctors as witnesses. Seeing this family memento fills the old couple with emotion. The Bible had been their Christmas gift to their son many years before. Whereas Old Brown welcomes his newly found granddaughter to his household, Mary refuses to recognize her, saying that Bill's marriage to Fenglian "does not count" because it was not a Catholic ceremony. To be regarded as a bastard by her own grandmother deals a heavy blow to Lotus's self-esteem. Moreover, she has to endure the older woman's prejudices toward China and the Chinese. Mary hates Chinese people because she believes that they killed her son. Being a stranger in America turns Lotus into a total Chinese, a change that surprises even herself. She had thought herself to be very cold, even hostile to China. In the end, she wins the acceptance of her American family when she volunteers to take care of her grandparents after Mary suffers a heart attack.

In a study of the exiles in Vladimir Nabokov and Isaac B. Singer's novels, Asher Z. Mibauer points out that these characters have to achieve a balance between their past and present in order to survive. If they are overwhelmed by their past, they cannot live in the present. If they cut themselves off from their past completely, they die a spiritual death.[64] Of the exiles in Nie Hualing's fiction, Mulberry is a typical example of someone who dies a spiritual death. Fortunately for Lotus, she manages to achieve a balance between her past and present. She owes thanks to people like Billy and Dr. Lin, who help her live in the present, and to her mother's letters, which help her understand her past. On the last page of one of her mother's letters to her, Lotus has written the following commentary: "When I know the history of my family, I will be able to identify with my family; when I know the history of my country, I will be able to identify with my country."[65] At the end of the novel, Lotus writes to her mother, using a hardbound volume of *Modern Chinese History* as a pad. Even though we do not know whether she eventually decides to stay in America or go back to China, we are certain that she will be able to find her way in life whatever her decision. The three divisions of the book, present, past, and present again, coincide with the heroine's efforts to transcend her exile.

From her stories about the mainland emigrés in Taiwan to her novels about Chinese immigrants in America, Nie Hualing has made the fate of Chinese exiles and the Chinese nation a central concern of her fiction. She told one interviewer that the longer she is away from the country, the more concerned she feels about it.[66] Lotus expresses a similar sentiment in *Far Away, A River*: "The farther I am from China, the closer I feel."[67] This concern is not so paradoxical or particular to the Chinese as it may seem. Malcolm Cowley, in his study of exiled American writers in Europe following World War I, noted that the sojourn abroad taught these writers to admire their own country. They eventually overcame their alienation and reintegrated into American society. The final stage of their exile was their homecoming.[68]

This homecoming is, of course, eagerly awaited by exiled Chinese writers. Nie Hualing is determined to be a bridge builder, helping to bring about this happy event, not only for the writers but for all the Chinese people living in exile because of their divided country. She concludes her novel *Two Women of China: Mulberry and Peach* with a Chinese fable. A little bird, which was transformed from the spirit of the Sun God's drowned daughter, tries to fill up the sea by dropping pebbles into it. To this day, the princess bird still flies back and forth between the sea and the mountain; with each trip, she takes another pebble.

As noted by Vladimir Nabokov, "the best part of a writer's biography is not the record of his adventures, but the story of his style."[69] In reading Nie Hualing's fiction of the past thirty years, we witness a definitive evolution in her style. Her early stories are realistic portrayals of life in Taiwan. In "The Several Blessings of Wang Danian," she successfully combines realistic descriptions with symbolic representation. The use of symbolism is further developed in her novel *The Lost Golden Bell*, in which the golden bell becomes an extended metaphor symbolizing the heroine's process of coming of age. Her manipulation of symbols in *Two Women of China: Mulberry and Peach* makes this book a powerful allegory of modern China's tragic fate. Her use of the diary and epistolary forms in this novel is a noteworthy accomplishment. The letters and diaries allow the characters to reveal themselves in an intimate and direct fashion, without any interference by a narrator or the author. It is "showing" at its most effective.

Nie Hualing's experimentation with language is also an innovation she introduces into this work. Instead of her usual lucid and lyrical
prose, she adopts a fragmented language shorn of all descriptive
embellishments to reflect and match the mental state of her characters.
*Far Away, A River* is similar to *Two Women* in that both deal with the fate
of the Chinese exiles against a background of modern Chinese history.
However, they differ in narrative technique. Whereas *Two Women* is all
"showing," *A River* is mostly "telling." Even the letters Lotus's mother
writes to her are designed not so much to reveal the character's inner
workings as to recount historical events, especially the student demon-
strations that marked the final days of the Chinese Nationalist government in Nanjing.

The treatment of history is also different in the two books. In
*Two Women*, the author chooses four scenes from the heroine's life
to represent turning points in Chinese history. In *A River*, she gives
a much more detailed account of the events over the past forty years,
from the Sino-Japanese War to the Cultural Revolution. The prepon-
derance of historical events tends to overshadow the drama of the
characters. Consequently, *A River* is not as successful in that regard
as *Two Women*. Nie has said that her motto is never to repeat herself:
"My next novel may not be a better novel, but it will be a different
novel."[70] While *A River* is not better than *Two Women*, it represents
the author's efforts to explore different modes of expression. So, as
we anxiously await her future works, we can anticipate the continued
development of her style and technique, as well as her exploration
of different thematic boundaries.

## Notes

1. C. T. Hsia, ed., *Twentieth Century Chinese Stories* (New York:
Columbia University Press, 1971), p. xi.

2. Peter Nazareth, "An Interview with Chinese Author Hua-ling
Nie," *World Literature Today* 55, no. 1 (Winter 1981): 11. See also Yan
Huo, "Nie Hualing de gushi" ("Nie Hualing's Story"), *Haiwai huaren
zuojia lüeying* (Hong Kong: Joint Publishing Co., 1984), p. 19.

3. *Taiwan yishi* (Beijing: Beijing chubanshe, 1980), p. 1. All translations in this article are mine, unless otherwise noted.

4. At that time forty New Taiwanese dollars were equal to one
U.S. dollar.

5. C. T. Hsia, p. 197.

6. This story is included in the book *Yanshan yehua* (*Evening Talks at Yanshan*). Deng Tuo paid dearly for his criticism of Mao. He was bitterly denounced and died in prison during the Cultural Revolution.

7. Ye Weilian, "Tuchu yishun de tuibian: Celun Nie Hualing" ("The Epiphany in Nie Hualing's Fiction"), in *Wang Danian de jijian xishi (The Several Blessings of Wang Danian)* (Hong Kong: Haiyang wenyi chubanshe, 1980), p. 278.

8. C. T. Hsia, p. 196.

9. Ibid.

10. Ibid.

11. *Taiwan yishi*, p. 11.

12. A *tatami* is the straw mat that lines the floor of a Japanese-style house. One *tatami* is about the size of a single bed.

13. *Taiwan yishi*, p. 7.

14. Ibid., p. 4.

15. Ibid., p. 9.

16. Ibid., p. 10.

17. *Wang Danian de jijian xishi*, p. 81.

18. "Am I the Heroine?", in *The Purse* (Hong Kong: Heritage Press, 1962), p. 91.

19. *Shiqu de jinlingzi* (Taipei: Linbai chubanshe, 1987), p. 5.

20. "Am I the Heroine?", p. 95.

21. See Nie's preface to *Shiqu de jinlingzi*, pp. 6–7.

22. Ibid., p. 20.

23. Ibid., p. 4.

24. Xiang Yang, "Xiongyongzhe de penquan: Du Nie Hualing xiaoshuo *Shiqu de jinlingzi*" ("Bubbling Fountain: Reading Nie Hualing's *The Lost Golden Bell*"), in *Shiqu de jinlingzi*, p. 273.

25. Ibid., p. 20.

26. The translation of this line and the information on Wangdi are all from the introduction to *Anthology of Chinese Literature*, edited by Cyril Birch (New York: Grove Press, 1965), vol. 1, pp. xxvi–xxvii.

27. *Shiqu de jinlingzi*, pp. 42–43.

28. Ibid., p. 241.

29. Ibid., p. 245.

30. Ibid., p. 264.

31. Ibid., p. 44.

32. "Tuchu yishun de tuibian: Celun Nie Hualing", pp. 275–76. See also the definition of epiphany in M. H. Abrams, *A Glossary of Literary Terms*, 3rd ed. (New York: Holt, Rinehart and Winston, 1971), p. 52.

33. For these opinions, see Ye Weilian, "Ping *Shiqu de jinlingzi*" ("On *The Lost Golden Bell*"), a reprint article that appeared in *Xin wenxue luncong*, no. 4 (1980): 194–97, and Xu Yu's introduction to the book *Yiduo xiaobaihua* (*A Little White Flower*) (Taipei: World Book Co., 1963), p. 3.

34. "Langzi de beige" ("A Sad Song of the Wanderer"), preface to *Sangqing yu Taohong* (Beijing: Zhongguo qingnian chubanshe, 1980), p. 1.

35. *Two Women of China: Mulberry and Peach*, translated by Jane Parish Yang and Linda Lappin (Beijing: New World Press, 1981), p. 41.

36. Ibid., p. 42.

37. Ibid., p. 46.

38. Ibid.

39. Ibid., p. 103.

40. Ibid., p. 129.

41. Ibid., p. 128.

42. Ibid., pp. 149–50.

43. Ibid., pp. 188–89.

44. Ibid., p. 159.

45. "The Wandering Chinese: The Theme of Exile in Taiwan Fiction," *Iowa Review* 7, nos. 2–3 (Spring–Summer 1976): 211.

46. *Two Women of China: Mulberry and Peach*, p. 1.

47. Ibid., p. 218.

48. For an English translation of this poem, see *Sunflower Splendor: Three Thousand Years of Chinese Poetry*, edited by Wu-chi Liu and Irving Yu-cheng Lo (New York: Anchor Books, 1975), pp. 34–35.

49. *The She King*, vol. 4 of *The Chinese Classics*, translated by James Legge (Hong Kong: Hong Kong University Press, 1960), pp. 12–13.

50. *Two Women of China: Mulberry and Peach*, p.115.

51.This passage is omitted from the English translation. The Chinese original can be found in *Sangqing yu Taohong* (Hong Kong: Youlian chubanshe, 1982), pp. 255–56.

52. *Two Women of China: Mulberry and Peach*, p. 214.

53. Ibid., p. 211.

54. Ibid., p. 140.

55. Ibid., p. 79.

56. Ibid., p. 198.

57. *Qianshan wai, shui changliu* (Hong Kong: Joint Publishing Co., 1985), pp. 106–7. English translation by Jane Parish Yang from the author's unpublished manuscript.

58. Ibid., p. 139.

59. Ibid., p. 128.

60. Ibid., p. 71.

61. Ibid., p. 285.

62. Ibid., p. 303.

63. Ibid., p. 123.

64. Asher Z. Mibauer, *Transcending Exile: Conrad, Nabokov, I. B. Singer* (Gainesville, Fla.: University of Florida Press, 1985), chapter 2, pp. 54–72; chapter 3, pp. 73–87, passim.

65. *Qianshan wai, shui changliu*, p. 251.

66. Peter Nazareth's interview, *World Literature Today* 55, no. 1 (Winter 1981): 11.

67. *Qianshan wai, shui changliu*, p. 274.

68. *Exile's Return: A Literary Odyssey of the 1920s* (New York: Viking Press, 1951), pp. 289–90.

69. Quoted in Mibauer, p. 54.

70. Preface to *Wang Danian de jijian xishi*, p. 2.

Li Li

李 黎

# Li Li

Li Li (b. 1948), nee Bao Lili, also writes under the pseudonym Xue Li. Born in Nanjing, China, she moved to Taiwan with her parents in 1949 and spent her childhood and adolescence in Gaoxiong, in the southern part of the island. She received her B.A. in history from National Taiwan University in 1969.

During the early seventies, Li Li studied political science at Purdue University. It was also during this period that she, like many overseas Chinese students then driven by patriotism and idealism, participated in the Protection of Diaoyutai Movement. Because of its Leftist orientation, she was blacklisted by the Nationalist government in Taiwan and was unable to return until 1985. In the late seventies, Li Li visited mainland China, where she was warmly received and is highly regarded. Her first collection of short stories, entitled *The Moon of the West River* (*Xijiang yue*), was published on the mainland in 1980. She now lives in Stanford, California.

Li Li's first story, "A Day in Professor Tan's Life" ("Tanjiaoshou de yitian"), was published in 1971. Its deft symbolism and psychological insight won the twenty-three-year-old author immediate recognition and critical acclaim. However, her second story, "Night Trees" ("Yeshu"), did not come out until five years later. By self-admission, she is not a prolific writer who writes on a regular basis. Nonetheless, over the last few years, there has been a steady flow of well-written stories. Her status as an overseas Chinese who has traveled from mainland China to Taiwan and then to the United States, and her personal experiences with the patriotic fervor and bitter disillusionment of the Diaoyutai incident, have influenced Li Li's primary concern with the Chinese identity in this unprecedented historical era. Although physically an exile living away from her homeland, she identifies completely with China intellectually, spiritually, and emotionally. This is clearly evident in her fiction, which explores the impact of a divided China and self-exile through personae ranging from families separated by the Taiwan Straits, to overseas Chinese students, to first-generation Chinese-Americans. Although the artistic value of a literary work does not rely solely on its theme, Li Li's work demonstrates that literature can be one of the most profound forms contemplating the universal themes of human life.

Li Li is the author of seven volumes of short stories and novellas, and of three volumes of prose and essays. She also has edited an overseas Chinese writers' anthology and has translated Aldous Huxley's *Brave New World* into Chinese.

# Homeward Bound[1]

## Li Li

### 1.

One by one, the train passed by stations with obscure names. He had never known that north of the crowded city of Kowloon existed such a vast stretch of half-urban, half-rural land.

The afternoon summer sun shone on the interspersed paddies, ponds, and houses outside the train window. Lush, subtropical vegetation flourished in the sun, extending beyond sight.

The train began to slow down. "It's approaching the border," he heard someone say. Suddenly, he felt his heart in his chest, sensing its existence and its palpable, heavy beat.

Perhaps feeling his uncontrollable quiver, Meijun lifted her head from his shoulder and asked, "Are we there yet?"

"Not quite. We're only reaching the border now."

"Oh, what do you know, I dozed off! How long have I been asleep?"

He paid no heed to her, his eyes still focused on the country outside the window.

"I didn't expect Hong Kong to be so warm, and I'm afraid Canton won't be any better," she said, yawning. "I slept less than three hours last night. This jet lag is just killing me. It's not as easy to adjust to this as it was when we went to Europe!"

He felt her weight shift away from his shoulder. Meijun straightened up, took out her purse, checkbook, and a minicalculator, and started to go through some receipts. He gave her a sidelong glance. She was still attentive, self-assured, and good-looking. She seemed to have changed very little over the past decade. Yet some of the expressions that had always made him feel removed from her were still there. They had not disappeared over the years. He directed his eyes out the window again.

There were pebbles alongside the railroad tracks, and beyond that was a dirt road flanked with shrubs and withered violet morning glories. Further in the background, he could see barbed-wire fences and a stream that despite its muddy water shimmered in the sun. Under the scalding sunlight, the dense vegetation was surprisingly full of life and moisture. As they went further inland, into the countryside of Canton, he wondered if the landscape would be the same as it was here.

His mind had been filled with numerous thoughts such as these, both before and during the trip. He thought of all the places, people, and things he could possibly think of, things that might or might not happen. . . . His thoughts had become so tangled up with old memories and fantasies, that even he could not sort them out anymore. At night he would dream, often of an endless stretch of land and glossy green rice paddies in the hazy morning light. Sometimes he dreamt of a wasteland in the midst of a howling wind, where he circled in the air like a condor, circling but never landing. A low voice was murmuring in his ear, as if someone were calling him from afar. It, too, sounded like the wind. . . .

"Chengzhi," Meijun called out to him. He turned around, lost in a daze. Her face was right in front of him, yet there seemed to be miles between them. "Let me take a closer look at the picture, so I'll be able to recognize them at the station later. That'll save us a lot of time looking around."

He opened his wallet to show her the pictures. Meijun pointed at the picture of their daughter and asked, "Why did you bring this old picture? It's three years old! Lisa's recent ones are much nicer."

It was his favorite picture of Lisa. At that time she still looked girlish, with two dark, shiny braids, like a China doll from a distant land. Now, her hair was short and permed, something he felt did not look right on her. Yet he never argued about these things with Meijun. Quickly, he continued turning the pictures over without saying a word. The one of their son was the same. He didn't want Meijun to know that it was an even older picture. He turned to the last one, a black-and-white photo, and pulled it out carefully.

Meijun scrutinized the picture and exclaimed, "I bet you won't recognize your cousin either. You say she's eight years older than you? She looks older than that, almost like an old woman."

"What did you say?" he leaned over and asked. He had heard her words, but lost in his own thoughts, he failed to comprehend them. It seemed as if they were always talking to each other from across a long distance.

"I said, you probably won't recognize her either. The station is so big, what if we don't recognize them or run into them? You should have listened to me and not asked them to meet us there. It would have been much better. . . ."

He had lost her again. Staring out the window, he noticed the train was slowly passing by a small steel bridge. He saw two different banners, first one, then the other, at the two ends of the bridge. In an instant, he was aware of himself sliding into the land. Suddenly, he had the urge to get off this steel car, take off his shoes and socks and all that separated him from the earth, and step on it, fly toward it. . . .

Yet he just sat there quietly, staring, his eyes embracing the vast landscape that was opening up before him.

He began to imagine how the land would look at night, under the soft glow of the moon and starlight. He had seen it before, but the memory had faded into the realms of his dreams. At this moment, however, in the broad light of day, with time and place so clearly defined, it all seemed unreal, even more so than his dreams.

2.

"Do you see that? That twinkling star over there? That's the Cowherd, and on the other side, that's the Weaving Maid. . . ."[2]

Auntie held onto his cousin with one hand and him with the other as they stood on the deck of the steamboat. The wind made him feel cold and want to go to the bathroom. He shivered. Although he looked up until his neck was sore, he still did not know which two stars Auntie was talking about.

That was almost all he could remember of the Yangzi River voyage. The rest was a blur. The steamboat had seemed gigantic to him as a child. The lower deck was stuffed with boxes and full of noises and the hazy sky indistinguishable from the mountains and waters.

At night, the ship rocked gently. He was sleepy, yet he was thinking of his home in North Pei. He snuggled up to his cousin and asked quietly, "How long will it be before we go back to Chongqing?"

"Silly, we're not going back!" His cousin lifted her head, and her hair spread over the pillow covering one side of her face. "We won the war, so we're going home now, silly!"

He clearly remembered how he had felt being called "silly" twice. He dared not ask anything else, but he was still confused. His father and mother had taken Little Brother back to Nanjing by plane. He never had a chance to ask them what was happening. Going home?

Was home in North Pei, the place where there were three brick walls enclosing the courtyard? The place where his five friends were? Every day, after school, he and the boys would play until dark. Their favorite game, the one they never tired of, was to steal half-ripe grapefruits from the courtyard and kick them around like a ball. They always got themselves all dirty and sweaty. Cousin would stick her face out from the window on the second floor and call him in to eat. Her moon-white blouse was the only bright spot in the darkening dusk.

During air raids, he would crawl into a deep shelter, and sleepily hold onto his mother's or Cousin's hand. Air raids became a routine part of life, accompanied by neither fear nor excitement, only drowsiness. Often he fell asleep leaning on his cousin and was awakened by the sound of his little brother crying in his ears.

All that was in the past, his cousin had informed him. She had told him just as if he were an adult: "The war is over, and everyone is going home." She even acted like an adult, especially in the manner she spoke to him. She was so tall he had to look up to her. How he wished he could stand on a stool and look into her eyes. She had always looked at him with lowered eyelids, her lashes fluttering like two dark shadows under a lamp. Her lips curled up at the corners, delighting him for no reason and making him smile with her. Then she would touch his nose with her forefinger and say, "Silly! What are you smiling about?" Gazing at the dimples at the corners of her mouth, he would continue smiling. Her fingertip felt cool, carrying an elusive scent.

He had stayed at his Uncle, Auntie, and Cousin's home in Shanghai for a long time. He could not remember how long exactly. Somehow, childhood years seemed short. Thus the days felt long in contrast—everything was long! Auntie's house was located in a long, long alley. Every day after school, when he walked back on an empty stomach, he felt the alley was endless. The staircase at the entryway was also long. The area under it was dark and damp like a mysterious den, one he never dared to explore.

The days after lunch were long, too, especially during the summer. One time, his cousin, wearing a white gauze blouse, was taking a nap in the rattan lounge chair. Her eyelashes lay quietly on her face, a few hairs stuck to the perspiration on her rosy cheeks. Not wanting to nap, he tiptoed down the stairs. Their neighbor was mincing meat in the kitchen, but its monotonous sound was not enough to wake anyone. Outside the sunlight was dazzling, brightening up the entire alley. He could hardly keep his eyes open. Someone on the block was playing the Chinese erhu.[3] They played the same tune over and over again.

*Yeeya* —*yeeya*—he could not help but memorize the tune. Later, whenever he did anything monotonous, he would find himself unwittingly humming the unknown tune.

Cousin held his hand whenever they crossed the street. It was always filled with people and cars. Once his palms were covered with sweat, and he was worried that Cousin would not like it. She was neat and clean. He had wanted to pull his hand away from her and wipe it on his pants, but he was afraid she might not want his hand back. He could still vividly recall the jitters he had felt at that moment.

A tram passed by jingling. Cousin pulled him back a little.

As they walked, the leaves on the trees along the roadside turned yellow, first a pale yellow, then gold. Palm-sized leaves fell gently; when they were about to fall on his face, they made a circle and dropped in front of his feet instead, lying perfectly still. He stepped on them, making a crackling sound.

Cousin had shoulder-length hair with ends that curled inward. Usually she fixed her hair into two braids and tied them with bows. She also had bangs. Once she told him that they were called *liuhai*. The name puzzled him. To him, it sounded like a man's name, so it was easy to remember.

One winter evening, he walked home with Cousin after seeing a movie. It was so cold they stuck their hands inside their coats for warmth. Cousin used the tip of her nose, which had turned red from the cold, and her chin to point out the direction to him. They exhaled puffs of white vapor from their nostrils, reminding him of the smoke-puffing dragons in Western fairy tales. When Cousin lowered her face to talk to him, their white vapors merged into one.

Children dressed in canvas bags walked up to them, begging for money. They were about the same age as he, perhaps a little older. He felt an unknown dread and a strange sort of guilt. He dared not look them in the eyes.

Then his father came to Nanjing to take him home. Going home again? He thought that either the house in North Pei or the one in Shanghai was their home. Father spoke with Uncle in the living room for a long time. Their voices would become very loud, followed by moments of prolonged silence. He walked into Auntie's bedroom. Auntie was talking to Cousin in a low tone of voice. Seeing him come near, she stretched out her hand to pull him close to her, but he had recently made up his mind that he was too grown-up to snuggle up to Auntie anymore. Still, he approached her until he was close enough to smell the scent of her clothes. It was a woodsy scent that was very clean and sweet. It made him feel at home.

Cousin's hair was hanging loose, with her bangs resting on her forehead. He remembered that moment very clearly. She reached out her hand and held his, saying gently, "You are leaving us soon."

"For Nanjing?" he asked, lowering his head and pursing his lips closed tightly.

"No, farther than Nanjing. You are going across the sea, to Taiwan."

He could tell by her expression that she was not joking. He panicked and persistently asked more questions. His heart sank. Even though that was thirty years ago, he could remember the way Auntie and Cousin shook their heads in response to his questions so well it seemed as if it were still happening right in front of his eyes.

He could not understand the adult world. He had no say in their decisions, so he had to accept them. A day later, he came home from school with a small piece of chalk and drew a circle in front of Auntie's front door. He wrote the day, month, and year in the circle, with the hope that someday he would come back to find it there.

He hoped, too, that when he returned, he would be as tall as Cousin, and he could almost look into her eyes at the same level. She would always stay the same age and never grow older. And someday he would be the same age as her, and he would stand before her, tall and handsome. It would be as if they had just seen each other for the first time. . . .

After he had ascended the train to leave, Auntie pulled out the handkerchief tucked in the lapel of her gown and wiped her eyes. "Go. . . come back. . . soon," her voice choked. He looked at his cousin, standing there with folded arms and her head lowered. She brushed aside the bangs on her forehead, but he could see that she was actually wiping something from the corners of her eyes. All this seemed so familiar and, yet, so helpless. He felt he could never leave them, but at this moment he told himself that he would leave with the assurance that they would wait for him. With the bed made and dishes warmed, they would wait for his return from a long, hard journey.

The train had started to move. Cousin's shape on the platform receded, first slowly, then quickly, farther and farther. Finally, the barely discernible moon-white of her clothes, and her dark hair and bangs became an unreachable beautiful shadow. She and her world swiftly faded out of sight.

His stay in Nanjing was very short, so short that later he had virtually no memory of it whatsoever. He could only dimly recall the endless stone steps leading up to Dr. Sun Yat-sen's memorial.

Then he was on a ship sailing for Taiwan. Holding onto his mother's sleeve, he walked along the railings on the deck. He felt her arm trembling, and all of a sudden, he was frightened. How he wished this ship was the steamboat on the Yangzi River and Auntie was there with him. How he wished he could turn back. He thought about the chalk circle and the writings in it, in front of Auntie's house.

The sea was rougher than the Yangzi River. He became seasick and felt miserable. At night it was windy, and as the boat tumbled on, he thought of what it must be like to be a tiny leaf in the infinite ocean. He did not go on the deck at night, so he did not even see the dark night sky. He wondered when he could have Auntie point out to him which star was the Cowherd and which one was the Weaving Maid.

3.

"Look, Lisa, that's the North Star, and the one close to it is the Big Dipper. . ." Roger said.

"It's the Seven Stars of the North Dipper," he silently corrected his son, in Chinese. Of course, he would not repeat his thoughts out loud. They spoke two different languages.

"Over there is the Little Dipper. There, look, the one that looks like a crown, that's the Cassiopeia."

"I can't tell," his younger sister replied impatiently. "It doesn't look like a crown to me. I don't know what you're talking about! You must be joking with me."

"You're stupid!" the boy retorted. "I learned that at summer camp. How could it be wrong?"

"Roger, don't talk to your sister that way," he interjected, gently reprimanding his son. "Look, the sky's so clear tonight. The only place it's clear like this is in the mountains. You can't see it in the city. Look over there, the stream of stars. . . ."

His son interrupted, "You mean the Milky Way."

"Oh, yes, the Milky Way. The Chinese call it the Silver Stream, or River of Heaven—"

"It's the Milky Way!" his daughter corrected him insistently.

He stopped talking. The thought of telling them the story about the Cowherd and the Weaving Maid disappeared as well.

Meijun was adjusting a new portable mini-tv without much success. He could not understand why anyone would want to watch television while camping out in the mountains.

"Meijun, do you know . . ."

He was going to ask her if she knew which stars were the Cow-herd and the Weaving Maid, but the sight of her grumpy face in front of the flickering screen made him swallow the rest of his question.

"I can't even get one single channel." Disappointed, Meijun turned off the television. "It's so quiet and boring here. Let's go back early tomorrow. There's so much more to do at home."

It was late. Meijun and the children had fallen asleep in the tent. He sat alone watching the smoldering campfire. All around there were insects chirping, making the great quiet night feel so empty and iso-lated. The stars were unusually brilliant. Gazing at the beautiful night sky, he was overcome by the loneliness that surrounded him, as if he were soaking in the solitude of still water.

He met Meijun during his first year of graduate school in the United States. Loneliness, school pressure, homesickness, language problems, lack of money. . . he was faced with all the common prob-lems shared by overseas students.

"Hello!"

The Asian girl who worked part-time in the library always gave him a sweet smile as she raised her head from her book to greet him. He thought that her profile looked Occidental. From her forehead to her nose, her lips, and her chin ran an outstanding, curvaceous line. He often sat reading at a desk not far from hers. When he felt tired, he would raise his head to admire her profile and watch her neatly check books out to the students.

After she got off work at night, they would go to the cafeteria in the student union to have a cup of coffee and french fries. Then he would walk her back to the dorm. Without her, he didn't know how he could have possibly made it through those days.

His younger brother had written to him, informing him that Mother was back in the hospital again. He squeezed the letter so hard that only when his nails cut into his palms did he feel better. Mother first became ill after he graduated from college. It was the first year of his military service at Phoenix Hills, in southern Tai-wan. At that time, he was preoccupied with going abroad. He could not think of much else besides application forms, reference letters, TOEFL scores, admissions, and teaching assistantships. A few days before he left, Mother was in high spirits. Believing his trip abroad would make her proud and happy, he held her bony shoulders and said confidently, "I'll return in two years, as soon as I get my master's degree."

However, Mother was unable to wait that long.

When Father's letter came, he was still writing his thesis. It was the first time his father had ever written to him himself.

". . . During the critical period of her illness, she was still concerned about your studies. Therefore, she repeatedly forbade me to divulge anything about it to you. She didn't want to disturb you. Besides, it would have been futile for you to worry across the miles. Who would have ever thought that within two weeks her illness would take an abrupt turn for the worse and she would be beyond cure. . . . In her last moments, your mother was unconscious and did not leave a word behind. That you were not here with her is an irreparable regret. . . ."

He sat in front of the only desk in his room. The draft of his thesis was spread all over it, but he could still see a corner of his father's letter. He swept the desk with his hand, and the pieces of paper dropped to the floor.

Meijun came into the room, holding a portable electric typewriter. He quietly picked the papers up off the floor and straightened them out one by one. Swiftly, she started typing for him. The crisp tapping sound on the keyboard, her agile fingers, her attentive profile—she was so close to him, yet she had no idea what he was thinking and feeling at the moment. She paused to correct a mistake and turned around to give him a smile. Then she attentively resumed her work, typing rapidly.

She had never seen his mother or his home—the courtyard in North Pei, the alley in Shanghai, the Japanese single-story house in Taipei, the steamboat, his high school basketball team, or the college classmates with whom he had gone mountain climbing. She would never know the most precious parts of his memories. But what did it matter? Those memories were so far away. Now she was the only thing close to him; she was the only thing real.

He walked up to Meijun and leaned over to embrace her from behind. Burying his face in the hair that rested on the nape of her neck, he asked, "Meijun, let's stay together. Will you marry me?"

He parked the car, turned off the engine, and looked at Meijun with a sigh.

"Let's not fight anymore; please don't be angry, okay?"

Meijun did not reply. She turned on the overhead light and took a compact out of her purse. Looking in the mirror, she dabbed some powder on her face. As he watched these familiar movements, he knew the storm was over. It had always been like this, a waste of time and emotion. They could never reach a conclusion, nor could they make

any progress. It was always the same, the argument and then reconciliation. Their arguments always ended like this, partly because he gave
in to her, and partly because Meijun cared a great deal about "losing
face." She would never let anyone, including herself, doubt that she
had the most wonderful family and the happiest of marriages.

"Let's go inside. We're already forty-five minutes late," he said,
glancing at his watch.

"So, what if we are forty-five minutes late? What if we didn't
show up at all?" she quipped at him.

He knew she would get out of the car. She just wanted to emphasize her reluctance. Tonight, his co-worker was having a party. They
had received the invitation two weeks earlier, the third one this year
from the Mos. This time, the celebration was in honor of Old Mo's
recent promotion to chairmanship of the Chemistry Department. Old
Mo had invited some Chinese friends, and it would have been very
impolite for them not to attend the party.

Meijun disliked socializing with his native friends. She had come to
America much earlier than he had. When the conversation turned to Taiwan, and they talked about high school or even college, she could not join
in at all. At first, he would go along with whatever she decided. He did not
like socializing to begin with, so he usually listened to her. But those cocktail
and tea parties of hers had become increasingly frequent over the years and
were as unbearable to him as his parties were to her. Therefore, tonight was
not the first night they had had an argument such as this one.

"Let's go in," he said wearily, getting out of the car. Meijun
followed suit, quickening her steps so she could walk ahead of him.
The Mos' house was brightly lit, and they could hear the sound of
voices and laughter. It was a cloudy starless evening in early autumn.
The air was cool and refreshing.

Meijun gently patted her hair at the doorway, glaring at him as
he walked up slowly. "Now that we're here, don't put on that quaint
face of yours and hide in some corner reading magazines! Don't make
me lose face!"

He had a funny feeling that he was the one who should have said
those words to her. However, this was one particularly good point
about Meijun. Because she would never reveal her emotions in front of
others, he never had to worry about her embarrassing him at gatherings she attended unwillingly. He knew that tonight, as always, Meijun
would smile and talk a lot, looking as graceful as ever.

Shortly after the musical doorbell rang, Mrs. Mo appeared, her
face kind and smiling. She invited them in while talking incessantly,
"You deserve a penalty, being so late. I was worried that you wouldn't

show up again, like the last two times. We all know your better half is a busy person. What if she had ten other parties to go to? Then we'd lose out again!"

She took the box Meijun handed to her and exclaimed, "Ah, you brought us something! You didn't need to do that. You know, we were just talking about you! Rarely do we see such a capable wife! One who's good at everything, has a successful career, raises great kids, and always looks so young and pretty."

Suddenly, Mrs. Mo turned around to face him, giving him a start. "Old Mo always says, Xia Chengzhi is one lucky guy!"

He smiled helplessly as he followed them into the living room. Immediately, Mrs. Mo led Meijun into the den to show her their newly purchased exercise equipment. He then relaxed and, out of habit, looked for a chair in the corner where the newspapers and magazines were placed. Then, suddenly recalling Meijun's admonishments, he picked up a drink instead and sauntered toward a group of people that included the host, Old Mo. Speaking amongst them was a young woman with whom he was unfamiliar. Old Mo introduced her to everyone as the new postdoctoral research fellow in the department. Her name was Tan or Tang. He was not paying much attention, however; what he did notice were her bright, clear eyes.

After dinner, Old Mo asked Meijun to join the bridge table in the den. At one corner of the living room, they had set up a mahjongg table. The people who were not participating in the games casually talked about the usual few topics: school, careers, real estate, inflation, while only lightly touching on domestic and international politics.

Aimlessly, he strolled toward the sliding glass door. Looking into it, he realized it was too dark outside to see the yard. Instead, all he saw was a vague reflection of himself and the living room. Then, mirrored on the glass, he noticed someone walking up to him from the crowd. He could not recognize the face from the reflection, but as soon as the person was standing beside him, he knew who it was.

"Mr. Xia, we've met before."

"Really? In Taiwan?" He turned around so they were facing each other. She was looking at him attentively, her clear, bright eyes attractive like the rest of her.

"No, in Washington. At the protest march defending Chinese sovereignty over the Diaoyutai Archipelago, that spring. . . ."

He looked at her, confused and surprised at the same time. He searched his memory. That was six or seven years ago. . . .

"You must not remember," she smiled slightly. He found her smile dazzling. "I'm Tang Ning's younger sister. That day, my brother. . . ."

"Yes, yes!" Pleasantly surprised, he cut her short. "Now I remember!" Piece by piece, he recalled that day's events. To his great surprise, he had run into his college friend, Tang Ning, during the biggest protest ever staged by overseas Chinese students.

"Well, well!" Tang Ning had cried, laughing and slapping his shoulder. "The 'Bookworm' is here, too!"

"And you, the 'Playboy,' you're here!" He had retorted, also laughing with delight and patting Tang on the shoulder. They had acted like a couple of children.

In the midst of all the excitement stirred by the protest and the delight of running into Tang Ning, he paid little attention to Tang's sister. She had been standing there next to him and had come to America from Taiwan less than a year before.

"What do you know! How's Tang Ning? Does he know I live here?"

She shook her head with a smile, "He doesn't. You two've been out of touch with each other for years! . . . After the protest, my brother still talked to me about you. He said," she paused momentarily, looking somewhat embarrassed. Perhaps it was because she suddenly realized that, after all, they were still strangers who had met only once. With a gentle smile he encouraged her to continue.

"Well, my brother said that in college you didn't care about anything except books. So, when he saw you there, holding that big sign, he was deeply touched. . . . Oh, yes, and I still remember the sign you held. It had more words on it than anyone else's: 'Chinese people can neither be killed, nor humiliated; Chinese land can neither be given away, nor sold.' Isn't that right?"

Bashfully, she smiled. Although she was at least ten years his junior, he noticed that her smile made her look even younger than her age. He remembered that Tang Ning also had a smile like that.

"Your memory is excellent!" he sighed. "If you hadn't mentioned it, I would have never remembered the sign I was holding that day."

"It's not my memory, it's just that the day was so unforgettable. I had never seen anything like it before."

"Me neither. Those days. . . ."

They both became silent, as if they knew what the other was thinking. They just stood there quietly.

After a few moments, he let out another deep sigh. "If Tang Ning could see me now, now it's the same old me again. I don't care about anything anymore, not even books." He reached his hand out to touch the sliding door, but the penetrating coldness made him draw it back.

Knowingly, she remained quiet. He suddenly had a very strange feeling, as if he had known her for many years.

"Where's Tang Ning now? I haven't heard from him for at least three or four years. I received some publications he edited a few years back."

"Well, he. . . ." She paused for a second. "How should I put it? Back then, he used to edit political newsletters, sponsor lectures, and so forth. He almost lost his job because of it. Our parents were still living in Taiwan and were scared. They begged him not to be so politically active, or at least to wait until after my father retired. He didn't really listen. But, later. . . well, as you know, later he felt lost and confused, like many other people. For a while, he was very troubled. Sometimes he would call me long-distance, but we didn't have much to say."

"Is he still like that?"

"He's working for a computer firm in Chicago now. He has a nice job, and everything seems fine. But not long ago he remarked to me, 'Once you have been the sea, it's hard to be a stream.'"

"'Once you've been the sea, it's hard to be a stream,'" he nodded slowly.

"I understand," he whispered, as if to himself. "I understand."

Although he was not sure when he would contact Tang Ning, he wrote down his address and phone number in the little notebook he always carried with him.

After conversing a while longer, he said in embarrassment, "I beg your pardon. I'm very careless, but your name is Tang . . . Tang . . ."

"Tang Jing. J-I-N-G."

"Oh, Tang Jing."

"I have another brother whose name is Tang Ping. I remember my father telling us their generation went through so much turmoil that they did not ask for anything other than peace for the country. . . ."[4]

"Tang Ping, I know him. Isn't he a year younger than Tang Ning and I?"

She nodded.

"Oh, now I remember!" he exclaimed happily. "I must have seen you in Taiwan before! I've been to your house!"

"It's possible, but I don't remember," she beamed. "I'm much younger than my brothers and sisters. When they were in college, I was only in elementary school. They hung around with their friends all day long and had very little time for me."

Leaning his forehead on one of his fingers, he thought about it for a few moments, and then smiled. "I'm right, I have seen you before.

You used to live in an alley off Jianguo South Road, right? One time, four or five of us went over to ask Tang Ning—that's right, it was Tang Ning—to go mountain climbing. Just as we were about to leave, a little girl ran out of the house and would not let go of him. I think that maybe she was even crying. Wasn't that you?"

She mused, "How can I possibly remember that? You could make up any story you wanted to, and I still wouldn't remember."

Now, the whole thing came back to him. He continued, "Back then, I was thinking on Tang Ning's behalf: How is he going to get out of this? You didn't hold on to him long though. After a while you let go. I still remember thinking, what a lovely, pretty little girl. . . ."

She was still smiling, but slowly lowered her head and started playing with the glass in her hands. Abruptly, he realized that the little girl he was talking about was the same grown woman standing in front of him. Suddenly, he felt awkward and could not go on, but the silence was even worse than not speaking. Apparently sensing his embarrassment, she came to his rescue.

"I'm the youngest in my family, so when I was little, I always demanded a lot from my parents and brothers. You probably saw me then. What a small world it is!"

They smiled as they looked at each other. He could tell that, like him, she was not talkative. But that night they stood there in front of the sliding door, with their backs to the noisy, brightly lit living room, and talked for a long time. He felt as if he had known her for many years, which, in a way, was true.

After the party, he went home and dug out the cardboard box buried in the corner of the closet in his study. It was filled with the old magazines and newspapers that he had not had the heart to throw away after he moved. He seemed to remember putting the publications Tang Ning had sent him there, too. He was right. They were there, along with copies of other handwritten publications and newspaper clippings. There were a few he could not remember having ever read. He tried to recall his state of mind when he first read some of the other articles back then. It was like walking on a road that seemed familiar, but somehow the things around it had all been changed.

After the protest, he had participated in a couple of activities sponsored by students at his school. At that time, he was an assistant professor fighting for his tenure and a promotion. He was experiencing a tremendous amount of pressure at work, and that winter, he felt especially torn between getting his promotion and changing schools. Snowflakes had blown on his face like razor blades in the cold, chilly wind. He was saddened by the thought of Meijun having to pick up their young children in the snowstorm after a day of hard work.

It was not for lack of passion that he did not get involved. Often scenes of the protest still floated up in his mind, but he had too much on his mind and never devoted himself to it again. The following year, he arrived at the present university he taught at as a tenured associate professor. When he lost contact with Tang Ning around that time, he also let go of his last link to those early days.

He settled in to his new position and Meijun also found a good job at a local bank. However, often he would awaken in the middle of the night for no apparent reason. And, often he saw an invisible self retreating farther and farther into the distant dark, retreating farther and farther out of life, meekly and without argument.

4.

Meijun had been promoted again and was now the assistant manager of her branch. As of late, she had been arguing less and less with him, especially about their social life. Perhaps she thought if it was so important to him, she might as well give in to it. He was somewhat touched by her efforts, but she failed to understand that the social engagements actually meant nothing to him. Perhaps she would never understand.

When spring arrived, the Chinese faculty and students hosted a barbecue by the lake, some twenty miles out of town. Meijun was in high spirits and cheerfully agreed to bring some food.

He parked outside the picnic area and helped Meijun carry a big box of marinated pork chops and chicken legs. When he raised his head, he caught sight of Tang Jing in the distance, wearing an oversized beige sweater and jeans. She was playing frisbee with two students. Suddenly the sun and breeze seemed unusually pleasant and the box in his hands felt extra light.

After meeting Tang Jing at the Mos', they had run into each other several times on campus and at a few Chinese gatherings. They did not have much chance to talk, however, since they were often interrupted by others after exchanging only a few sentences. But he had formed the habit of searching for her on such occasions anyway. Once he found her, he would quietly wait for her to turn around and see him, and then she would give him a gentle smile. That was all. Many times, when he drove on campus, he saw her back from afar. Sometimes, when he saw her, she was still wearing her white lab coat, setting off the beauty of her dark, shoulder-length hair. She almost always walked alone, hurriedly. Her solitude bespoke a silent loneliness and pride, which for some reason restrained him from talking to her. Perhaps he didn't want to disturb her; perhaps her shape was only a pale reflection that he had projected on the glass sliding door. . . .

He did not want to analyze his feelings. He could vaguely sense something deeply hidden and formless inside of him. It was better to let it be buried there, not to bring it to life. Perhaps he should never have met her.

But now she was coming his way. She was laughing, running in his direction after the frisbee. When she brushed her hair from her face, she saw him. For an instant, it seemed that her eyes revealed something. Then she smiled at him, picked up the frisbee, and walked away.

Boys from several of the families were playing soccer together. Fourteen-year-old Roger, already almost as tall as himself, was handling the ball nimbly. Lisa was under a tree, chatting with the Mos' daughter, and every now and then a chuckle could be heard. A graduate student from his department was playing badminton with Old Mo. With his beer belly, Old Mo had a hard time picking up the birdie. The aroma of barbecue wafted in the air. Everything seemed so right and pleasant, yet he could feel waves of anxiety surging up inside of him, until they could almost no longer be suppressed. Inside his pocket was a small piece of paper that he had kneaded into a soft ball with his fingers.

Meijun and several wives were standing around the barbecue. He heard Mrs. Mo saying, ". . . an old maid of almost thirty, yet still so proud. Two American professors in the department are interested in her, but she doesn't pay any attention to them. Who knows what she has in mind?"

"She's pretty all right, but her age! Besides, she has a Ph.D., too good for some men!"

A higher wave of anxiety washed over him. He walked away quickly, but the sound of Meijun's voice stopped him. "Chengzhi, would you go find some twigs? We don't have enough charcoal here."

"You have the best husband!" It was Mrs. Mo again. "So nice and quiet. He listens to everything you say."

He walked toward the lake. The early spring wind was still chilly and felt stronger by the shore. He saw Tang Jing standing alone, facing the lake, her hair billowing in the wind.

He immediately wanted to ask, "Are you cold? Be careful you don't catch cold." And it suddenly occurred to him that he had not felt or shown such concern for another person in a long time. He felt a gentle prick in his heart, but it was beyond his reach.

She turned around to look at him and did not seem at all surprised. He walked closer to her. His intuition told him she was tired and lonely.

They walked along the lake for a short while, neither of them uttering a word. The silence was disturbing, like a noise, making them both uneasy. He did not know how to break it, nor did he really want to. For some reason, sensing her uneasiness comforted him.

She stopped and spoke gently, "Let's go back. It's getting cold."

He stretched out his arm and grasped her shoulder. Immediately, he felt it quivering. He could not refrain himself from exerting more pressure, and he held her tighter. She walked with him quietly for a while; then, as if her mind was made up, she pulled away from him. Brushing her hair away from her face, she said hurriedly, "The wind's too strong. I'll go ahead first."

His arm was still extended, and he could still feel the warmth of her shoulder and body on his palm. But her back was turned, and she was already way ahead of him. She walked in a sea of gently swaying green grass and twinkling yellow flowers, drifting farther and farther away.

After their encounter, he had picked up the phone in his office several times, longing to call her, but he always hung up with great self-control. He was aware that he was approaching a turning point, the turning point of the unknown or perhaps, as it was, the knowable. Would he risk predictable chaos and pain for the happiness of reawakening after a winter hibernation, for the ecstasy and rejuvenation of rebirth? Still, he refrained from going to see her.

This self-restraint, he thought, was actually nothing more than proof of the fact he was too cowardly to pay the price and face the consequences. When he looked at himself in the bathroom mirror in the morning, it was like looking at the face of a stranger. His life still revolved routinely with this world, and the gray hair on his temples increased day by day. "Coward!" he spat at himself vehemently. "You coward!" Then he smiled at his reflection sarcastically.

Tang Jing did not show up at the Mos' last big party. However, during the course of dinner, he overheard she had decided to go back to Taiwan that summer to teach at her alma mater.

"Didn't you tell me what a fine researcher she is?" one of the Chinese professors asked Old Mo. "Why didn't you ask her to stay?"

"Everyone has their own mind. Even the department chair can't do anything about it. She's a very independent girl."

"Women, nowadays, they're really something. . . ."

That night, as soon as he returned home, he rushed into the bathroom and threw up. Even tears came streaming down his face.

Meijun was upset, and blamed it on his drinking and the greasy food those Chinese wives had cooked.

He pondered on it for days and concluded that it would be better to let the whole affair pass. Time was a marvelous thing anyway. No matter how great the pain, time would heal it. It was just that he didn't know how long this pain would last. He remembered a movie he had seen many years ago. The hero was riding on a train that stopped at a station during the night. Another train stopped next to it. In the dim lamplight of the window, the protagonist caught a glimpse of the heroine's face. It was the same face that had constantly appeared in his dreams. Just as they discovered each other, the trains started to move again, despite them frantically calling out to each other from behind the window panes. The trains ran in opposite directions, farther and farther, until they both finally disappeared in the dark night.

*The trains that carried him and Tang Jing should not have crossed their paths in the first place,* he thought.

One afternoon, after school, he ran into her again. He saw her walking alone on the sidewalk, and all his resolution crumbled in a second. He let his car slide by her slowly, as if for fear of frightening her.

"Let me take you home," he said, as he rolled the window down.

"No, I . . ." she paused, looking frightened anyway. "I'm used to it, walking, that is. It only takes twenty minutes, it's not far. . . ." She rarely talked in this mumbo jumbo fashion.

"I'll take you home," he repeated stubbornly. He leaned over to open the door for her. After some hesitation, she got into the car.

Her eyes did not leave his face until she sat down. "You've lost weight."

He smiled bitterly, not saying a word.

"Did you know that I'm leaving?" she asked after a brief silence.

Looking ahead, he spoke almost rudely, "Tell me how to get there, to your place. I don't know how to get there!"

When they arrived at her apartment, she stepped out of the car. Without waiting for an invitation, he also got out and followed her. Standing behind her, he watched as she looked for her key and fumbled at the door nervously. It was a small studio. There were a couple suitcases and some cardboard boxes scattered around on the floor, making the place look even more crammed. Seeing that she was packing angered him. His hand released the fury of his rage on the doorknob as he slammed the door closed with a loud bang.

Again, she seemed to be frightened, and said hurriedly, "I'll go make us some tea. I always drink tea after I get home."

She had always looked so calm and composed, never showing any timidity or confusion. Thinking of her trembling shoulders, he felt so full of love for her it began to hurt.

She brought out two cups of tea from the kitchen and stood in front of him. The tea cups clattered on the tray. He saw the hand holding the tray quivering slightly. He took the tray and set it on the table. Then, grasping her hands in his, he pulled her into his arms. His brain was humming loudly. It was the sound of the world retreating until there were only the two of them left.

The light curtains fluttered in the summer breeze, and outside the window, far away, children were playing and laughing. It was so quiet around them he could almost hear both of their pulses. The boxes were still lying on the floor; a few stacks of books and journals sat on the desks; and a tapestry of the Great Wall hung on the facing wall. There was a watermark on the ceiling near the corner of the closet. Now everything seemed so peaceful and natural. The agitation, passion, and rage of the past few days was gone, and all that was left in his heart was a calm, clear tenderness. He smelled her hair. It had a distant yet familiar scent, but he could not remember where he had smelled it before.

It was getting dark outside. She lifted her head up from his shoulder and took his left hand to look at his watch. He pulled it back, not wanting her to see it.

Time had a way of passing on its own—a few hours, a few years, a few decades. Life also passed by on its own. She did not catch up with him, and he did not catch up with . . . with what, he did not know.

It was completely dark now, and he had to leave. She did not ask him to stay, just as he did not ask her to stay. She had her own path; he had neither the right, nor the power, to keep her with him. He just could not bear the thought of her becoming another him ten years from now.

When he was outside, he turned around to see her standing at the door, surrounded by the thick dusk. Her face was a hazy white spot of light. As he raised his head before getting into the car, he saw the most beautiful starry summer sky that he had ever seen. He turned around wanting to point it out to her, but she was already gone.

5.

He dreamt he was walking on a street that was familiar, yet strange. Each side of the street was lined with shabby buildings, and a woman stood at the end of it. He started walking toward her. As he drew closer, he saw she was wearing a loose-fitting moon-white blouse and skirt, and had dark shiny hair that hung on her shoulders, with bangs on her forehead. He was unable to see her face clearly. The clothes and body were so familiar; he must have seen her and known her many years ago. She turned and walked toward a row of houses. At that moment, he saw her face clearly. It was Tang Jing. He chased her, screaming her name, but he did not know which door she had gone through. Behind him he could hear a bell ringing, *dong-dong-dong,* each peal louder and more hurried than the one before. Amid the deafening roar of the bell, he looked for her in a panic, pushing open one door after another. Inside each door was nothing but deep darkness, filled with dust and spiderwebs, resembling the space under the staircase of an old house, from long time ago. He was terrified and felt as if he was unable to take another step.

However, he still searched for a door, a door with writings beneath it. He couldn't find it. It was getting dark, and suddenly he realized the bell was no longer ringing. The dreadful silence surrounded him. He turned around abruptly, and she was standing behind him, in the twilight. Her moon-white blouse glowed against the dusky shadows. He slowly approached her. His legs seemed to be bogged down by weights, every step so difficult. In the gloomy evening light, he stared at her face and the long lashes under her bangs. It was not Tang Jing, it was his cousin. He reached out his hand, signaling her to give him her hand. He could not go on anymore. He was weeping. Yet she was still standing so far away, their hands never touching.

He was awakened by the feeling of Meijun pushing at him, "Wake up! What's the matter with you, you're mumbling and crying. Did you have a nightmare?"

He laid there in a daze, feeling wetness in his eyes and on his cheeks. He was not completely out of the dream yet, but he knew he could never return. Unable to go back to sleep, he put his robe on in the dark, went downstairs, and walked on the patio in their backyard. The night was cool like water, the moon was bright, and the stars were few.

It had been two weeks since Tang Jing left.

On the other side of the world, she was sixteen hours ahead of him, his tomorrow. What was she doing now? He could call her from his office, but did not know her phone number. Actually, if he really wanted to find out, he could get it. He wondered, if it were ten years ago, would he buy a plane ticket and fly to Taipei? He didn't know. Well, then, how about twenty years ago? He did not know about that either, just as he didn't know what he would be doing ten or twenty years from now. All he knew was that, at this moment, he felt trapped in his house. His wife and children were asleep upstairs, and his diploma, a pile of lecture notes, and his dissertation were downstairs. Thirteen miles away was the university where he had a guaranteed lifetime position. These things composed his world of system and order. He did not have the courage to break out of it after all. He assumed that if he lived until he was eighty, then he was already halfway through his lifetime. He thought of his life since childhood and of how he would live it if he could start over again.

He stood there, allowing his thoughts to drift most of the night, until the few sparkles of starlight faded into the light of dawn.

Before she left, Tang Jing asked him to keep in touch with her brother. He remembered her words, and the following evening, he dialed Tang Ning's phone number. When it rang, he suddenly became nervous, not knowing what to say. He was unsure as to whether or not Tang Jing had said anything about them to Tang Ning—most likely not. What difference would it make anyway? At first he was speechless. It was Tang Ning who was pleasantly surprised and talked a lot. As he listened to the sound of Tang's voice and laughter, he began to feel at ease. He even felt like crying. He was exhausted and finally he could rest, because Tang Ning was there.

After that, he talked to Tang Ning on the phone often, whether he was happy or sad, or when he missed Tang Jing badly. Gradually, he calmed down somewhat.

One day, Tang Ning called him at the office. "I'm going back next month."

Immediately, he thought of Tang Jing.

"To Taiwan? For how long?"

"No, to the mainland. It's a business trip. My company's sending me. Of course, I don't feel like it's a business trip. You know what I mean."

He remembered what Tang Jing had told him: Once you have been the sea, it's hard to be a stream. He repeated it to Tang Ning. Tang laughed heartily at the other end.

"That's true, that's true."

"That was then, so what about now?" he pursued further.

"'Since you've been the sea once, why can't you go back to being the sea again?' Little Jing said that. Didn't she already go back? Our seas were originally one and the same."

Two days before Tang Ning left, he called Xia, asking if he could do anything for him. Without hesitation, he gave Tang the names of his uncle, auntie, and cousin, and asked him to inquire in Shanghai about their whereabouts.

Three months after Tang Ning returned with their address, he sent the first letter he had ever written to Auntie and Cousin.

Even after he had Cousin's reply and photograph in his hand, he still could not believe it was possible. He would wake up in the middle of the night and go to his study. Turning on the desk lamp, he would reread the letter and look at the picture again carefully. Every time he did that, it was like the first time, as if they were a dream that would vanish any moment.

One person was missing from the picture, but was replaced by two others he had never seen. Uncle had passed away twelve years ago. The old woman in the picture was Auntie, and the woman whom he at first took to be Auntie turned out to be Cousin. The middle-aged man beside Cousin was her husband, and there was also a young girl. He looked at her for a long time. He knew it was not Cousin, but her daughter, An'an.

As he gazed at the black and white shapes of Auntie and Cousin, his eyes began to tear. Even with his vision blurred, he could still see what time had done to them. He walked into the bathroom and looked at himself in the mirror. Like them, he too had waded in the river of time for thirty years. Thirty years! Yet, there they were, still waiting for him with the bed made and the dishes warmed. They were waiting for him to return after his long voyage.

6.

"... I don't know where to begin telling you about those thirty years. Mother asked me to tell you in my letter that she is old and her legs are bad. Her eyes are getting worse and worse, too. She only hopes she can see you and make your favorite desserts before she is unable to see or use her legs to walk. I remember how you used to love dumplings and roasted chestnuts. Back then, Mother always worried about you getting indigestion if you ate too much. So, every time we went to the shopping area near the temple of the local deities to eat dumplings, we always kept it a secret from her. . . ."

As he stared out the train window, he recited Cousin's letters one by one. A vast stretch of verdant fields could be seen outside. The subtropical landscape was so familiar that he almost forgot where he was. The year he served at the Infantry Academy in South Taiwan, after graduating from college, he traveled on the north-south railroad many times. How similar it was—the rice paddies, hills, windbreaks, the ponds reflecting the blue sky, and even the farmers walking on the ridges. But, at that time, preoccupied by the business of going abroad, he was in no mood to appreciate the land to which he would soon say goodbye. Nor did he pay much attention to the abrupt deterioration of his mother's health.

"... The greatest regret Mother has is that she will never see your mother again. They were closer than sisters. It is comforting to learn from your letter that Uncle is in good health. That makes Mother feel relieved. She's hoping she can see her brother again someday."

By the time he went back to Taiwan for a visit, after receiving his doctoral degree that summer, Mother had been gone over three years. He sat in the house, face to face with his father, both of them burdened with apology and guilt as well as silent blame and anger toward each other. Finally, unable to stand the tension any longer, he took Meijun and their son to southern Taiwan for a week.

The night before he returned to the United States, he had to bid his father farewell. That night, under the light, he suddenly realized Father was very old. When Father shed tears in front of him, he was so shocked that it almost took his breath away. He had never imagined, in his wildest dreams, that his father, who had always seemed so self-assured, was really a lonely old man. They talked until the wee hours of the morning, and he boarded the plane without a minute of sleep.

Father had never before shown his weak side in front of him. It was not until that night he felt close to his father. But it was all too late. At that time, he was close to thirty, a new father himself. During his adolescence, when he needed his father to talk to him the most, his father was always in his office, at a banquet, or in the lecture hall, energetic and appealing, talking eloquently to others. It was not until he reached adulthood and became a father himself that his father reappeared, as it were, to tell him that he actually loved him and his mother very much. It was too late. It was regrettable, like a missed train. It was too late for Mother and him, for Father and Mother and him. It was all too late.

"... How Mother would like to write to you herself! But, she really can't see very well. She said for you to write to your father often and go back to see him when you have the time. Or maybe have him come spend some time with you and his grandchildren. You are a busy man, but you should remember that Uncle is old and alone. . . ."

He wrote a letter to his father telling him about his planned trip to visit Auntie. Father's reply came quickly. In his letter, he repeatedly asked him to convey his concern to them. Obviously lost for words, his ink was blurred by the stains of his tears. He could imagine how Father must have felt when he wrote the letter and felt closer to him than ever before. The letter was now tucked in a briefcase to be shown to Auntie. He planned to take many pictures this time. After he returned home, he would ask someone to deliver them to his father. If his father was interested, his father could come live with him in the United States for a while and decide where he would like to go from there.

"... You asked me about my husband, your cousin-in-law. After being married over twenty years, I can't really answer that question. Over the last few years, he did quite a bit of hard labor, but now he is teaching again. He is a man of few words, except in the classroom. I have spent half my life with him, and we've endured a lot of hardship together. I'm used to his company. ... When you arrive, you can see for yourself. Maybe you will like him. ..."

He did not know. "Cousin-in-law," what an incredible term! He always felt that Cousin would never grow up, get married, and grow old. Yet, there was a man who, during all those years he was away, walked the road of life with her. What did it matter whether or not he liked that man? It was he who could not keep time from passing. Time did not wait for him, and he could not be everyplace he would like to be. There was no one to blame for that. Take Meijun, for example, could he blame her for showing up too late in his life? She had been trying very hard to walk toward him. He, too, should walk toward her. He should meet her halfway. He turned around to look at her, so close to him. The same face that did his typing in the dorm that year was this close, too. They had been traveling together for so long, and the road from now on would be even longer. Since they had to go on together, why not do it well? He was lost in a reverie.

"... You said An'an looks like me. It's only in appearance. Her generation is beyond us. When she graduated from junior high, she was not even sixteen. She roamed the countryside with a production brigade.[5] I still remember the day I saw her off. After all those years, she was no longer the little girl who held on to me, crying when we said goodbye. She seems to have lived a whole life. ... But, there are times when suddenly I see the old me in her. I'll let you find out for yourself. ..."

The broadcast on the train announced that it was approaching the station. Meijun checked their tickets, visas, and carry-on bags in an orderly fashion, and then she held his hand gently. He realized that his hand was sweaty and trembling slightly. He gave her a grateful look. How composed and relaxed she was. Loneliness and agitation suddenly overcame him, making him feel as if he were about to fall apart.

As the train approached the platform, the first thing he noted was the clock on the wall. He realized it was also sixteen hours ahead of his time at home in the States, as was Tang Jing's home in Taiwan. Tang Jing, Auntie, Cousin, and An'an were all in the same time zone; and now he was here, too. He felt a warmth flow through his heart and into his eyes.

The train had come to a complete stop. He looked out the window and saw among the crowd a middle-aged woman standing on the platform not far away. He caught sight of her immediately, as if answering her call, inaudible and gentle. Then he saw a young girl standing next to her. She did not have bangs on her forehead or shoulder-length hair and was not wearing a moon-white blouse and skirt either. But, as she stood there, her figure was exactly like that of the young girl standing on the gradually receding platform thirty years ago, that indelible memory in his mind. He gazed at this short-haired girl, dressed in a short-sleeved white blouse and gray pants. She seemed to notice him and started walking toward his window, looking at him attentively. Then he saw her eyes, a pair of bright, well-defined eyes. He must have seen this pair of eyes—such clear and beautiful eyes—on another face, at another time, at another place.

He stepped off the train and walked toward them.

### Notes

1. "Homeward Bound" ("Jinxiang") was translated by Michelle Yeh with the permission of the author and the publisher, and is published here in English for the first time. This translation is based on the story's original in the collection entitled *Tiantangniao hua* (Taipei: Hongfan, 1988), pp. 25–68.

2. "Cowherd" and "Weaving Maid" are the Chinese names for Altair and Vega. According to Chinese legend, the celestial Cowherd and Weaving Maid fell in love with each other and neglected their heavenly duties. Consequently, they were punished by the Jade Emperor, who made them live at opposite ends of the Milky Way, never to see each other except on the seventh night of the seventh month of the lunar calendar.

3. The *erhu* is a traditional Chinese musical instrument with two strings, often used in the Beijing opera.

4. The three names, Ning, Ping, and Jing, all mean peace.

5. During the Cultural Revolution, unofficially but popularly dated from 1966 to 1976, many youths who joined the Red Guards lived in the countryside with their "production brigades" to learn from the peasants and help with agricultural production.

# The Divided Self and the Search for Redemption: A Study of Li Li's Fiction

## Michelle Yeh

In the fictional world of Li Li, we often encounter a moment of solitude and confusion, agonizing and incomprehensible, a vertiginous moment of probing into the deepest recesses of one's consciousness and the core of one's being. This moment appears in "A Day in Professor Tan's Life" when the aged Chinese literature professor reaches into buried memories of his youthful idealism, love for his mentor, and tension between the unbending mentor and his opportunist disciple, who is now a powerful colleague in Tan's department:

> The shrill cry of cicadas made Professor Tan open his eyes. Outside the window the sky was still dazzlingly bright—so bright that it blurred his vision—and the loud cicadas still cried relentlessly without fear of losing their voices. It all was so pressing, pressing one to uncover those things of long ago, to hang them out like airing old clothes in the blue sky and sun. Professor Tan's head no longer felt like it was boiling, but a ball of heat had moved into his chest and was stuck in his throat.[1]

In "Night Trees," a frustrated teenage runaway takes refuge at her school and experiences similar emotions, although couched in almost opposite, sensuous images:

> She stood still, then slowly slid down the wall till she squatted on the ground. She felt cold, as if soaked in cold water, boundless cold water, boundless fear and helplessness. She was under a spell, squatting immobile at the foot of the wall, staring at the light overhead. Gradually hypnotized by the hazy light, she was drawn into its halos, a whirlpool, a bottomless vertigo.[2]

In "The Moon of the West River," the hero, feebly rebelling against the past glory of his family, dreams of the dagger that symbolizes his dying father's military prowess:

> The dagger seemed very thin, giving off a pale blue glint under the dimming light; however, the spots of rust on it appeared rather thick, maybe because of its age. He wasn't sure; he could only vaguely see the dagger lying still in the dark, perhaps it had blood stains on it. He could not see it clearly. He tried to walk away, but his legs were so weak they could hardly move. He heard a ring by his ears. He tried to marshall up some strength to wake up—he told himself it was a dream, wake up! . . . Possessed, he struggled to awaken.[3]

The nightmarish past exerts an equally obsessive power on Xia Chengzhi, a professor who compromises his quest for his emotional and intellectual ideals, for security and family unity:

> He was unable to see her face clearly. The clothes and body were so familiar; he must have seen her and known her many years ago. She turned and walked toward a row of houses. At that moment, he saw her face clearly. It was Tang Jing. He chased her, screaming her name, but he did not know which door she had gone through. Behind him he could hear a bell ringing, *dong-dong-dong*, each peal louder and more hurried than the one before. Amid the deafening roar of the bell, he looked for her in a panic, pushing open one door after another. Inside each door was nothing but deep darkness, filled with dust and spiderwebs, resembling the space under the staircase of an old house, from long time ago. He was terrified and felt as if he was unable to take another step.

> However he still searched for a door, a door with writings beneath it. He couldn't find it. It was getting dark, and suddenly he realized the bell was no longer ringing. The dreadful silence surrounded him. He turned around abruptly, and she was standing behind him, in the twilight. Her moon-white blouse glowed against the dusky shadows. He slowly approached her. His legs seemed to be bogged down by weights, every step so difficult.[4]

Finally, for Shen Chang'an, a student from China studying in the United States, the attempt to recall the past is always accompanied by a piercing headache:

> He didn't really know when this headache and ringing in his ears had begun. It developed so gradually—at first just an infrequent mild pain, sometimes without the ringing—he didn't pay attention to it. By the time he began to take notice, the headache had already become unbearable. It felt as if clusters of fine needles were being shot randomly through the inside of his head, and the next moment, ultra-high frequency sound waves, like those produced by scratching glass, would pierce his ears. . . . He held his head in his hands, but couldn't touch the sore spot the way he could touch and massage pain in the skin or muscle, however severe it might be. The pain came from a source so deep, so far away that it was completely out of reach and totally unthinkable.[5]

The above passages have been cited at some length because they not only illustrate an important device Li Li uses to lead the reader into the inner world of her characters, but also bespeak a dominant theme in her stories. In the above examples, the characters experience fear, confusion, helplessness, and pain. These experiences, evoked by memories, are ultimately inseparable from their personal family and educational backgrounds, or even their life experiences as a whole. The moment often arrives unexpectedly and is beyond the control of the characters; they come under its power without warning or defense, hence making more conspicuous their own helplessness and confusion. Artistically, the device often signals a stream of consciousness where the past and present intertwine with dreams and reality. Thus, it serves the purpose of delving into the characters' innermost being, beyond time and space, presenting it in its naked truth. Descriptions of such moments are thematically crucial to the expression of the author's central concerns.

The cause of the "moment of vertigo" lies in the dichotomies between reality and conscience, and the external and inner self, of which the characters are acutely aware. Such a dichotomy creates a tension between the characters' perception of what they would like to be and what they are, or what they have to be for various reasons that will be examined later. In the case of Professor Tan, it is clear that his youthful idealism and deep love for his mentor, Kang Yue, have never really died even though, by all appearances, he has shown little of

either. That is why, after reading the vituperative article on Kang by Xia
Chenbai, his present colleague and former fellow disciple under Kang,
he stays up late writing a retort. The crux of the story occurs at the end
when the professor shoves the retort he has spent hours writing into
the drawer and tears up the envelope he meant to use to deliver it. He
returns to school the next day with a lowered head and his usual
cautious steps. The sting of conscience that prompts him to defend his
beloved teacher eventually yields to the security and peacefulness of
his humble and lonely world which he hesitates to destroy.

In "Night Trees," Du Juzhu is ashamed of the wide gap between
her self-image: intelligent, sensitive, loving, and yearning for love; and
the image her family ruthlessly forces on her: poor, shabbily dressed,
lacking social grace, and sexually naive. The immediate cause of her
running away from home can be attributed to her failure to request
money for the class picnic, and the jeering and scolding she receives
from her parents. However, her act of running away more aptly represents the explosion of pent-up discontent with her surroundings and
life in general. Her sense of disillusionment and frustration is intertwined with her simultaneous fears and fantasies about sex. For instance, she falls in love with a history teacher who disappears
mysteriously; political reasons are intimated. At the same time, she is
repulsed, curious, and even attracted to obscene writing on the girls'
restroom walls, as well as the unfounded speculation about the sexual
perversity of the homeless janitor, Old Wei. The story ends dramati-
cally with Old Wei, who kindly takes her in and gives her food and
shelter, being falsely accused of taking advantage of her by her hysteri-
cal mother and brought to total disgrace. It is an ironic comment on the
perceptual dichotomies between reality and appearance, and an individual's self-image and society's image, all of which are often perpetu-
ated by superficial assumptions and societal prejudices.

Du is unique among Li Li's characters in that, befitting her role as
a teenage student with little worldly experience, her self-under-
standing is incomplete. Her rebellion against the oppressive environment and her attempt to achieve a sense of autonomy and pride are
emotional, impulsive responses rather than the result of self-introspec-
tion and moral conviction. However, most of Li Li's heroes and heroines are mature intellectuals. They are painfully conscious of their
divided selves, but feel helpless to change the situation. For instance,
Xia Chengzhi, in "Homeward Bound," feels "trapped in his house. His
wife and children were asleep upstairs, and his diploma, a pile of
lecture notes, and his dissertation were downstairs. Thirteen miles
away was the university where he had a guaranteed lifetime position.

These things composed his world of system and order."[6] Shen Chang'an in "The Last Subway Train" tries to bury his past of mindless cruelty and wasted time during the Cultural Revolution. However, "after coming to America, he realized that he could travel to the end of the earth, yet he still could not escape from himself or those vivid and obscure memories. They followed him stubbornly, constantly reminding him with physical pain."[7]

In a broad sense, the theme of the divided self is found in all of Li Li's fiction to date. In addition to the stories discussed above, "The Wedding Feast"[8] exposes the pitiable hypocrisy of many overseas Chinese whose snobbery and materialism camouflage their deep-rooted feelings of insecurity and inferiority. In "The Lost Dragons,"[9] the successful physics professor is rendered helpless by his other less successful roles as father and husband. In "Snow Field,"[10] two pregnant women, one from Taiwan studying for her doctorate in America and the other living in rural China, are torn between their maternal instinct to protect their unborn babies and the pressure, not entirely from external sources, to get an abortion. "Spring Hope"[11] depicts the long-term guilt of an old man separated from his children in mainland China, and his successful attempt to be reunited with them. In "The Grand Ceremony,"[12] a mental patient who lives in the past manages to escape from the asylum and puts on his old general's uniform to inspect the troops. Even in "Under the Fortress Wall,"[13] the young professor struggles to protect his independence and supremacy in his small kingdom against what he perceives to be the menacing forces of love and marriage.

Throughout her writing career, beginning in 1971 with the publication of her first story, "A Day in Professor Tan's Life," Li Li exhibits consistent concern with the integrity and unity of the self. This ideal of man living in perfect accord with his conscience, aspirations, and environment, however, remains a vague and distant dream vis-à-vis the stark reality of the broken self, the divided consciousness. Under her objective and realistic scrutiny, Li Li refuses to provide us facile endings by simply manufacturing happy resolutions to man's most universal basic conflict, the conflict within oneself and the world. Consequently, her stories are more often pessimistic than optimistic, more often heavy-handed than light and witty. A writer rather than sociologist, she is interested above all in examining the complexity of this conflict and its impact on man rather than suggesting solutions to the problem. In her sensitive explorations, she delineates the various forces behind man's failure to achieve the totality of the self, pinpointing three of the major sources of anguish: family, politics, and culture.

Born into a low-income military family that lives in a military housing community, Du Juzhu in "Night Trees" experiences a microcosm of society that is "primitive and cruel."[14] Parental neglect and financial difficulty imbue her with a deep sense of insecurity and inferiority. Although she attempts to develop herself as fully as possible, such as by insisting on going to a regular high school instead of vocational school, she is nonetheless frustrated and lacks self-confidence, as indicated in the following passage:

> She hated her home, not only because it was small, filthy, and disorderly, without one good thing, one thing that belonged to her, or one person that needed her, but also because it was unpresentable and it shamed her. She felt the same about the entire compound. But, it was precisely because her home and compound were so unpresentable that she enjoyed a sense of superiority. The unpresentability almost set off her strong points, even if she did not have any. She felt that she was gray, which only looked white amid pitch black. Thus, the black environment proved to be necessary for her, which made her even angrier.[15]

The story sensitively portrays the identity crisis, sexual or otherwise, commonly experienced by adolescents, a crisis aggravated in this case by Du's strained circumstances and loveless home environment. The central symbol in the story, the young trees planted near the entrance of her school in perfunctory observance of Dr. Sun Yat-sen's birthday, also known as "Tree-planting Day," is thus given an ironic twist. A motto quoted in the story states: "It takes ten years to rear a tree, a hundred years to rear a human being." Young trees are a traditional Chinese symbol of youth as the pillars of future society. Just as trees need constant care and pruning, youths need abundant love and patient guidance. Therefore, it is only natural that the motto is used to emphasize the importance of education. However, in our story, there is serious doubt on the part of the author that our heroine, growing with a distorted, unfulfilled sense of self, will grow into a strong tree. Besides her oppressive home, the overall school environment is described in similarly negative terms. This is symbolically expressed in Du's nightmare after she falls asleep completely exhausted on Old Wei's cot:

> It was the history teacher, his feet also in shackles. . . . She was struck by sadness and just when she was about to call out, she saw Father run up with a leather whip in his raised hand, and

slash!—it hit Old Wei instead. With shackles on his feet, Old Wei's blood dripped, forming a long clear bloody trail on the concrete. By the road was a row of young trees . . . instantly dyed by the crimson blood. . . . Then, she heard Mother screaming shrilly: "Kill him! Kill him!" Her younger brother was writing on the wall like crazy as he, too, screamed: "Kill her! Kill her!"[16]

The negative impact of family on the individual is also present in "The Moon of the West River." The title's image is probably an allusion to the quatrain entitled "Reflections on the Past at Su Pavilion," written by Li Bo (701–762). In the poem the glory of King Wu, Fu Chai, in the fifth century B.C., and his love for the famous beauty, Lady Xi Shi, are contrasted with the "old garden and deserted pavilion" on the Gusu Mountain, the only remnants of the past. The poem concludes with this couplet:

> Now there is only the moon over the West River,
> Which once shone on the one in King Wu's palace.[17]

People come and go, and the only thing that survives the constant flux of time is the lonely moon shining over the West River, another name for the Yangzi River. Drawing upon the poem, the title gives a hint of the story, which is related to nostalgia and the sense of futility accompanying nostalgia. This idea well describes the old man who, once a famous general and powerful politician, has been living in seclusion in Los Angeles and is now dying. The pathos of his indulgence in the memory of his glorious past and the yearning for his homeland is conjured up in the image of the dagger, which, according to the old man, "is our family heirloom. Back in those days, I depended on this dagger to get me through. From now on, descendants of the Chen family will pass it on and hold it in reverence."[18] His pride and obsession with the past, however, imposes an unnecessarily heavy burden on his sons to carry on the family tradition. The hero, whose name, Yaozong, literally means "glorification of the clan," lives in self-abandonment and cynicism as a form of passive protest against the dominance of his tyrannical father. The author also seems to draw a correlation between the absence of parental guidance and the homosexuality of the elder son, Yaozu, meaning "glorification of the ancestors." The detrimental impact of family on Yaozong's sense of self comes to the fore in his girlfriend Mansheng's comment: "I've been thinking . . . you shouldn't be called Chen Yaozong, or Tony Chen. You should have a name of your own."[19] Lacking "a name of his own,"

Yaozong oscillates between giving up on life completely and seeking help to pull himself out of the abyss. Love is viewed as a possible source of salvation. However, Mansheng thinks to herself: "She had loved him once, but loving a person did not mean being buried with him. Then, what could she do for him?"[20] Although the possibility of reconciliation and redemption is suggested at the end of the story by the positive image of a little boy, probably Yaozong's nephew, basking in the sunlight, it is by no means certain in view of the hero's indecisiveness and apathy.

In "The Lost Dragons," family tragedy is depicted in a different setting: the pressure that divorced parents subtly and perhaps unconsciously place on their only child. The frustration of handling that pressure and the anxiety of losing the love of either parent makes Little Jie precocious, insecure, and moody. Although the story has been interpreted as giving an optimistic view on human nature and the redemptive power of love,[21] an alternative interpretation should be considered based on the following several factors. Little Jie's statement that he will probably never get married,[22] psychologically innocent but artistically significant; his inquiry, motivated by frustration and anger, as to whether or not an orphanage will take someone like him;[23] and, most importantly, the association of the extinction of dinosaurs with the jokingly predicted extinction of mankind,[24] all strongly suggest a negative outcome to the situation. The dinosaurs became extinct because, according to Little Jie, "they were too stupid. . . . The volume of their brains was very small compared with their bodies. They were too big and needed a lot of food. When there was not enough food, they couldn't work it out except fighting with and killing one another. . . ."[25] There is clearly an analogy between the dinosaurs and the modern couple who are too suspicious and selfish to save their marriage and end up "killing each other" and perhaps their child, too.

Li Li is one of the first contemporary writers to examine the impact of China's political situation on the Chinese consciousness. In her fiction, politics is not extraneous to one's sense of self but a major source of it. It is subtly interwoven into "Night Trees" in the two minor characters. The young history teacher's disappearance is most likely linked to his voiced discontent with the political situation in Taiwan, and Old Wei's poverty-stricken, lonely life is also related to the turbulent history of modern China over the last four decades. As a young husband and father, Old Wei was drafted and taken away against his will, thus involuntarily abandoning his wife and sick daughter. After retiring from the army in Taiwan, he receives little financial support in his old age and lives a minimal life on campus. These two incidents, although secondary to the plot, are indicative of Li Li's concern with politics and human dignity. The history teacher may be poor under the heavy burden of supporting a bedridden wife and two children, but there is pride and dignity in his intellectual and moral independence. Having taught modern Chinese history up to the republican revolution, he says to the class:

> "There's nothing to talk about after this. If I were to talk about it, I'd have to read from the textbook. So, you may as well read it yourselves." The corner of his mouth curled up slightly, "It's okay if you don't read it. Maybe even better." Having said this, he lifted his head to look out the window and gave a slight, cold smile.[26]

The cynicism described above provides a clue to the subsequent disappearance of the young teacher, who was apparently taken away under extraordinary circumstances because he did not even take the time to cap his red-ink bottle. As to Old Wei, when Du naively retorts that the wooden shed *was* his home, the illiterate janitor

> Suddenly stopped laughing and stood up abruptly, speaking ferociously to her: "How can you say that? Do you think I was born for this kind of place? Was I supposed to live like pigs and dogs from the moment I was born? Frankly, rich people's dog houses are better than this!" The exhaled scent of alcohol filled her nostrils. "Home? You call this home? Is your home like this? Is the school principal's home like this?" After taking a breath, he spoke somewhat mildly: "You young girls, what do you know!"[27]

Minor characters in Li Li's fiction, such as Old Wei and the history teacher, are memorable because the author endows them with a real sense of dignity in spite of external adversity, a strength that remains intact despite economic and political pressure.

The Communist takeover of the Chinese mainland and the evacuation of the Nationalist government to Taiwan in 1949 are directly responsible for the two family tragedies described in "Spring Hope" and "Bird-of-Paradise Flowers." The situations depicted in these stories are similar in that both husbands, separated from their wives, remarried even though they already had wives and children on the mainland. Although they share an underlying tone of helplessness, a reaction to the larger sociopolitical forces, they differ in many other aspects. "Spring Hope" is one of Li Li's few stories that has an undoubtedly positive ending, already adumbrated, in this case, by the title. With the lifting of restrictions for mainland Chinese to travel abroad in recent years, this story's seventy-year-old hero is able to go to Hong Kong and see his children, from whom he has been separated for more than thirty years. His feelings of guilt are considerably relieved in this happy reunion by the confirmed bond between the father and children, his love for them, and their understanding and forgiveness. Taking the title from Du Fu's famous poem, which also deals with the separation of a family by war and the anticipation of reunion, the author focuses on the positive aspects of the experience. Although the political development of modern China over the last forty years has contributed to many family tragedies, at least love and forgiveness have the capacity to provide a source of solace and redemption.

In "Bird-of-Paradise Flowers," however, the angle shifts once again from the optimistic to the pessimistic. The reunion of father and children in "Spring Hope" is replaced here by the reunion of husband and wife. The author seems to be asking the following questions: After forty years void of communication, after another marriage and family, how much of the bond is left? How much can be reestablished between the couple? Although there is much reminiscence and even love between them, there is even more silence, sadness, and loneliness in the story. From the eyes of the twelve-year-old Weien, his recently reunited grandparents "merely watched television, seemingly attentive, but he knew that neither understood English. . . ."[28] He also observes the old couple "sitting facing the sliding glass doors, without looking at each other, talking as if to themselves."[29] The only visible sign of love or lingering bond between them is the bag of knickknacks that Grandma diligently carries with her everywhere she goes. It contains, among other things, mementos of Weien as a baby, a photograph of Grandpa, and the leather slippers he left behind after he went back to China. The old brown checkered plastic bag is symbolic of the memories dear to Grandma, the only thing that truly belongs to her because it cannot be taken away, and it grows heavier as she becomes more dissociated and withdrawn from her loved ones. The pathos of the story does not really come from the fact that she cannot be reunited with her husband who has another family on the mainland, but is derived from the grim realization that time irrevocably changes all human relationships. It is the ultimate insurmountable barrier to which man must submit himself.

"Bird-of-Paradise Flowers" is more complex than "Spring Hope" in the sense that, unlike the latter, which deals with life in two Chinese societies, it is situated in the milieu of American culture, which exerts a certain amount of influence on the relationships between the characters in the story. The increasing isolation of Grandma is significantly due to the decrease of communication with her grandson, Weien, who has shown an aversion to learning Chinese and is less able to understand it as time passes. Language becomes a barrier between them, even though they were once very close. In addition, there are hints of other contributing elements, such as a busy life-style, including a new job and overtime work; materialism, as implied by Weien receiving a new ten-speed bike for his birthday after his mother changes her job; and lack of family unity in American society as a whole, illustrated by Weien's American friend, Anita, whose parents are getting a divorce. The author is not only commenting on the tragic situation of the old woman, but she is equally concerned with the breaking of cultural ties for people in general, such as for Anita, who is of Jewish descent, and for today's Chinese in particular.

In the final analysis, Li Li's depiction of the role of familial and political dimensions in the shaping of an individual's sense of self cannot be separated from her emphasis on the nurturing and unifying power of culture. It is in one's culture that one finds the most fundamental enduring basis for one's identity and the richest source of self-fulfillment. The severance of this tie inevitably leads to the sense of division and contradiction from which many of her characters suffer. In "The Last Subway Train," Chang'an was once caught up in the political frenzy and fervor over his country's heritage, symbolized by his spur-of-the-moment decision to change his name. Chang'an, literally "everlasting peace," is the name of the capital of many Chinese dynasties. Thus, it evokes the splendor and glory of Chinese culture. However, he rejects this name during the Cultural Revolution in favor of "Changzheng" or "Long-March,"[30] an explicit display of loyalty and identity with the Communist regime. Along with his name, the antique incense burner he smashes during a raid with the Red Guards; his Granny, who personifies traditional Chinese virtues; and Huang Jue, whose Chinese qualities distinguish her from American women, all represent Chinese cultural heritage. The story focuses on the hero's loss of cultural roots, its detrimental impact on his sense of self, and his effort to retrieve that essential link. His fond memories of Granny, his love for Huang Jue, and the fatal act of rescuing the Chinese woman who reminds him of the victimized owner of the incense burner are all related to his coming to terms with his conscience and culture. In the final analysis, personal, familial, political, and cultural factors are all inextricably related in forming the core of one's identity and consciousness. For Li Li, culture not only transcends political labels and geographical divisions; it transcends time itself. Although Chang'an and Huang Jue come from two Chinas, they belong to the same culture and share the same Chinese identity.

Cultural identity even goes beyond nationality. In its broad and profound sense of affinity, both emotional and spiritual, to people, their customs, beliefs, and history, culture also constitutes the theme of the story "Jews in the City of Kaifeng." Although Mingjin and her husband Jiaqi are both from Taiwan, they have grown apart under the pressure of life in America, and their marriage ends in her total disillusionment and near suicide. Later, she establishes an intimate relationship with Xiao Cheng, a middle-aged man from the same Henan province as her mother, and whose maternal grandmother was a Muslim. Their love is doomed, however, since he must return to his wife and family in China, and she later marries Gordon, an American Jew who cares very much for her. As Gordon's father flips through the pages of the family album, showing her pictures of Jews in Henan, feelings of empathy and identification emerge more strongly in Mingjin's heart than ever before. He explains to her:

> Yes, that is the city Chinese Jews chose to settle in. They say that even now there are still Jewish descendants in the city of Kaifeng; they still observe the old customs, even though they do not know why they do it, or what they are.... Can you imagine that, over a thousand years ago, those people traveled along the Silk Road and arrived in the Orient, in a country totally unknown to them, and settled down? Generation after generation, they have tried to carry on their tradition, and the result.... Can you imagine that?[31]

Despite their differences in nationality and other respects, Gordon and Xiao unite as one, symbolizing a profound respect for culture.

The concern for culture as the major source of self-identity is also expressed in "Homeward Bound." Xia Chengzhi is equally drawn to the memory of his female cousin, who loved him as an older sister, and to Tang Jing, who shares his ideals. Tang's love for China is shown by her participation in the movement to defend Chinese sovereignty over Diaoyutai, an archipelago off the Asian continent in the East China Sea, during the early seventies; her late disillusionment with the political intrigues in mainland China; and, finally, her restored confidence and renewed commitment to a better China as a cultural entity. As such, her Chinese identity is no different from that of Chengzhi's cousin, whose simplicity, maternal kindness, and warm earthliness bespeak a natural bond with the ancient land. Thus, in the story, the images of his cousin, Tang Jing, and his cousin's teenage daughter are all superimposed, their distinctions intentionally blurred:

> The train had come to a complete stop. He looked out the window and saw among the crowd a middle-aged woman standing on the platform not far away. He caught sight of her immediately, as if answering her calls, inaudible and gentle. Then he saw a young girl standing next to her. She did not have bangs on her forehead or shoulder-length hair and was not wearing a moon-white blouse and skirt either. But, as she stood there, her figure was exactly like that of the young girl standing on the gradually receding platform thirty years ago, that indelible memory in his mind. He gazed at this short-haired girl, dressed in a short-sleeved white blouse and gray pants. She seemed to notice him and started walking toward his window, looking at him attentively. Then he saw her eyes, a pair of bright, well-defined eyes. He must have seen this pair of eyes—such clear and beautiful eyes—on another face, at another time, at another place.[32]

For Chengzhi, his homecoming is both physical and spiritual. He returns not only to visit his cousin whom he has not seen for over thirty years, but also to retrieve his lost self and mend his broken identity.

It is clear from the above discussion that the theme of the divided self is inextricably related to the search for redemption and wholeness. Whereas the heroes in "Spring Hope" and "Homeward Bound" succeed in their quest, other characters are less fortunate. Chang'an, in "The Last Subway Train," may enjoy a deep rapport with Huang Jue, but his hope to be with her is shattered at the end when he loses his life while saving a Chinese woman from a black man who is mugging her. Committed on the spur of the moment, he acts on a sudden flashback to the incident where he mercilessly shattered an antique incense burner during the Cultural Revolution, despite the owner's desperate pleas. Thus the present situation is almost a total reversal of the past, with Chang'an now playing the role of the brave hero rather than the violent Red Guard, the victim rather than the predator. Although this redemptive act costs him his life, he gains peace of mind and restores the link with his past, both personal and cultural, as suggested in the last image of Granny waiting for him in the beautiful starry sky.

In "The Moon of the West River" and "The Lost Dragons," as discussed above, the prospect of redemption is more ambivalent and uncertain. Indeed, in the case of "Bird-of-Paradise Flowers," the search for redemption is even more futile. Despite the love and goodwill of everyone involved, it probably only enhances the pain the grandparents have experienced. This again exemplifies the author's somewhat pessimistic refusal to provide facile endings to her stories. Each character and situation she describes is unique, and their psychological complexities are explored to the fullest extent. The sensitive objectivity and probing realism underlying Li Li's fiction are demonstrated in the wide scope of her vision as well as in her style.

As an overseas Chinese intellectual who herself participated in the Diaoyutai political movement in the early seventies, Li Li has a profound insight into the background and mentality of the people involved. Xia Chengzhi, Tang Jing, and her brother Tang Ning in "Homeward Bound," and Huang Jue and her boyfriend, who died of liver cancer, are some of the characters drawn from that particular historical context. Patriotism, disillusionment, castigation of the Cultural Revolution, and concern for the future of Chinese culture are all part of the historical experience vividly described in Li Li's fiction. Thus it is understandable that critics tend to emphasize the political dimension of her work.[33] However, this emphasis may distract our attention from the themes that are of a more universal and, I believe, eventually a more profound nature. The divided self is a dominant concern throughout her career as a writer. This theme is presented in the most critical light in stories that focus on Chinese intellectuals. Most of the heroes and heroines are highly educated people; indeed, many are university professors. Professor Tan's decision not to publish his refutation of Xia Chenbai's slanderous remarks about their mentor may not exactly be an act of cowardice, which Tan's friend bluntly accuses him of on a previous similar occasion. It could be interpreted in the Confucian sense as an act of answering to one's conscience regardless of worldly opinions. However, there is little doubt in the reader's mind that the old professor lives a life of compromise and evasion, symbolized in the way he walks, with his head low, staring at the space immediately in front of his feet, and taking each step cautiously.

Intellectuals come under similar attack in other stories such as "The Wedding Feast," "The Lost Dragons," "Homeward Bound," and "Snow Field." In "Snow Field," the couple from Taiwan decide on abortion, not because of social pressure, as would their counterpart on the mainland, but because of the more immediate, personal concern for the husband's doctorate. Selfishness and apathy are clearly detected in the husband's attitude: "Of course, it won't matter whether you get your degree or not; but mine can't be stalled any longer. Why don't you find a job? It will be hard on you for the first few years. . . . Anyway, whoever wants to keep the baby will be responsible for raising it."[34] His selfishness is reiterated when they leave the clinic and he complains: "The whole day today is wasted!"

There is a wide spectrum of perspectives from which intellectuals, mostly overseas Chinese and university professors, are portrayed in Li Li's fiction. At the positive end, we see them as idealistic, compassionate, patriotic, and farsighted; at the other end, they are selfish, hypocritical, self-righteous, and shallow. The critical lens under which they are examined reflects the author's high expectations for them and their important role in the future of Chinese culture. Comparing her Chinese identity to the "Chinese knot," a popular decorative item from Taiwan made of satin strings hand-knotted into intricate designs, Li Li poses this question: "The tightly knit knot at the bottom of my heart, when will it be unravelled?"[35] Although her stories may not represent the unraveling itself, they certainly reveal the various beautiful, complex, and thought-provoking designs in the Chinese consciousness today.

On the artistic achievement of Li Li's fiction, William Tay once commented: "In some of her works, there is a fine, natural balance between art and ideas."[36] While our present discussion is primarily concerned with the thematic significance of her stories, it is also important to point out a few outstanding features of her art. A conscientious craftsperson and wordsmith, Li Li excels in forging perceptive images, symbols, and puns to express her themes. Images help set the tone and ambiance for Li Li's stories. For instance, in "Night Trees," the author inserts a legend circulated at school that tells of two students who fell in love against the rules and got married, but under financial pressure the girl later committed suicide with her baby. It is said that her ghost still haunts the campus. The legend conjures up a Gothic atmosphere in the story and enhances the heroine's fantasy of love and sex; furthermore, it contrasts sharply with the unromantic reality where the "rowdy, cropped-haired, rude filthy boys all stood at a distance, like a horde of earth-colored animals."[37] Similarly, before meeting Yaozong's father, Mansheng imagines herself to be the young scholar from the classic collection of ghost stories, *Record of Fantastic Tales from the Liao Studio*, who "followed the ghost of his lover to the non-existent mansion in a deserted graveyard, to visit a host of non-existent spirits." [38] The image not only prepares us for the pitiful sight of the shrunken old man, but also enhances the theme of decay and vanity.

The symbols that frequently appear in Li Li's fiction can be termed "primal" symbols in that their sensuous nature carries universal emotional connotations. Strong, intense colors such as red and black are used to evoke oppressive negative forces: red being associated with blood, and black with darkness. We have already observed the use of black in Du's description of her home in "Night Trees." Red appears in "Snow Field," where, resting in the recovery room, the woman from Taiwan sees

> gentle ripples emerging before her eyes; the sunlight showered down, like golden rain, on the river, on the smiling face of a little girl. The little girl turned around and walked toward the river, with sunlight on her hair, her shoulders, and her skirt. The tiny body went into the water. The sunlight turned into a scarlet sunset, the river was instantly dyed red. . . .[39]

Black appears again in "The Last Subway Train," when Chang'an envisions that the train he is riding is heading into infinite darkness. Similarly intense and oppressive is the color white in "Snow Field," which ends with the mother hearing a little girl's voice coming from far away, during a particularly bitter winter:

> Outside the window, the snow fell in hurried profusion, yet it was perfectly still. Suddenly, in this boundless dead silence, she heard a tender voice: "Mommy . . . Mommy. . . ." . . .She felt a warm stream surge in her chest, into her eyes and head. She rushed to the door in a frenzy and jerked it open. Snowflakes scraped her face and hands like knives. The earth was shrouded in white; there was nothing to be seen. She covered her face and slowly sank to her knees. On the snowy field in front of her there seemed to be a few tiny footprints. When she strained her teary eyes for a better look, however, there was not a trace. Her tears had already congealed into ice.[40]

The identity of the mother in this section is intentionally vague and may be identified as either of the women presented in the story. Whereas Li Li uses arabic numerals to designate the five sections on the woman from Taiwan, Chinese numerals, also from one to five, are used to designate those for the woman on the mainland. However, the conclusion of the story is given the enigmatic number zero. Thematically, by blurring the distinction between the two mothers, it suggests the tragic fact that despite political, social, and educational differences, they suffer the same irreparable trauma of losing a child.[41] Symbolically, zero connotes emptiness and deprivation, which aptly describes the women's state of mind. Like darkness in the other stories, white in "Snow Field" is equally impenetrable and suffocating, ruthlessly cutting the characters off from their loved ones.

In contrast to the intense images of color or other senses, such as the unbearable heat in "A Day in Professor Tan's Life" or the piercing ringing in "The Last Subway Train," Li Li uses gentle, soothing images to depict positive feelings and ideas. In "The Last Subway Train," as Chang'an lies dying on the sidewalk, he sees the azure sea and blue sky associated with Huang Jue, who lives on the California coast, as well as stars in the clear sky, associated with Granny. These images suggest the peace of mind he finally achieves, although at the expense of his life. Equally positive are the stars in "Homeward Bound" associated with Xia's happy childhood with his cousin and later with Tang Jing. Likewise, sunlight and children have positive connotations in "The Moon of the West River" and "Snow Field."

As demonstrated, the names of some of Li Li's characters are highly symbolic, as is the care with which she chooses the titles for her stories. In addition to the titles that have already been discussed, the title for the story, "Under the Fortress Wall," is taken from the proverb "The army is under the fortress wall" (junlin chengxia), to describe the imminent threat of military attack. Thus it creates a hyperbolic comic effect in the story, where the young professor eventually surrenders to the charm and cunning of the beautiful editor, Shen Ruoshan. Ouyang Zi has identified four connotations of "The Lost Dragons."[42] First, the title literally refers to the extinction of dinosaurs, a subject in which Little Jie is very interested. Second, Little Jie was born in the year of the dragon; the word dragon or lung is the same character as dinosaur (konglong) in Chinese. From the father's viewpoint, he not only loses custody of his son to the mother, but the boy seems to be closer to her as well; thus, for him, the boy is the "lost dragon." Third, the story also suggests the dominance of technology in modern society and the fear that, like dinosaurs, mankind or humanity might be destroyed by overdependence and undue emphasis on machines and cold intellect. Finally, the Chinese see themselves as the descendants of the dragon, a powerful majestic creature; the author expresses her concern with the future of Chinese culture versus the technological, American culture in which Little Jie grows up.

The adroit use of puns is evident in "Under the Fortress Wall," where the "end of the carpet" refers to both the carpet on the boarding aisle in the airport and the aisle in the wedding chapel. The author also uses the word *tuiqiao*, a compound literally meaning "push or knock," but semantically meaning "to consider or ponder" for its imagistic effects: "Thus, one good marital prospect after another was 'pushed away' or '[knocked] broken' by his unparalleled cautiousness."[43]

The attention to language is further demonstrated by Li Li's use of parallelism as a major technique. Often two images or situations are juxtaposed side by side to suggest either similarity or contrast. Many of the passages already examined present such parallels as between past and present, memory and reality, life and death, and hope and despair. One other example that should be noted is in "The Lost Dragons." Little Jie tells his father how he once, after a particularly fierce argument between his parents, cried and wished that he would die so as to stop the fighting. Upon hearing this, his father "turned his face away abruptly, facing the model dinosaur eggs and newly hatched baby dinosaurs."[44] The juxtaposition reinforces the parallel between the young boy and baby dinosaurs, driving home the theme that it is worrisome to predict the future of Little Jie growing up in the shadow of a broken family.

The major portion of this study has focused on the theme of the divided self and the search for redemption in Li Li's short stories, however, it is clear from this brief analysis that the techniques she uses are inseparable from her thematic concerns. Exhibiting a felicitous unity of form and content in her fiction, Li Li rightfully deserves her high stature among other remarkably accomplished contemporary Chinese writers.

## Notes

1. *The Last Subway Train (Zuihou yeche)* (Taipei: Hongfan Shudian, 1986), p. 21. Unless otherwise indicated, all passages cited in this essay are my translations.

2. Ibid., p. 55.

3. Ibid., p. 101.

4. *Bird-of-Paradise Flowers (Tiantangniao hua)* (Taipei: Hongfan Shudian, 1988), pp. 58–59.

5. *The Last Subway Train*, p. 131.

6. *Bird-of-Paradise Flowers*, p. 60.

7. *The Last Subway Train*, p. 143.

8. Ibid., pp. 77–99.

9. Ibid., pp. 165–91.

10. Ibid., pp. 193–212.

11. Ibid., pp. 213–44.

12. *Bird-of-Paradise Flowers*, pp. 1–24

13. Ibid., pp. 153–207.

14. *The Last Subway Train*, p. 36.

15. Ibid., pp. 36–37.

16. Ibid., p. 74.

17. *One Thousand Tang Quatrains (Qianshou Tangshi jueju)*, edited by Fu Shousun et al., 2 vols. (Shanghai: Xinhua Shudian, 1985), vol. 1, p. 168.

18. *The Last Subway Train*, p. 117.

19. Ibid., p. 108.

20. Ibid., p. 121.

21. See Ouyang Zi's analysis of the story in the "Redemption of Human Nature" ("Renxing de jiushu"), in *The Last Subway Train*, pp. 245–63.

22. *The Last Subway Train*, p. 190.

23. Ibid., p. 189.

24. Ibid., p. 190.

25. Ibid., p. 187.

26. Ibid., p. 48.

27. Ibid., p. 65.

28. *Bird-of-Paradise Flowers*, p. 102.

29. Ibid.

30. *The Last Subway Train*, p. 139.

31. *Bird-of-Paradise Flowers*, p. 96.

32. Ibid., pp. 67–68.

33. See, for example, Chen Yingzhen, "Dissolution of the Diaoyu-tai Movement and Its Emotional Complex," in *The Last Subway Train*, pp. 1–12; and Ku Ling's review of the volume in *Literature and Arts Monthly (Wenyi yuekan)*, no. 209 (November 1986): 68–71. The author was urged to broaden her historiopolitical concerns in Wang Dewei's review in *Unitas (Lianhe wenxue)* 3, no. 8 (June 1987): 213–14.

34. *The Last Subway Train*, p. 201.

35. Li Li, "The Chinese Knot: A Preface," *The Last Subway Train*, p. 16.

36. Quoted by Liu Binyan in his preface to *Bird-of-Paradise Flowers*, p. 8.

37. Ibid., p. 47.

38. Ibid., p. 108.

39. Ibid., p. 208.

40. Ibid., p. 212.

41. In the case of the woman from Taiwan, it is clear that she had an abortion. As to the woman in mainland China, it is intimated that her little girl was murdered by her husband's family so that she could give birth to a boy without violating the law stipulating one child per family. The vagueness seems only to enhance the horror of the episode.

42. Ibid., pp. 262–63.

43. *Bird-of-Paradise Flowers*, p. 157.

44. *The Last Subway Train*, p. 186.

Zhong Xiaoyang

锺晓阳

# Zhong Xiaoyang

Zhong Xiaoyang (b. 1963), who achieved literary fame when she was still in high school, had an unusual educational background. The daughter of an Indonesian-Chinese father and a mother who came from Manchuria, Zhong went to an English Catholic school in Hong Kong, after which she came to the United States to study film at the University of Michigan.

Ever since she was a child, Zhong was attracted to classical Chinese poetry and fiction, a precocious interest that she pursued and eventually developed into a writing style which became noted for its rich use of imagery and allusions. Between 1979 and 1981, she won in succession a number of literary awards in various youth contests, a feat that swiftly brought her to the attention of critics in both Hong Kong and Taipei. In 1981, at the age of eighteen, she published her first fictional work, a novel entitled *Halt, May I Ask . . . (Tingche zan jiewen)*. Serialized in three newspapers in Hong Kong and Taipei, the novel drew immense admiration from the public for the compelling poetic pathos and sophisticated literary style contained within the tale of a simple romance. Her short stories, a total of fourteen to date, are mostly concerned with the ardent efforts of youth in the pursuit of love, a quest that does not attain romantic fulfillment and in the end leaves the reader with a sense of existential pessimism.

Zhong is the youngest writer in this collection and is the author of an award-winning novel, four short story collections, and three volumes of prose, poetry, and essays.

# The Wedding Night[1]

## Zhong Xiaoyang

Sitting on the edge of the huge bed in her bridal chamber, she felt uncomfortably warm. A piece of red silk was draped across her face.

She really hadn't been sitting this way that long, and yet she could almost feel the prime of her life fleeting by. She placed her hands on her lap, fingers crossing like strings stretched over a lute.

*I should never have agreed to play this silly game with the groom*, she thought; her feelings were a mix of regret and resentment. *What is this? Veiled in red and clad in a wedding gown, sitting upright on the edge of this newly purchased Simmons mattress?* She was his bride, but not yet awarded with his compassion. He was more like a stranger to her now. But, just a short while ago, they had been in each other's embrace, overwhelmed by kisses that seemed to last forever.

At that moment, the sight of the fire that had broken out just a few blocks away flashed back through her mind.

In the future, when she was in the company of her husband's friend's wives, it would be amusing to recapitulate this experience to them and reminisce on it. *The first fire I ever witnessed was on my wedding night.* Surely, they would all courteously grant her the attention she deserved. It seemed as if she had just set a new record.

Before the game had begun, she had been engaged in a long and passionate kiss with her husband. The setting was draped by two panels of new crimson curtains that reached to the floor. The room was illuminated by a pair of red candles sculptured with dragon and phoenix reliefs that stood aflame on a chest of drawers. It was the groom who had suggested this arrangement. He had wanted to create an atmosphere he considered befitting the romantic occasion, a taste he shared with his generation. In the heat of their embrace, their sweat dripped onto each other's bodies.

Then, the urgent sirens of fire trucks began to wail. The shrieking peals madly forced their way into the bridal chamber. It couldn't be this floor that was on fire, could it? The groom stretched out his right hand and used two fingers to lift a corner of the curtain. He peeked out somewhat timidly. He turned his head, first to the left and then to the right, almost as if he were about to cross a street. After looking out the window a few moments, his eyeballs began to feel like they were rolling to the rhythm of the glaring siren lights, swirling rapidly around.

"Look!" he exclaimed.

She looked out the window. Not far away, she could see a building on fire. The blaze was raging out of control, and firemen were fighting to contain it.

"It looks like. . . ." His words came to an abrupt stop.

She felt a sudden tightening in her throat, and it dawned on her. She gasped, "Isn't that. . . ?"

It was the restaurant where they had entertained their guests that same evening.

"It looks like it," the groom concluded. Or, was he merely repeating himself?

It was a truly unfortunate coincidence. For a few moments, they remained silent.

In an impulsive move, the groom picked up the champagne they had saved for that very evening, and stuck the bottle out the window. Aiming it at the fire, he uncorked it. *Pop!* A stream of creamy liquid gushed out in a straight line, shooting far and high. The groom had satisfied his obligation as a citizen with his effort to put out the fire.

"Spiritual blessings from God!" the bride chuckled. Standing on her toes, she stretched out her body like a plant that grew outward from the wall. She looked down. There, a few floors below them, were numerous pedestrians. Their heads looked like they were strung together, forming an expansive smooth surface upon which one could easily imagine running about swiftly. What a tumultuous scene, a commotion perhaps as alarming as what would happen in the midst of major warfare.

"What a crowd! All out there gawking at a disaster like that!" the bride said to herself with a sigh.

It was a rather unusual phenomenon to see an entire street swarming with excited people acting as if it were some kind of convivial celebration. But was it? She could not be sure. The crowd flushed a feverish red; the color of the devastating fire was reflected in the expressions on their faces.

The din of the crowd spread, and the air was filled with the ever thickening smell of incineration. It became increasingly hot.

The sight of the fire and the people fighting it radiated a glow on the newlyweds' faces. This was the auspicious day of their wedding.

The groom chose this particular moment to whisper into the ear of the bride.

"You must be joking!" The bride stared at him, her eyes open wide, trying to understand the real man inside this visage beside her.

"It's just a game," said the groom.

For a moment she was confused about the distinction between a joke and a game. But, collecting her thoughts, she maintained the same tone of voice as the groom and replied, "You're a nut!"

"Come on," he pleaded persistently. "Do it for me!"

"That was only done in the old days when marriages were arranged by matchmakers. Now, we live in a different age altogether. Besides, you already know what I look like. So, why do you want me to do this? Are you nuts?"

"No, that's not true. You saw the play *Dinühua,*[2] right? Zhou Shixian and Princess Changping had known each other long before they were married. Yet, on their wedding day, the princess veiled herself just the same."

She didn't want to hear anymore about it. She stepped away, and then a few steps more.

The groom came forward with a smile. "Why don't you play the part of Princess Changping, and I'll be the imperial husband Zhou Shixian?"

The request baffled the bride, and she sensed something ominous. She didn't say anything, although by this time she was already a bit angry with him.

The groom continued with words of love. "You never knew this before, but I have dreamed of this ever since I was child. If only I could do what they did in the old days, unveil my bride on my wedding night, I would be the happiest man alive. And, now, the day is finally here. I am about to fulfill my fantasy. If you will change into the traditional gown now and put on the red veil, then I will have a chance to remove the veil and look at you as if for the first time."

His words touched her. She thought to herself: *Not a fight on the first day of our marriage, let him have it his way. He's been waiting all these years, why disappoint him now?* Thus, it wasn't much of a protest when she said, "If I had known you were so old-fashioned, I wouldn't have married you."

"This is just a convention. It has absolutely nothing to do with whether I'm old-fashioned or not. To me, the bridal veil possesses magical power. As soon as I lift it up, I know you will become even prettier."

The bride laughed with delight. "What do you think you're going to perform? A magic trick? I will always look the same, and nothing is going to change that."

"Are you really sure?" The groom looked into her eyes, his gaze full of profound feelings.

Slightly perplexed, the bride looked at him, and for no apparent reason, she felt her heart begin to pound.

The gaze lasted for just a brief moment. The groom gently motioned to her, "Go put on the gown first."

She had ordered two specially made gowns for the wedding banquet: a traditional full-length gown with a vest, and a *cheungsam*. Presently, she was wearing the white brocade *cheungsam* with shimmering red trim. The high collar was like a chain around her neck, clumsy and burdensome. The traditional garment was even worse.

She returned wearing the new costume. Holding a red square kerchief by his waist, the groom stood smiling like a matador. He said, "I have saved this especially for tonight. And this, too." He turned around, and there, in his hand, was a sandalwood fan with a red tassel. "I wasn't able to find another, so I guess I'll have to settle for this one." A sign of embarrassment tinged his smile.


Such was the backdrop for the scene in which the bride now found herself. Sitting on the edge of the bed, she thought of the fire and their silly game. The garment she was wearing was embroidered with a pair of phoenixes and strung with colorful sequins. She had never imagined that she would have to put it on again—twice in one night! Incredible. Was there any special significance? This was the outfit she wore at the wedding banquet when she knelt in front of his parents to offer them tea. It took place at that very same restaurant, the one that was just in flames. It hadn't been that long ago, and yet the site of the festivity was now burned to the ground.

She carefully placed her hands on the bed, enjoying the warmth and softness of the bedspread as much as she could. This was the bed where she would share a blissful night with the groom. Having never been to bed with a man, she was lost for a moment in her fancy. Why isn't he here yet? If waiting meant nothing more than counting the passage of time, it would be an ultimate form of meaningless and futile action. Besides, she recalled a line from an ancient poem that said, "A night of romance, a thousand pieces of gold."[3]

She tried to figure out where he was standing. She pricked up her ears, but there wasn't a sound. The carpet must have muffled the sound of every step. The groom seemed to have assumed an omnipresence. His presence was usually difficult to define, and yet, now she could sense his invisible presence pressing towards her. His breathing in her direction felt as if a future world were closing in on her with an insurmountable force. She took a deep breath. The red veil had no smell.

If only there wasn't anyone else in the room and this was all but a dream.

Was it possible that this was nothing but a dream? The perplexed groom wavered between his rational mind and his emotional fantasy. The moment he lifted up the veil, would he find himself in bed just waking from a dream? Dreams often ended at their climatic points. If such were the case, he'd rather restrain himself from making any move. How often would he have such an amorous dream? The mere rumination on it engaged the groom with even more amorous thoughts.

He was about ten feet away from the bride. He moved slightly forward, but then quietly withdrew himself as if he had to deliberate on every step he was about to take. He seemed to have exhausted all of his inner strength making that very small move; he felt too feeble to even lift up the veil. How he wished he could raise that crimson curtain, the silk screen behind which he would find tenderness in a bed of brocade opulence.

How well did he know this woman in front of him? From their courtship to the wedding, the degree of his familiarity with her had always been dictated by their environment, fluctuating as changes emerged around them. The environment seemed to have the absolute power to change anything and everything. Even now, despite great effort, he failed to connect the face of the woman in his memory to the body now sitting under the veil. A very puzzling phenomenon. Her head and body were like two independent entities. A headless corpse.

The veil became an unbridgeable separation. He remembered that just a short while ago, when she entered the room wearing the traditional gown, he felt as if he were witnessing a woman emerging from thousands of court beauties, pacing forward over petals of golden lilies. It was a scene of startling glamor, a sight he would never forget. *What pleasure in life doth thou seek? A romantic encounter, an amorous peek.* Waiting behind that red veil was a promise of mystery and beauty.

*Where is he? What is he waiting for?* The dead silence around her began to grate on her nerves. She'd rather have him say something, anything. Preferably, of course, something she'd like to hear. "When the veil is removed, you will become even prettier." The words were delivered with such confidence that even she began to believe in what he had said.

When a magician performed a trick, often he would first cover his props with a huge handkerchief and then pull out from under it a rabbit, a pigeon, or a string of handkerchieves tied together in knots. Had the groom been practicing magic without ever telling her about it? This red veil might be serving the same function as the handkerchief in a magician's hand. The bride became all the more anxious. Why hadn't he first asked for her opinion on the matter? He should have consulted with her and asked what features of her face she would like to have corrected. She had always wanted to have double eyefolds, a tall and prominent nose, and lips that were slightly fuller.

Would she be transformed into a more beautiful woman? His next move would determine it. She raised her hand and touched her face gently. Moving her palm closer, she studied it as if it were a mirror, a glass in which she was examining her reflection. Her cheeks were burning. The red veil encircled her in flames, a peril of red. She gasped for air, fanning the blaze into an even more violent red in front of her eyes. She felt thirsty and restless; the mystical power of the red veil, the power the groom had spoken of, began to take hold of her.

Shadows flickered under the illumination of the two red candles in the room. The red veil wavered slightly as she breathed. Indescribably eerie, the room was permeated with a haunting atmosphere. He felt especially frightened because he couldn't see her face. At that moment, he realized he had never been confronted by a person whose head he couldn't see. His doubt increased as his fear thickened. Could she be a ghost? He recalled the many stories about ghostly wives. A skull behind the red veil. It wasn't until the wedding night that the groom discovered that the woman with whom he had just exchanged nuptial vows was in reality an avenging ghost.

The groom panicked. He wanted to run and turn on the light.

She had never been in the same room with someone who couldn't see her face; it was an experience tantamount to that of removing one's own head from the torso. The bride began to have a strange vision: She saw herself as an invisible person, with an imagination much like that of an ostrich trying to shut out the rest of the world by hiding its head. According to Greek mythology, there was such a magical object, an article that would render invisibility the moment it was donned. That article, however, was not a red veil.

During all this time there had not been the slightest move on the part of the groom. If the inconsideration of this man she had just married had upset her in any way, her anger was now long gone. What was left was a feeling of estrangement. *Had she known the groom long enough to be his wife?* she questioned herself. Veiled under the red silk, she could only envision how the candlelight fluttered its shadows over the face of the groom. As in a horror movie with special lighting effects, the visage foreboded evil and bane. It wouldn't come as a shock if such a man would now murder her. There were stories in newspapers reporting how psychotic husbands tortured their wives with bizarre schemes and killed them in the end. Before this night, she would never have believed that the groom could be psychotic or insane. But now, when all circumstantial elements converged at this very moment, anything seemed possible. Yes, he insisted on having her change into the gown and put on the veil, solely for the pleasure he would achieve in removing it. A night of nuptial celebration had turned into something sinister and macabre. Nothing could be more miserable than to be killed in a room of silence. She tried to remember the layout of the room, preparing herself to dash for the doorway at the slightest sign of alarm.

Brooding seemed to have given life to her imagination, and she became all the more scared. Her heart pounded like the fist of an unborn baby against a mother's rib cage. Even though she still wouldn't be able to see anything, she desperately hoped that the groom would turn on the lights. She lowered her head. The first thing to catch her eyes was the sight of her breasts jutting out like two mounds. The front lapel of her gown seemed to be there for the sole purpose of draping her breasts. Here was her world, restricted to all that was directly in front of her. In uncompromising terms, the red veil had defined her alienation and distance from the groom, a man who belonged to the world outside. The world without boundaries.

How would the world look at him? The question crossed the groom's mind as he sniffed the fan under his nose. He felt that this was a convention of great historical significance. For generations, he thought, grooms had followed in each other's footsteps, walking up with great courage to unveil his betrothed on the wedding night, and his destiny. The curtain was about to be ceremoniously raised for the commencement of a new marriage.

How did she know that it was her and not the groom who would undergo a transformation? The act might bring forth some welcome surprises. Why was it that only the groom had the right to inspect his bride and not vice versa? Unconsciously, the bride began to compose her thoughts. Suppose this was their first encounter. When Princess Changping met with Zhou Shixian for the first time, she had never laid eyes on him during their exchange of words. It wasn't until he offended her with his arrogance that

> Changping slowly turned around to glance at
> Shixian. Startled by his looks, she smiled
> and said listlessly, "Bring the wine."[4]

The red veil continued to stretch itself, expanding swiftly into a huge screen. The groom seemed able to walk straight behind the red curtain. What would ensue had actually been arranged in advance. A kiss was to be followed by the sharing of the nuptial drink. She could imagine the faithful Zhou Shixian now lifting the red veil, gazing at the bride, exchanging the nuptial cups. . . .

> From the golden goblet he received, he lightly
> sipped the wine;
> With tears, he sprinkled poison on the sweet
> juice of the vine.

Would the groom put poison in the wine? The bride became suspicious. Why had he referred specifically to this particular play *Dinühua*? A double suicide on the wedding night. She had heard of such incidents before. According to history, Princess Changping and Zhou Shixian had died for the fall of the Great Ming Empire. That was about three hundred and fifty years ago. Yet it may have been nothing but a fabricated tale.

Would he kiss her after he removed the veil? A kiss that would signify new life like in *The Sleeping Beauty*? Even in the West, a wedding ceremony always included a scene in which the groom would unveil his bride and give her an endearing kiss.

The bride began to feel a subtle sense of attachment to this red cloth that hung from her forehead. Now the game seemed to have taken on new meaning. Just then she sensed a sudden and complete transformation of thought in herself.

*The Red Turban Movement!*[5] The bride grinned in silence. She had never thought of doing this before, and yet here she was christening the night with a name that greatly delighted her. It was like an historical event, a movement, a revolution. The entire world might change as soon as the veil was removed. She saw herself traversing through time to a scene of smoke and disintegration. Surrounded by broken tiles and piles of debris, she had been transposed back to the Ming dynasty, in the year A.D. 1644. . . .

In the stillness, the waiting bride vicariously felt the magnitude of the resentment that had haunted Princess Changping in her cloistered palace. She felt the anger of her new husband, a loyal subject of the court, the death of her royal father on Mount Mei, the trepidation of the people who fled like injured creatures. . . . When Princess Changping veiled herself behind the red silk, she must have thought of her father who had hung himself with his hair veiled over his face. It was an indication of shame, a failure so grave that he could not face his ancestors in the next life. In this regard, death with her groom was a martyrdom she had chosen of her own free will. In the face of a national crisis, every man and woman had obligations to fulfill, with courage and dignity. . . . Lingering on thoughts of ancient misfortunes, the bride felt a strengthening force growing within her. Thousands of years of history now guarded her with an eye of compassion.

Draped in red, she waited in silence, the air permeated with tranquil heat. The noises from the street grew louder. It would take some time to contain and extinguish the fire that had broken out a few blocks away. She regained her posture, crossing her fingers like musical strings stretched over a lute. *From whence came those almost inaudible strains of music?*

> Enchanted shade, the willow twigs shall make,
> Behind there lies a face my eyes cannot forsake.
> O, Princess of Ming, my wife-to-be,
> A lamp in hand, a glance of thee.

*Is he coming?* Gazing at the tip of the fan that slowly touched the veil, the groom felt deeply in love with the woman before him.

From within this red domain were a pair of watching eyes, carefully focused on the tip of the fan as it slowly approached from beyond. A whiff of subtle fragrance arose from the sandalwood. Slightly dizzy, the bride, so vulnerable.

## Notes

1. "The Wedding Night" ("Liangxiao") was translated by Samuel Hung-nin Cheung with the kind permission of the author and publisher, and is published here in English for the first time. This translation is based on the original that appeared in the collection entitled *Aiqi* (Hong Kong: Tiandi tushu, 1987), pp. 243–55.

2. *Dinühua*, a Cantonese opera first presented on stage in Hong Kong in the 1960s, was particularly known for its lyrics written by Tang Disheng. The story describes the tragic love between Princess Changping, daughter of the last Ming emperor, and her betrothed Zhou Shixian, who mourned the fall of their country by committing double suicide on the night of their wedding.

3. The line is from a poem by Su Shi (A.D. 1037–1101), a northern Song poet.

4. All of the following quotations are from the opera *Dinühua*.

5. The designation *Red Turban* is evidently derived from a historical term, the *Yellow Turbans*, which refers to a peasant revolt in the second century A.D. Under the leadership of some Daoist masters who claimed to perform miracles, peasants in eastern China rose in rebellion against the declining Han court. Because they all wore recognizable yellow turbans, the incident has come to be known as the Yellow Turban Rebellion.

# Beyond the Bridal Veil: The Romantic Vision of Zhong Xiaoyang[1]

## Samuel Hung-nin Cheung

> When did the moon begin to shine?
> Lifting my cup I ask of Heaven.
> I wonder in the heavenly palaces and castles
> What season it is tonight.
> I wish to go up there on the wind
> But am afraid the crystal domes and jade halls
> Would be too cold on high.
> So I dance with my limpid shadow.
> As if I were no longer on earth.[2]

This is the first half of a celebrated Su Dongbo *ci* poem which is recited to Jiang Chaoxin, a frustrated young dreamer, in a final scene from "The Fleeting Years" ("Liunian"), a 1983 short story by Zhong Xiaoyang. Despite its sublime metaphors, the poem ironically returns a soaring soul yearning for higher aspirations back to the world of mundane reality. The celestial palace with its crystal dome and jade halls represents a realm beyond the reach of man, whose home is to be found nowhere but in this mortal world. Recurrent in Zhong Xiaoyang's stories is the vision that man will forever be haunted by the anxious desire to break away from his irksome routine and sterile environment, and that all human attempts ultimately prove absurd and in vain as the irrevocable cycle of life and death presses onward. These are themes that few other young modern Chinese writers are able to handle with comparable sensitivity and poetic pathos.

"The Fleeting Years" is a ninety-page romance in which Zhong Xiaoyang symbolically examines the poignant suffering of a man torn between spiritual love and worldly desires. Jiang Chaoxin is a foreign student studying architecture at the University of Michigan. One day, while looking over some old photographs with his girlfriend, Yu Xianglun, an economics student, he finds a picture of himself and Ye Chen, a next-door neighbor in Hong Kong with whom he had shared an innocent childhood romance. The shining smiles in the picture arouse cherished memories of the past and rekindle his fancy for the ethereal and unobtrusive beauty he sees embodied in the image of Ye Chen. This emotional upheaval consequently prompts and, in turn, intensifies a series of confrontations with Yu Xianglun, toward whom he bears ambivalent feelings. He feels both flattered and threatened by her officious words as she wards off potential rivals, including her own cousin, Yao Qianyun, who comes to visit one Christmas. He believes that his relationship with Yu Xianglun developed only as a result of his isolation in a foreign land. He claims no especially fond feelings for her; he has merely grown accustomed to her company since they first met a year ago. The delicate and graceful qualities he remembers in Ye Chen, on the other hand, project an image of perfection, a source of love, to which he still aspires. However, the more he tries to break away from the clutches of Yu Xianglun, the more he finds himself attached to her companionship and enjoying the material comfort she provides him. Even during a fierce argument over Ye Chen and Yao Qianyun, his anger dissipates when he remembers that he needs to borrow her car for the graduation ceremony. When he returns to Hong Kong, he drives Yu Xianglun's family car to pick up Ye Chen for a date. The name Xianglun, homophonous with the word *xianglun*, meaning "fragrant wheels," signifies her importance to him in the practical world. When he secretly takes a picture of a Taiwanese girl, whose daintiness reminds him so much of Ye Chen, it is again Yu Xianglun's camera that he uses to capture the entrancing image. That Ye Chen's image forever remains an unattainable ideal in the real world dominated by Yu Xianglun is best illustrated in the following passages where Jiang Chaoxin tries to convey his feelings to Ye Chen as they sit together in Yu Xianglun's car.

Chaoxin was somewhat nervous when he said, "I feel that . . . you're kind of unusual, and I'm . . . very proud to have a friend like you." It was quite obvious what he wanted to say. His heart began to pound; even his thoughts stammered.

He could not see her face as she was looking outside. The air conditioning in the car was turned on and all the windows were tightly closed. Ye Chen's face was reflected on the window, a pale, thin face, detached and aloof, as if it were merely an apparition forming on the glass. Even if Ye Chen was gone forever, the illusion would still remain. He would always find it there, etched on the glass window.[3]

Yu Xianglun's surname is also functionally significant in that it is indicative of the means and convenience she provides toward Jiang Chaoxin's social mobility. Her presence in the story is ubiquitously accompanied by some form of reference to *yu*, "fish," a word homophonous with her surname Yu. Both her room in the Michigan apartment and her house in Hong Kong are decorated with bowls of goldfish. When she first appears in the story, she is munching on dried squid, *youyu*, as she listens to Jiang Chaoxin recount his story about Ye Chen. In another instance, she wears a bright blue woolen cloak to a student party, which makes her look like a devil fish, *moguiyu*, gliding on the floor, ready to ensnare all that is within touch of her fins. Her lips are described like those of a whale, *jingyu*, and even her laughter is compared to the explosion of *yulei*, a torpedo. *Yu*, "fish," is also phonologically related to the word $yu^4$, meaning needs and desires in the mundane world, a world in which Jiang Chaoxin finds himself trapped, contradicting everything Ye Chen stands for: spiritual fulfillment rather than material satisfaction. It is indeed no coincidence that Ye Chen's appearances in the story are always marked by a touch of "green." The word *qing*, "green," is a near homophone for *qing*, meaning "love, sentiments."[5] One example of this is the pot of evergreen, *wannianqing*, growing on her veranda. Moreover, what is even more indicative of this characteristic feature is her own name, Ye, which literally means "leaf."

Attached to both the worlds of spiritual aspiration and material possession, Jiang Chaoxin attempts to bring them together by seating himself between the two women at a wedding banquet. His efforts, however, fail hopelessly as Ye Chen refuses the shark fin soup, *yuchi*, and the sizzling fish, *tieban shiyu*, which he offers her. She claims to be allergic to fish, and throughout the entire evening, all she eats are some greens, *qingcai*. There can be no compromise between the two worlds, and a choice is imminent. Jiang Chaoxin confesses to Ye Chen that he can never realize the vision of true love that he had once aspired to, and he also cannot relinquish what he now possesses. That life is marred with imperfections is a fact that one must resign oneself to. As the story draws to an end, we see Jiang Chaoxin dash off in Yu Xianglun's car, first casting out of the window a Hallmark card he purchased for Ye Chen professing his love, and then her picture which he had kept close to him during his years abroad and at home. The source of his emotional conflict and disturbance is now dismissed. One year later, he marries Yu Xianglun.

As an architect, Jiang Chaoxin dreams of one day building his own skyscraper, perhaps one similar to the heavenly castle in Su Dongbo's poem; yet, in reality, he recognizes the fact that any house he builds for himself will be constructed on the land provided by Yu Xianglun. In the beginning, Jiang Chaoxin tries very hard to resist the physical temptations offered by Yu Xianglun. He refuses to eat an apple-flavored donut that Yu gives him; but, as pressure begins to mount, his will weakens. When a woman supervisor hands him a piece of apple pie, he finally succumbs. "The lady boss gave the piece to Chaoxin. He felt his adam's apple swelling. The apple pie was really very delicious. He gobbled it down."[6] The use of the biblical inference is a subtle but effective means of characterizing Jiang Chaoxin's final surrender to the realities of life. Once having eaten the apple, he is forever banished from the garden of celestial grace.

The same theme of discontentment with reality and the ultimate resignation to it is recurrent in another of Zhong Xiaoyang's stories, entitled "Green Sleeves" ("Cuixiu"). Cuixiu is a middle-aged woman in Shanghai who marries an elderly businessman from Hong Kong, not out of love but because she sees a chance to escape from an enclosed world in China. No sooner has she attained security and affluence as wife of Wo Gengyun than she feels bored with life on the island. She looks for excitement and falls prey to her own desire for Lu Zhichong, a handsome young stockbroker. One day, the broker pays her an unannounced visit, and she welcomes him with flirting smiles and suggestive remarks. The broker looks especially captivating wearing his safari outfit; and, garbed in a sleeveless, black and white striped dress, Cuixiu moves like a zebra and wriggles like a serpent. This seduction scene is skillfully described as a hunting game, a game one plays according to instinct and need. Both Cuixiu and Lu Zhichong indulge themselves in the sport; but, as soon as the curtains in the room are slightly lifted, they instantly find themselves assaulted by busy skyways and roaring traffic. Reality intrudes into their make-believe land of romantic wilderness. However, her own fantasy convinces Cuixiu that she should leave her home and pursue a new life with Lu Zhichong.

In the dark, she climbed seven staircases to reach Zhichong's floor. All eight members of the family got out of bed and crammed into the small sitting room to see who had come.

Zhichong looked extremely upset and hurriedly put her in his sister's room. When no one was around, he blamed her for being rash and not having let him know about her visit in advance. Things could have been worked out differently. She came to a completely new understanding. He had a big family and was poor. She wouldn't want to hurt him or herself. So early next morning, she went home.[7]

She returns home a wiser woman. The charming dimples, which distinguished her initial appearance like delicate crescents on her slightly round face, are now gone forever from the corners of her mouth.

"Green Sleeves" begins with an intriguing portrayal of Cuixiu trying to pull off a loose thread that dangles from her green sleeve; and, likewise, it ends with a similar incident. The thread symbolizes her tempting thoughts of passion, as abundant as those in the green garment she wears or in the handkerchief she tucks under her sleeve; such thoughts have to be resisted in order for her to return to a state of equilibrium. Thus, when her brother cuts off the loose thread in the first scene, Cuixiu is promised to Wo Gengyun by her family, thereby putting an end to her emotional vulnerability. Yet, when she consents to Wo Gengyun's proposal as he takes her for an evening stroll on a nearby bridge, a sudden gust of wind blows her handkerchief away. Despite several anxious attempts, neither of them are able to retrieve it. Thus, from the very beginning, the marriage is doomed to be void of passion or intimacy. The thought of venturing into an adulterous affair with Lu Zhichong, however, is stimulated by their playful banter with handkerchieves. Yet, as soon as Lu Zhichong's poverty is taken into account, she passively succumbs to the banality of life, especially in the approaching days of her husband's retirement. She resigns herself to her lot, a volition expressed symbolically by her readiness to reach for a pair of scissors when Wo Gengyun complains that a loose thread hanging from her peppermint-colored pajama sleeve is irritating his hand.[8]

"Green Sleeves" concludes with Cuixiu turning off the light and fading into obscurity. When Jiang Chaoxin bids his last farewell to Ye Chen in "The Fleeting Years," we see the approach of darkness engulfing the young architect as he stands motionlessly at a street corner. Resigning oneself to reality and accepting the status quo without any urge to challenge or change it is, to Zhong Xiaoyang, like crossing the threshold of darkness and entering death. Zhong Xiaoyang often characterizes this kind of compromise in life as a process of gradual death.

To fail in what one strives for is a painful experience, but it is only when one feels pain that one knows one is still alive. The discomfort of a bare hand in the freezing cold, Zhong Xiaoyang claims, is paradoxically a comforting sensation that reassures us the hand is still full of life. When numb, the nerves are already dead.[9] When a man is stripped of the passion to struggle against his lot in life, he is spared failure; yet he is also reduced to a meaningless existence of simply eating, sleeping, and awaiting death. If intellectual maturity is defined in terms of a man's readiness to recognize and accept the limitations and imperfections of life, Zhong Xiaoyang sees death in this mental growth, a process she metaphorically compares to the ripening of litchis in the next story. When ripe, the red skin is to be peeled off the fruit, its meat to be eaten, and its pit to be spit out.

Though not an account of romantic entanglement, "When the Litchis Ripen" ("Lizhi shu") revolves around the same issue of human discontent. This story features a forty-year-old servant who is on the verge of resigning from her current employment. Cao Shao'e is an Indonesian-born Chinese woman who has spent a number of years working on an agricultural farm in China. She moves to Hong Kong and, with few marketable skills and limited knowledge of Cantonese, finds shelter in her cousin's house, where she has been working as a servant ever since. She envies her friend, Yanrong, who is also from the mainland, is married, makes more money than she as a factory worker, has more free time at work, and now owns a small wooden shack. She knows that with her present salary she could never afford to buy a similar hut for herself. She is encouraged by Yanrong to resign from her maid position, and yet she fears losing the enjoyment of such luxuries as air conditioning, a gas stove, television, a washing machine, and the other amenities in her master's home that have become basic conveniences in her daily routine. Unable to make a decision, Cao Shao'e turns to her brother, Cao Hongxiang, for advice. The brother, busily involved in his own wedding plans, offers little assistance. Ironically, however, his sudden death a week later pushes Cao Shao'e to a decision. Since Cao Shao'e understands little of procedural matters or how to cope with bureaucracy, she becomes a victim of circumstance, relying solely on her cousin to take care of the funeral and other family-related business matters. As a result, she finds it even more difficult to forgo her dependence on her all-protecting kin. In exchange for her submission to service, she can continue living a comfortable life in an orderly uncomplicated manner, free of worries.

When Cao Shao'e was a young girl in Indonesia, she went out fishing with her brother one day. They caught a long black fish, which, though still hooked to the fishing line, flapped its tail and struggled for its life. The brother stretched out one hand, grabbed it firmly by the middle, and squeezed it into a basket. Cao Shao'e's fantasy to live as an independent person, perhaps like her friend Yanrong, sparks off excitement in her otherwise humdrum life. However, when the passion is abandoned, she is forced to share a similar fate with that of the fish, forever trapped in the house of her cousin, Wei Jianbi, *jianbi* literally meaning "solid wall." A comfortable and orderly life is composed of a set of documents recording the birth, marriage, and death of a person, and each person in turn claims such certificates. Her brother understands and accepts this pattern of life without the least eagerness to challenge it. On his deathbed, his last words are "This is what life is all about."[10]

In spite of her initial and naive wish to change the course of her life, Cao Shao'e also eventually comes to the understanding that life is like a bus ride: the destination point clearly shown on a sign hung high in the front window even before the journey begins. The red dress she wears in her last appearance in the story indicates that she has reached maturation in her outlook on life. The litchis are now ripe, ready to be plucked, bought, and eaten. What awaits Cao Shao'e is a gradual but inescapable death. The use of litchis to symbolize death is especially evidenced by Zhong Xiaoyang's conscious choice of the numeral *si*, "four," which is a homophone for the word *si*, meaning "death." In this story it is ironically used as a quantifier for the fruit, such as the selling price of litchis at around four (*si*) dollars a pound, and the description of "four (*si*) litchis lying stiff on the table."[11]

The essence of life is nothing more than a stark cycle of birth, aging, and death. It is a pattern that we are all too familiar with, and yet we continue to look beyond it for more meaning in life. We have convinced ourselves that there is a higher goal to strive for. Jiang Chaoxin finds his inspiration in the picture of Ye Chen, and both Cuixiu and Cao Shao'e fantasize about their idols on the TV screen. It is always that fanciful but intangible image or momentary urge that induces a train of exciting but unattainable thoughts. Human effort to alter the course of life ultimately proves to be absurd and in vain. Yet such effort, however superfluous or painful, makes the assertion of one's existence and identity possible. Life, in the final analysis, is meaningless; thus the meaning of life, if there is to be one, is supplied or projected by individuals.

In another of Zhong Xiaoyang's stories, "The Second Sonata" ("Erduan qin"), a young boy is puzzled by the expression *fengjing ruhua*, "the scenery is like a picture."[12] Since scenery in the natural world is real and what one finds in a picture is false, the boy wonders why the real is compared to the false and the natural beauty not used as a metaphor for the tableau. The answer that Zhong Xiaoyang gives in her stories is that beauty is a human concept and does not exist in the natural world. A picture represents the human effort to capture and manifest one's ideal of beauty. It is an image that man aspires to, but nature itself is void of such human values. Similarly, man struggles, and regardless of his success or failure, the attempts are meaningless to life, which operates on its own immutable and impersonal course. Thus, on one extreme, Zhong Xiaoyang bemoans the spiritual death of resigning oneself to a passive role in life; and, on the other, she emphatically underscores the impossibility of those counter-endeavors. This is the eternal paradox that bewilders all men and women, and is beyond reconciliation.

Like all great writers who deal with the paradoxical nature of life, Zhong Xiaoyang provides no definitive answers or solutions in her stories. She deftly sets the scene before her readers and lets the drama unfold as the characters act out their fears and love. She is sensitive to the twists and turns of emotion in the human psyche; she stands aloof from the entanglements in the narrative, but her compassion for their vulnerability infuses her words and her play on homophonic sounds. Her language is embedded with a poetic pathos that many critics have compared to the writing of Zhang Ailing (Eileen Chang).[13] However, unlike most writers who sharpen their senses and refine their craft for many years before gaining recognition in the literary world, Zhong Xiaoyang attained almost instantaneous fame for her brilliance when she began her writing career at the young age of fifteen.

Born in Canton in 1963, Zhong Xiaoyang's father is Indonesian Chinese and her mother is from Manchuria. She attended an English Catholic school in Hong Kong and received little formal training in Chinese classical literature.[14] In 1981, she left for the United States to begin her college education at the University of Michigan, majoring in film. Though her schooling lacked an emphasis on her native language, her writings, which have won her prizes since she was sixteen,[15] demonstrate a remarkable familiarity with Chinese poetry, drama, and fiction. By her own admission, she is a fervid reader of *Honglou meng*,[16] the eighteenth-century Chinese masterpiece that examines the paradoxical nature of love and life in the romance of a declining aristocratic family. The novel, as critics have noted, placed an indelible imprint on Zhong Xiaoyang's writing, as it did on many other twentieth-century authors, including Zhang Ailing, who is, in fact, the contemporary writer Zhong most admires. Her aspiration to emulate Zhǎng's novel, *Bansheng yuan*, which she claims to always carry with her,[17] may account for the general impression that she composes in the footsteps of Zhang Ailing.[18]

However, it is unquestionably her own precocious curiosity about life and nature that has drawn her to the great works of the past, compelling her to explore philosophical concerns in her own fictional world. She owes much of her lyrical style to Chinese poetic traditions, and not only is she well versed in the genre, but she has also experimented since childhood with rhyme and meter in other various poetic styles. She is sensitive to sounds as well as images, a gift that enables her to play with words and symbolism, as amply illustrated in the previous discussion. Since the early 1980s, she has published two collections of essays and poetry.[19] She draws ideas for her prose and verse primarily from her own life experiences and immediate surroundings; her essays, mostly written in narrative style, are character portrayals of those who are close to her. Her first published work of fiction, a novel in three parts, was inspired by a visit to northeast China in 1980 with her mother, a native of that area. Her experiences as a student in America have also formed a rich source of inspiration and materials for her stories, even after her return to Hong Kong, where she now resides and continues to write for publications in both Hong Kong and Taiwan.

*Halt! May I Ask . . . (Tingche zan jiewen)*, the only novel she has written thus far, is a romance that spans a politically chaotic period of twenty years, shifting geographically southward from the Japanese-occupied Manchuria, in 1944, to the British Crown Colony, in 1965. The core of the novel revolves around postwar China during the late 1940s. The saga begins with the accidental meeting of a sixteen-year-old Chinese maiden, Zhao Ningjing, and a young Japanese college student in an air-raid shelter in a northeastern town, Fengtian. Racial animosity sparks a strange sort of attraction between the two, but the relationship, more innocent affection than passionate involvement, is cut short because of the political situation. As the Japanese retreat in 1945, following military defeat, a male cousin of hers from Shanghai enters the stage as the new hero in the second part of the Zhao Ningjing's drama. However, the romance is beset from the very beginning by a host of human factors that interfere with and eventually destroy their trust in each other. The cousin has been previously engaged to someone else, a family-made arrangement that makes it almost impossible for the audacious affair to be accepted by either family. Further complications arise when the cousin's career is sabotaged by a love-stricken doctor who schemes to marry Zhao Ningjing. The amorous intrigue finally fails under external pressure. In both of these amative adventures, first with a foreigner and then with someone else's fiancé, Zhao Ningjing has been playing the role of a defiant but impractical dreamer. In the third part of the novel, however, she becomes a schemer herself, deliberating every move she makes in order to divorce the doctor husband she loathes and to win the love of the man, her cousin, she has been waiting for all her life. She succeeds on all counts but makes one miscalculation: the man whose dedication she is so sure of leaves her at the last moment, a betrayal not due to fickleness but rather to a fear that he, beleaguered by poor health and impoverishment, will prove a burden to her. The romantic quest of Zhao Ningjing over two decades proves only one thing in the end, namely, the treacherous nature of life itself. However true love is professed to be, its permanence is beyond an individual's control. External conditions, be they political, societal, or familial, may eventually be overcome or ignored, but a genuine love can also destroy itself. The theme of the inexplicable mystery of life and the futility of human efforts to comprehend or alter it is best captured in the concluding scene in this biography of Zhao Ningjing:

> She looked out of the window, her mind drifting afar. An old-fashioned building stood in front of her, the window frames all painted green and the panes each invariably bearing a huge cross in white masking tape. It was a precautionary measure taken in typhoon season. From inside, there emerged the vague reflections of a great many bottles and vases of various sizes and shapes. Around the lower floor a long veranda was built, also painted in green, with metal railings arching out in succession. It was like a bird cage, a tunnel, a confine. Stretching across behind the railings were some ragged old clotheslines and hanging poles. Also, there was a child's bike, a few pots of dying plants, and other miscellaneous things. But, unexpectedly, one of the clay pots displayed a delicate hibiscus blooming a brilliant red. It was a dazzling sight. A misfit, a reincarnation in the wrong place, a bleak future. Presently, a slouchy little old woman found her way onto the balcony to use the clothesline. She hung one garment at a time, walking back inside to get the next item. Why didn't she bring out the entire load of laundry? It puzzled Ningjing as she stared at the scene in a daze. As if in slow motion, the woman put out a pair of grayish underpants of a boy; not too grayish, perhaps a worn out color of what used to be a clean

white. When the old woman appeared again, she held in her hand, not clothes this time, but a roll on which she munched piggishly. She then squatted down and scanned the street scene below her, her mouth still busily chewing. As she looked up, she noticed by chance that Ningjing was staring at her. She shook her head and ignored her. She kept on munching and occasionally side-glanced at Ningjing. This went on several times. Then, as if irritated, she went inside, shaking her head, not coming out again. The clothes flapped and fluttered idly in the open air.

It was a clear, brisk day. The clothes would be dry in no time. So would the tears of Ningjing. Very soon, they were all gone.[20]

As the defeated heroine drifts away in thoughts of her romantic past, the author introduces a two-tier structure to restage her story in symbolic terms. Her memory of the young boy she met in the air-raid shelter is now as blurry as the reflections on the storm windows on the top floor of the building now confronting her. The scene of a fenced-in long balcony on the lower flight with clothes hanging on ropes readily recalls the extended and tumultuous involvement she had with a man who used to manage a fabric store. The out-of-place bright red hibiscus represents the willful and passionate Zhao Ningjing, who seems forever unable to find her lot in life. Who is the old woman? Her seemingly irrational deeds puzzle the curious heroine. Is she the projection of Zhao Ningjing herself in the future, a being who lives in tedium and indulges in basic gluttonous needs? Or is she the almighty god whose enigmatic behavior is beyond comprehension and whose control of individual beings is so complete that each life hangs as meaninglessly as a garment on a clothesline, "flapping and fluttering idly in the open air?" Viewed either way, life is a meaningless existence, and the earlier one comes to terms with this truth, the sooner one resigns oneself to the dictates of fate. The name of the enamored dreamer, Ningjing, literally means "peace and tranquility," an envious state of mind which one never attains until, in the words of her cousin, one dies. When the protagonist finally comes to this realization, she takes on a new form of being, a woman named Ningjing and a face without tears.

Zhong Xiaoyang spent two years writing this novel, publishing the first part in a newspaper in 1981 and completing the rest of it in 1982 when she was nineteen years old. Praised by critics in both Taiwan and Hong Kong as a work of genius,[21] the novel quickly found her a niche in the literary world, where her writing talent and ability to create romantic worlds laden with pessimism have continued to produce works in a unique style of lyrical pathos. *Halt! May I Ask . . .* crystallizes the primary philosophical concern that recurs in her later stories, where the characters, regardless of gender, age, or background, all encounter some kind of despair similar to that which jolts Zhao Ningjing to a choking realization of her place in life. In the short stories we have examined above, we have seen portrayals of Jiang Chaoxin ("The Fleeting Years") and Cuixiu ("Green Sleeves") as dreamers who stop dreaming when night falls at the end of their tales. To dramatize the struggle between fantasy and reality, the ideal and the mundane, titillation and ennui, Zhong Xiaoyang often constructs a love triangle in which the protagonist strives and frets but ultimately fails to find a way out of the emotional entrapment. "My Beloved Wife" ("Aiqi") is a sorrowful confession of a married man, a travel agent by profession, who is involved in an adulterous affair with a woman whom he does not really love and returns home too late only to find his wife already on her deathbed. "Thinking of My Beloved Husband" ("Yi liangren") recounts the confusing thoughts of a housewife who fantasizes about marrying two men either simultaneously or in succession. "Coming and Going" ("Lihe") describes an amorous woman who fails twice in marriage, both for reasons beyond her comprehension.

Romantic dilemmas may also be posed in the form of a lingering tension between the present and the past, the real and the fictional. We have seen in "The Fleeting Years" how the attachment to the memories of a childhood romance interferes with Jiang Chaoxin's perception of and ability to deal with the present. In "Calling Her Name" ("Huan Zhenzhen"), a young artist spends years looking for the impish neighbor girl who once modeled for him. By the time he finishes a portrait of her from memory, which he entitles "A Maiden in Stone," the young woman succumbs to prostitution. In "A Vow by the Clasp" (Shichai meng"), a young film student falls in love with the image of a girl he sees through the camera lens when she performs an exquisite ancient dance on stage. He picks up a pearl hairpin that she has dropped and sticks it "in the soil in a flower pot, attending to it daily with the passion of a gardener, wishing it would grow and, one day, bloom against the luxuriant green of the plants around it."[22] A few years later, when he finally musters enough courage to propose, carrying the hairpin as a token of his love, he finds that his nymph idol is, in real life, a petty social dance instructor in a community center, mechanically repeating "slow, slow, quick, . . . slow, slow, quick, . . . slow, slow, quick. . . ." Metaphorically, the ghastly displacement of fantasy by hard, cold, or even ugly facts is an experience that dawns on Quehua, the twice-divorced woman in

"Coming and Going." In it, she awakes one morning to find it is a leaking faucet responsible for the sounds of flowing water she mistook in her sleep as the murmuring streamlet where she had soaked her feet in a spring frolic with the two men whom she eventually married. The water metaphor is extended to an even deeper level of signification when Cao Shaoe, the maid in "When the Litchis Ripen," turns on the water faucet only to find that the water supply has been temporarily suspended; outside the window, however, there is a downpour. That man is unable to tap the torrential rain for direct faucet use is an unequivocal statement proving the futility of human undertakings. Repeatedly and laboriously, Zhong Xiaoyang manipulates various devices, structurally as well as rhetorically, to construct a world in which there is no hope. She voices a bleak outlook on life, the only significance of which seems to lie in the paradox between aspiration and resignation, both leading ironically to the same resolution. Romance is one manifestation of this paradox; and, by implication, any deliberate efforts to achieve it, with the exception of perhaps only one account in Zhong Xiaoyang's fiction, are bound to fail.

"The Wedding Night" ("Liangxiao"), the last story to be examined in this discussion, brings a breath of fresh air into Zhong Xiaoyang's world of romantic pessimism. First published in a Taiwan newspaper, in 1985, the tale probes into the minds of a newlywed couple, who, moments after the wedding ceremony, are already haunted by doubts and questions as to their readiness for each other. Much in the same vein as in her earlier attempts, she makes abundant use of paradoxical images and ironic twists; but, unlike "The Fleeting Years" and others, this story concludes with an affirmation of the matrimonial bond, an open willingness to share and face the challenge of uncertainties in the course of this new life. As the night begins, the bride sits quietly on the bed, fingers crossed "like strings stretching over a lute."[23] The Chinese word for lute, *qin*, is a near homophone for *qing*, meaning "love, feelings"; an interplay between these two forms has long been observed in the Chinese literary tradition.[24] The story ends with the same lute metaphor when the bride crosses her fingers once more like the musical strings. In between, however, the mind of the bride drifts and wavers between the past and the future. As she raises her palm close to her eyes, she gazes into it as if into a mirror in which she sees only her immediate present: her confinement behind a red bridal veil.

Traditionally, a Chinese bride would wear a red veil as she was brought to the house of her betrothed. Led in and guided by the matchmaker and other assistants, the bride would perform and participate in the entire matrimonial ritual behind the veil. Her physical inability to see indeed characterizes the nature of a blind marriage, *manghun*, a nuptial contract between two strangers as arranged and signed by their families. Only on the wedding night, when the groom lifts off this bridal headdress in their private chamber, do the couple see each other for the first time. Our groom ponders upon the significance of this historical custom: "For generations, he thought, grooms had followed in each other's footsteps, walking up with great courage to unveil his betrothed on the wedding night, and his destiny. The curtain was about to be ceremoniously raised for the commencement of a new marriage."[25]

The surprise beyond the veil was actually predestined for the groom as well as for the bride. For, from behind each side of the red silk, there would emerge a stranger, to whom one had been promised and with whom one would live from that day onward. The surprise could be a happy one, or it might be the unmasking of a hideous face, a sinister future, or both. The veil indeed possesses such magical powers of transformation over one's life that Zhong Xiaoyang readily compares it to the kerchief that a magician utilizes when performing a trick. The moment before the magician reveals what is in store for the audience is a moment of suspense, a suspense that fills a groom and bride before the critical act of unveiling. It is a suspense Zhong Xiaoyang tries to capture and recreate in "The Wedding Night," where the contemporary couple opt for this ancient connubial practice out of playful curiosity.

The couple, referred to in the story only as the bride and the groom, have been in love for some time before finally entering into matrimonial union. Their wedding ceremony essentially follows a traditional style, including a feast in which the bride, dressed in a gown "embroidered with a pair of phoenixes and strung with colorful sequins,"[26] presents the ceremonial tea to her parents-in-law in prostration. The bridal costume, however, does not contain a veil, and the veil is first introduced as an amusing suggestion by the husband, who has always fantasized about seeing his bride covered with a red veil.

> You never knew this before, but I have dreamed of this ever since I was a child. If only I could do what they did in the old days, unveil my bride on my wedding night, I would be the happiest man alive. And, now, the day is finally here. I am about to fulfill

my fantasy. If you will change into the traditional gown now and put on the red veil, then I will have a chance to remove the veil and look at you as if for the first time.[27]

The bride initially rejects the idea as being old-fashioned, out-dated, and downright "silly," but she concedes as he pleas with sweet words of coercion. Even though they were kissing passionately until that moment, "their sweat dripping onto each other's bodies,"[28] the notion of wearing a veil puts an instant halt to their physical embrace. Through a quick flow of internal monologues and random associa-tions, the couple's doubts are revealed. Once the red veil is put on, it becomes an impenetrable screen drawn between the two, creating a sense of distance that soon turns into estrangement. The groom finds it difficult to connect the face in his mind to the body now sitting under the veil. The bride begins to wonder if she knows him well enough for matrimonial commitment. Unlike their predecessors in the *manghun* era, our couple has chosen their own matrimonial course, yet the thin veil casts as much doubt, anxiety, and alienation as it did in the past. It conjures up various images for the groom as he tries to imagine what awaits him behind the red silk: a night of romantic bliss, a headless corpse, or a ghost wife who has come to prey on him. The bride envisions murder as she tries to see through the cover: is the man beyond her visionary world a bullfighter tucking a red scarf by his waist or a psychotic husband who schemes to torture her to death? The longer the suspense, the more bizarre their imaginative wanderings become and the less faith they find they have left in each other. The auspicious objects in the room that once stood for nuptial blessings have now abruptly and ironically turned into artifacts of evil. The candlelight, which the groom thought to be the most conducive ro-mantic illumination, now flickers ominously on his face. The sensual attraction of the red veil has turned into a suffocating force like flames burning around the bride's head. As foreboded by the fire that devas-tated the restaurant where they held their wedding feast earlier that evening, their "night of nuptial celebration" turned, in the couple's imagination, into a morbid fearful experience.

Through courtship, the couple may have acquired great famili-arity with each other. However, as they are about to take their first step in building a life together, a commitment that requires absolute faith in one another, they falter as they realize that the enterprise carries unknown prospects. As the bride sits motionlessly on the bed, "now she could sense his invisible presence pressing towards her. His breathing in her direction felt as if a future world were closing in on her with an unsurmountable force."[29] The anxiety prompts second thoughts: "If only there wasn't anyone else in the room and this was all but a dream."[30]

As for the groom, whether it be an amorous dream or a nightmare, he simply wants to end the game, not by lifting the veil, but by turning on the light. At the moment of pledging the matrimonial bond, our anonymous couple, hence assuming a generic representation for newlyweds of all lands and ages, suffer from "cold feet." Rather than confronting the confusion, they let their suspicions run wild and are tempted to escape from the unknown. This momentary admission of fear and misgiving is a universal experience that Zhong Xiaoyang eloquently captures in this seemingly innocent game. By hiding herself behind a red scarf, the bride feels as if she has put on a mythical garment that has rendered her invisible. In effect, by entering wedlock, one has effaced one's individual identity and assumed a new form of life as a conjugal unit. Whether physically veiled or not, whether betrothed to a total stranger or someone she thinks she is deeply in love with, a woman releases control of her future on her wedding day. Likewise, a man has yet to find out the true mind of the woman whose visage he may or may not have previously seen. Marriage is a betting game that one may win or lose, an outcome that no one can foretell. Zhong Xiaoyang chooses a blazing fire as the setting of the story to dramatize the ambivalent and paradoxical nature of the marriage institution. The fire breaks out when the couple finally finds their moment of privacy, embracing each other on the bed. The fire not only disrupts their intimacy, but also destroys the restaurant where they celebrated their nuptial festivity. The color of the fire, a dangerous red, contrasts with the auspicious hue of the draperies, the candles, the bedspread, and even the veil. The beaming red of the candles is set against the glare of swirling siren lights. The crowd on the street bustles around, radiating "a feverish red." The narrator questions whether they are celebrating merriment of calamity. "Red" has taken on contradictory meanings, imbuing the matrimonial relationship with an enigmatic quality. Nonetheless, the wedding is an enticing beginning, alarming and obfuscating, while at the same time promising "tenderness in a bed of brocade opulence."[31]

Through the chaotic stream of the newlywed's thoughts, vacillating from a contemporary local restaurant to the ancient Ming court, from traditional China to Western civilization, from mythology to poetry, from newspaper reports to stage performances, Zhong Xiaoyang connects the experiences of one couple to the history of humanity. In the West, the bride reminds herself, "a wedding ceremony always included a scene in which the groom would unveil his bride and give her an endearing kiss."[32] The two cultures differ only in the choice of color, the Western veil being white. The groom alludes to the legendary romance of Princess Changping and Zhou Shixian as justification for his insistence on a veiled bride: "You saw the play *Dinühua*, right? Zhou Shixian and Princess Changping had known each other long before they were married. Yet, on their wedding day, the princess veiled herself just the same."[33]

*Dinühua*[34] is a Cantonese opera adapted from a Qing play by the same title. It tells of the tragic love of Princess Changping, daughter of the last emperor of the Ming dynasty, who was ordered by the newly established Qing sovereignty to marry Zhou Shixian, a young scholar she had known and to whom she had been promised by her father before the fall of the Ming dynasty. To express their uncompromising loyalty to the Ming empire, they took their lives on their wedding night by sharing a poisoned nuptial drink. The tragic turn of events in this royal ceremony rings an ominous tone when Zhong Xiaoyang restages the drama in her narrative with the groom's whimsical proposition: "Why don't you play the part of Princess Changping, and I'll be the imperial husband Zhou Shixian?"[35]

The bride, though sensing something foreboding in the request, is unwittingly drawn more and more to the thought of her newly assigned role. With operatic songs echoing like a chorus singing in the background "From whence came those almost inaudible strains of music?"[36], the story delves into historical discourse, revolving around the same paradox, the enticing and yet perilous nature of marital commitment. Like the use of color symbolism, the story within the story achieves a double entendre. By joining two individuals together in matrimony, the imperial wedding also pronounces death. Is what awaits a conjugal union something to be welcomed or feared? The lyrics of *Dinühua* elaborate on the tantalizing beauty of what one wishes to see behind the red veil, but they also reveal, in dramatic terms, the most unambiguous and ultimate form of fear, the fear of death itself. Yet what distinguishes the imperial couple in the parallel story is their faith in each other, their readiness to face any consequence of the step they are to take together. With faith, they embrace each other in death, thereby dissolving any doubt or fear they may have initially harbored. "In this regard, death with her groom was a martyrdom she had chosen of her own free will."[37] As the bride sees herself being transposed back in time to the year 1644, when the Manchus broke open the Ming palace gate, she enters the mind of Changping and acquires a new understanding of the meaning of matrimony. With "thousands of years of history now guarded her with an eye of compassion,"[38] the bride finally gains the courage and strength to confront the unknown. As symbolized by the red veil under which the bride feels invisible, marriage marks the end of an individual's identity. What ensues in the joint venture remains a mystery.

The renaming of the veil as a "red turban," an allusion to the third-century "Yellow Turban" rebellion that toppled the rule of the Han dynasty,[39] underscores the precarious nature of the occasion. Or will the kiss that follows the unveiling be a miracle of resurrection, as in the story of *Sleeping Beauty*?[40] No one knows what the outcome will be, but, at the same time, no one can alter the course that Princess Changping chose to take. The bride is awakened to a new understanding of love: it is the will of the person to decide how the unknown is to be faced. The role-playing of the newlyweds as the star-stricken princess and her husband seems to portend a catastrophe; yet, ironically, the omen turns into a source of optimism. It is essentially through the vicarious suffering in the tragic drama that the couple finds the power to dispel their fears. Doubts once removed, bewilderment dissipated, they are once again enveloped in amorous thoughts of one another: "From within this red domain were a pair of watching eyes, carefully focused on the tip of the fan as it slowly approached from beyond. A whiff of subtle fragrance arose from the sandalwood. Slightly dizzy, the bride, so vulnerable."[41]

As in Zhong Xiaoyang's other works, "The Wedding Night" initially laments the inability of man to take charge of his destiny, destiny here represented in the realm of romantic endeavors. When Li Tianliang seeks the hand of Jianyu in "My Beloved Wife," her father agrees to the proposal by saying: "I'm now turning Jianyu over to you. But, as to what lies ahead of you, it depends on what you are going to put in and what fate has in store for you."[42]

In the stories of Yu Xianglun and of Zhao Ningjing, we witness the futility of human effort to shape the course of life to what is seen as appropriate or desirable. What one puts in has little to do with what one receives in the end. One after the other, the romantic heroes and heroines in Zhong Xiaoyang's world fall prey to higher forces that flatly negate any arduous effort. They find love which is soon to be taken away through events beyond their control, and they enter marriage without making conscious choices. Life becomes a form of meaningless existence as there becomes nothing left to pursue aside from the fulfillment of physical needs. We see the unwilling resignation on the part of Zhao Ningjing as she is compelled to face the projection of her future in the old hag squatting in the balcony across from her apartment. We see the sudden aging of the restless soul in "Tender Love" ("Rouqing"), a story that transforms a light comic romance into a theater of the absurd. "The Wedding Night" seems to follow essentially the same thematic pattern. Even though marriage is an imminent reality for the young couple who have attained their union, not through *manghun* but via courtship, what lies beyond the wedding ceremony is yet another course they do not have the vision to see or the ability to steer from within the bounds of their bridal chamber. Their fears, doubts, suspicions, and anger are all manifestations of an universal experience, the anguish of the unknown.

However, instead of ending the tale on a despondent note as in her other fictional compositions, Zhong Xiaoyang introduces a new message into her writing: a positive assertion on human endeavor. Even though we cannot anticipate what is in store for us in the future, the will to stride toward the unknown, regardless of the consequences, constitutes a new meaning for life. It represents hope and faith, a unifying force for those who join hands together to embark on the adventure. Zhong Xiaoyang chooses not to give the newlyweds names, thereby underscoring the universality of their brief but intense emotional trauma. In contrast, she provides specific details regarding the imperial couple, including their names and the year and locale of their tragic wedding. The switch from the anonymous to the identified, from the general to the specific, seems to lend convincing substance to this newfound faith. Yet, upon close scrutiny, the specific is again a legendary romance, a tale embellished in drama and poetry. The official history registers the death of Princess Changping as occurring a year after her marriage to Zhou Shixian. There is no record of a double suicide on the imperial wedding day.[43] The very fact that the suicide is a fabrication undermines the validity of this newfound faith. Much as the newlyweds aspire to the perseverance and conviction of the ancient princess and her husband, so the aspiration is just another illusion. In effect, the introduction of this poetic lie serves to further enhance the pessimism in Zhong Xiaoyang's fiction. However, by giving false hope to her world already full of despair, she sets up both her characters and her readers for another titillating suspense. Until the moment of truth arrives, that hope and faith in love, however false it may eventually prove to be, encompasses the entire meaning of life, asserting its influence even if it is only for a flashing instant. This paradox of the impermanence of love is perhaps what Li Tianliang tries to explain to himself in his delirious confession in "My Beloved Wife": "What we've been looking for all our lives is neither ecstasy nor agony, but rather that brief glimpse of love we catch as we run between ecstasy and agony."[44]

Jiang Chaoxin once taught Ye Chen a *ci* poem by Su Tongpo, only the first half of which, as cited at the beginning of this discussion, is what the young couple can enjoy reciting from memory. It is not by accident that Zhong Xiaoyang chooses not to give the second half of the song, which ends on a note of hope and optimism:

> I only wish that you and I may be ever well and hale.
> That both of us may watch the fair moon, even a
> thousand miles apart.[45]

The lines conjure up a romantic vision that true love can transcend the limits of time and space. In Zhong Xiaoyang's world, love is only meaningful to those concerned; it has no permanence or bearing on the passage of time. Time is the ultimate arbitrator of fate; it generates life and brings all to oblivion. It hastens the cycle of life and death, blotting out all traces that human endeavor leaves behind in the world. It is perhaps because of this understanding of the indifference of time that Zhong Xiaoyang chose to name the Jiang Chaoxin story as well as her first collection of short stories "The Fleeting Years."[46]

## Notes

1. This project was in part supported by a University of California, Berkeley, faculty research grant. I wish to thank L. Wang and W. Lu for their assistance in preparing the paper, as well as Ms. Wei-luan Lu, of the Chinese University of Hong Kong, who has kindly provided me with Hong Kong newspaper clippings on Zhong Xiaoyang. An early version of the paper was presented at the Asian Studies on the Pacific Coast (ASPAC) Conference in Los Angeles in 1984.

2. A *ci* poem, to the tune of "Shuidiaogetou" by Su Shi, a Song poet, better known as Su Tongpo, included in Cyril Birch, ed., *Anthology of Chinese Literature* (New York: Grove Press, 1965), pp. 355–56.

3. "The Fleeting Years" ("Liunian") in the collection by the same title (hereafter abbreviated as *LN*) (Hong Kong: Hongfan shudian, 1983), p. 105.

4. The two characters are pronounced differently in Cantonese: *yuh* (in Yale romanization) versus *yuhk*. They are, however, only distinguished by tone in Mandarin: the former, $yu^2$ versus the latter, $yu^4$.

5. Except in tone, the two characters are identical in pronunciation in both Mandarin and Cantonese.

6. *LN*, p. 86.

7. "Green Sleeves" ("Cuixiu"), *LN*, p. 19.

8. The punning on the homophone between *si* "silk; thread" and *si* "thought; sentiment" has long been a standard practice in the Chinese lyrical tradition. The choice of the color "green" also plays on the homophone between $qing^1$ and $qing^2$, as noted above. "Green Sleeves" was made into a movie in Hong Kong in 1987. For a discussion on the adaptation, with a particular emphasis on the symbolic meaning of the loose thread, see Ye Si's "Wenxue he yingshi di duihua" ("A Dialogue between Literature and the Video Media") in *Xiaoshuo jiazu* (*An Anthology of Short Stories*) (Hong Kong: Tiandi tushu, 1987), pp. 6–7.

9. "The Second Sonata" ("Erduan qin"), *LN*, p. 170.

10. "When the Litchis Ripen" ("Lizhi shu"), *LN*, p. 220.

11. Ibid, p. 206.

12. "The Second Sonata," *LN*, p. 125.

13. See Chen Qinchuan, "Zhong Xiaoyang ersan shi" ("Notes on Zhong Xiaoyang"), *Xianggang shibao* (*Hong Kong Daily*), August 22, 1981.

14. For sketches of her family and schooling, see her collection of essays entitled *Chun zai lüwuzhong* (*Spring in Luxuriant Green*) (Hong Kong: Tiandi tushu, 1987). In one of these articles, she mentions a history teacher who said, "That I am teaching you Chinese history in the English language is something that I don't know whether I should find ludicrous or I should be angry about" (p. 4).

15. In early 1979, she won honorable mention in the junior category of essay writing in the Sixth Hong Kong Annual Youth Literary Awards Contest. In 1980, she participated in the Seventh Hong Kong Annual Youth Literary Awards Contest and won a second place award in the poetry category (junior level). In 1981, she reaped two first-place awards, both in the senior category of essay writing: the Eighth Hong Kong Annual Youth Literary Awards Contest and the Second Annual Writing

Contest sponsored by the Hong Kong Government. The double victory brought Zhong to the limelight of the literary world; *Damuzhi*, a literary magazine in Hong Kong, devoted its May issue that year to her, generating much public discussion on the rise of this gifted writer.

16. See Chen's newspaper article cited in note 13.

17. Ibid.

18. In his discussion of Zhang Ailing's fiction, C. T. Hsia observes, "Actually, in the bulk of her short fiction, she is more apparently drawn to the vulgarities and ironies of everyday life, the compromises one makes in order to preserve sanity and stave off the pressure of reality." *A History of Modern Chinese Fiction, 1917–1957* (New Haven, Conn.: Yale University Press, 1961), p. 413. The thematic concern is evidently shared by Zhong Xiaoyang in her writing.

19. One of the collections is *Chun zai lüwuzhong*, first published by the *Damuzhi* magazine in Hong Kong in 1983; in 1987, the Tiandi tushu, Hong Kong, released a new edition, by the same title, with two additional articles. The other collection, which includes sixteen poems and twelve essays, appeared in 1983 under two different titles: *Xishuo* (*In Reminiscence*), published by the Sansan shufang in Taiwan, and *Zouguo* (*To Pass By*), published in 1984 by Nushen chubanshe in Hong Kong.

20. *Tingche zan jiewen (Halt! May I Ask . . .)* (Hong Kong: Tangdai wenyi, 1983), p. 253.

21. In his raving review of the novel (Part I) in *Xianggang shibao* (*Hong Kong Daily*), August 9 and 10, 1981, Zhu Xining describes Zhong Xiaoyang as a genius in her ability to write, despite her spatial and temporal restrictions as a young woman reared in Hong Kong, a novel of such length set in Manchuria in the 1940s. Sima Zhongyuan compares the work to Qian Zhongshu's *Wei cheng* in its use of symbolism. His comments are quoted in the introduction to the novel.

22. "A Vow by the Clasp" ("Shichai meng"), from the collection entitled *The Mourning Song (Aige)* (hereafter abbreviated as *AG*) (Hong Kong: Tiandi tushu, 1987), p. 31.

23. "The Wedding Night" ("Liangxiao"), from the collection entitled *My Beloved Wife (Aiqi)* (hereafter abbreviated as *AQ*) (Hong Kong: Tiandi tushu, 1987), p. 232.

24. The conscious use of *qin* to stand for the word *qing* "love" was already quite prevalent in Ming fiction. For example, in "Maiyolang duzhan huakui" (*Xingshi hengyan*, No. 3), both the hero and heroine in the romantic tale are named with words that are pronounced as *qin*: Qin Zhong and Shen Yaoqin. The latter is also accompanied by a lute. The name Qin Zhong, with a different character for the second syllable, also appears in *Honglou meng*.

25. *AQ*, p. 241.

26. Ibid., p. 237.

27. Ibid., pp. 235–36.

28. Ibid., p. 233.

29. Ibid., p. 238.

30. Ibid.

31. Ibid.

32. Ibid., p. 242.

33. Ibid., p. 235.

34. See note 2 in the translation. Zhong Xiaoyang seems to be particularly fond of this opera, as she has not only seen it both on stage and on the screen, but also knows the lyrics by heart. See her discussion of "Dinühua" in "Lixiang zhige" ("Songs from the Street"), *Chun zai lüwuzhong*, pp. 141–43. The Cantonese drama was adapted from a Qing play by Huang Xieqing (A.D. 1805–1864).

35. *AQ*, p. 235.

36. Ibid., p. 244.

37. Ibid., p. 243.

38. Ibid. See note 4 in "The Wedding Night."

39. Ibid.

40. Ibid., p. 242.

41. Ibid., p. 244.

42. "My Beloved Wife," *AQ*, p. 2.

43. According to *Mingshi*, the dynastic history of Ming, Emperor Chongzhen slashed at Princess Changping with his sword when the

city fell to the Manchu invaders. The princess lost an arm but recovered consciousness five days afterwards. The next year, she submitted a petition to the Qing ruler requesting permission to become a nun, thereby annulling her betrothal to Zhou Shixian as arranged by her father. The court, however, ordered an immediate wedding. A year later, she died of illness.

44. Ibid., p. 126.

45. Translated by Ch'u Ta-kao. See note 2 for further information.

46. The profound pessimism as evidenced in Zhong Xiaoyang's stories has often puzzled critics: however precocious and sensitive she may be, her bleak and distressing outlook of life seems to be beyond the comprehension and experience of a twenty-year-old student. According to the autobiographical sketches in her collection of essays, Zhong Xiaoyang was raised in a caring and supportive family conducive to optimism rather than resignation. Yet the colony in which she grew up is faced with the approaching expiration of the Sino-British lease, which, to many of the residents, is an imminent and devastating threat to all dreams of prosperity. Was Zhong Xiaoyang making a conscious attempt to reflect this emotional upheaval in her fiction? Or is the political climate there indirectly responsible for her cultivation of a style of pessimism? One can only guess. The only hint we might draw from her fiction is a play on the lexical word meaning "red" in "The Wedding Night." When the bride feels a suffocating fear hiding behind a red veil, a screen that blocks out her vision from the immediate surroundings as well as from her future life, the red drape is compared metaphorically to a blaze, "a peril of red." The word for "red," *chise,* is often used to refer to Communism. The historical subplot featuring Princess Changping also has some bearing on the conclusion of a political era and the foreboding of death in the beginning of a new dynasty.

# Contributors

**SAMUEL HUNG-NIN CHEUNG**, associate professor of Chinese studies at the University of California at Berkeley, received his B.A. and M.A. from the Chinese University of Hong Kong and his Ph.D. from the University of California, Berkeley. He has written extensively on Chinese linguistics and has also authored a book on Cantonese grammar, a translation of a compendium on historical phonology, and many papers on dialectology and grammar. His research in vernacular and contemporary Chinese literature has produced a variety of studies on colloquial short stories and classical novels such as *Shuihu zhuan* and *Honglou meng*; his latest project, entitled "Structure, Style, and Symbolism in Ming Fiction," is a literary study of folktales from the seventeenth century. His studies have appeared in *Journal of Chinese Linguistics, Journal of the Chinese Language Teachers Association, Journal of the Institute of Chinese Studies of the Chinese University of Hong Kong, Chinese Oral and Performing Literature Papers, Literature of the People's Republic of China*, and *Qinghua Journal of Chinese Studies* [Ch'ing-hua Journal of Chinese Studies].

**HSIN-SHENG C. KAO** is associate professor of Chinese studies at California State University at Long Beach. She received her B.A. in English from the National Taiwan University and her Ph.D. in comparative literature from the University of Southern California. She is the author of *Li Ju-chen* and translator of *The Grass of the Returning Souls*. Her articles and translations on both classical and modern Chinese literature have appeared in *Waiting for the Unicorn, The Indiana Companion to Traditional Chinese Literature, Tamkang Review, The Unbroken Chain, Women Writers of Twentieth-Century China, Renditions*, and *Literature of the People's Republic of China*. She is also the guest editor of and contributor to a full-length study entitled "Taoism in Chinese Literature" for the *Journal of Chinese Philosophy* 15, no. 2 (May 1988). Currently, she has completed a volume of translated short stories entitled *A Woman Writer at the Crossroads: The Short Stories of Chen Ruoxi*.

**MICHELLE YEH** received her B.A. in English from the National Taiwan University and her M.A. and Ph.D. in comparative literature from the University of Southern California. She is associate professor in the

Chinese and Japanese program at the University of California at Davis. Her publications show a wide range of interests, including comparative poetics, modern Chinese and American poetry, contemporary Chinese fiction, and translation. A few representative works include "Metaphor and *Bi*: Western and Chinese Poetics," *Comparative Literature* 39, no. 3(Summer 1987): 237–54; "Circularity: Emergence of a Form in Modern Chinese Poetry," *Modern Chinese Literature* 3, nos. 1–2 (Spring–Fall 1987): 33–46; and "Shapes of Darkness: Symbols in Li Ang's *Dark Night*," in *Modern Chinese Women Writers: Critical Appraisals* (1989): 78–95. She is the author of *Modern Chinese Poetry: Theory and Practice since 1917* (1991) and the co-editor (with Dominic Cheung) of a volume of contemporary stories from Taiwan, entitled *Exiles and Native Sons*.

**SHIAO-LING YU** received her Ph.D. in Chinese literature from the University of Wisconsin, Madison, in 1983. She is an associate professor in the Department of Foreign Languages and Literatures at Oregon State University. Her articles and translations on both classical and modern Chinese literature have appeared in *Renditions, Tamkang Review, Journal of Chinese Philosophy, The China Quarterly, Honglou meng yanjiu jikan,* and in anthologies such as *The Unbroken Chain, Contemporary Chinese Literature* (M. E. Sharpe), and *The Indiana Companion to Traditional Literature*. She is currently doing research on the literature of the People's Republic of China produced since 1976.

# Selected Bibliography

## Part One: On Individual Writers

### Chen Ruoxi 陈若曦

#### I. Primary Sources

A. Novels

*Zhihun* 纸婚 *(Paper Marriage)*.
Taipei: Zili wanbaoshe, 1986.
Hong Kong: Joint Publishing Co., 1987.
Beijing: Wenlian chuban gongsi, 1987.

*Er Hu* 二胡 *(The Two Hus)*.
Taipei: Dunli chubanshe, 1985.
Hong Kong: Joint Publishing Co., 1986.
Beijing: Youyi chuban gongsi, 1987.

*Yuanjian* 远见 *(Foresight)*.
Taipei: Yuanjing chuban gongsi, 1984.
Hong Kong: Boyi chubanshe, 1984.
Beijing: Youyi chuban gongsi, 1985.

*Tuwei* 突围 *(Breaking Out)*.
Taipei: Lianjing chuban gongsi, 1983.
Hong Kong: Joint Publishing Co., 1983.
Beijing: Youyi chuban gongsi, 1983.

*Gui* 归 *(The Repatriates)*.
Taipei: Lianjing chuban gongsi, 1978.
Hong Kong: Mingbao chubanshe, 1979.

B.  Short Stories

*Guizhou nüren* 贵州女人 *(The Woman from Guizhou).*
Taipei: Yuanliu chubanshe, 1989.
Hong Kong: Xiangjiang chubanshe, 1989.

*Chen Ruoxi zhongduanpian xiaoshuo xuan* 陈若曦中短篇小说选
*(Selected Short Stories and Novellas by Chen Ruoxi).*
Fushou: Haixia chubanshe, 1985.

*Chen Ruoxi xiaoshuo xuan* 陈若曦小说选
*(Selected Short Stories by Chen Ruoxi).*
Beijing: Guangbo chubanshe, 1983.

*Chengli chengwai* 城里城外 *(In and Outside the Wall).*
Taipei: Shibao chuban gongsi, 1981.
Hong Kong: Bafang chubanshe, 1981.
Hong Kong: Tiandi tushu, 1983.

*Laoren* 老人 *(The Old Man).*
Taipei: Lianjing chuban gongsi, 1978.

*Chen Ruoxi zixuan ji* 陈若曦自选集
*(Selected Works by Chen Ruoxi).*
Taipei: Lianjing chuban gongsi, 1976.

*Yin xianzhang* 尹县长 *(Mayor Yin).*
Taipei: Yuanjing chuban gongsi, 1976.

C.  Prose

*Qingzang gaoyuan de youhuo* 青藏高原的诱惑
*(The Temptation of the Tibetan Plateau).*
Taipei: Lianjing chuban gongsi, 1989.
Hong Kong: Publications Ltd., 1989.

*Xizang xing* 西藏行 *(Trip to Tibet).*
Hong Kong: Xiangjiang chubanshe, 1988.

*Caoyuan xing* 草原行 *(Trip to Inner Mongolia).*
Taipei: Shibao chuban gongsi, 1988.

*Tianran shengchu de huaduo* 天然生出的花朵
*(Flowers Grown Naturally)*.
Tianjin: Baihua chubanshe, 1987.

*Wuliao cai dushu* 无聊才读书  *(Reading to Kill Time)*.
Hong Kong: Tiandi tushu, 1983.

*Shenghuo suibi* 生活随笔  *(Random Notes)*.
Taipei: Shibao chuban gongsi, 1981.

*Wenge zayi* 文革杂忆 *(Reminiscences of the Cultural Revolution)*.
Taipei: Hongfan shudian, 1979.

D.  Works Written in English by the Author

*Democracy Walls and Unofficial Journals*.
Berkeley: University of California Press, 1982.

*Ethics and Rhetorics of the Chinese Cultural Revolution*.
Berkeley: Center for Chinese Studies,
Institute of East Asian Studies, University of California, 1981.

"Formosan Literature,"
*China Quarterly* (July-September, 1963).

*Spirit Calling: Five Stories of Taiwan*.
Taipei: The Heritage Press, 1962.

E.  Works Translated into English by Others

*The Execution of Mayor Yin and Other Stories from the
Great Proletarian Cultural Revolution*, translated by Nancy
Ing and Howard Goldblatt. Bloomington: Indiana
University Press, 1978.

"The Last Performance," translated by Timothy A. Ross and
Joseph S. M. Lau. In *Chinese Stories from Taiwan: 1960-1970*,
edited by Joseph S. M. Lau, 3-14. New York: Columbia University
Press, 1976.

"My Friend Ai Fen," translated by Richard Kent and Vivian L. Hsu.
In *Born of the Same Roots*, edited by Vivian L. Hsu, 276-302.
Bloomington: Indiana University Press, 1981.

*The Old Man*, edited by John Minford and T. L. Tsim. Hong
Kong: Renditions Books, 1986.

"Ting Yun," and "The Tunnel," translated by Chi-chen Wang.
In *Two Writers and the Cultural Revolution: Lao She and Chen Jo-hsi*,
edited by George Kao. Hong Kong:
Renditions Books, 1980.

F.  Novels Translated into Other Languages

*Borgmester Yins Henrettelse.*
Danish translation.
Denmark: Albatros, 1980.

*Haradshovding Yins.*
Swedish translation.
Stockholm: Atlantis, 1980.

*Le Prefet Yin.*
French translation by Simon Leys.
Paris: Editions Denoel, 1980.

*Mayor Yin.*
Dutch translation.
Amsterdam: B.V. Uitgeverji de Arbeiderspers, 1980.

*Mayor Yin.*
Norwegian translation.
Oslo: Dreyer Florg, 1980.

*Die Exekution des Landrates Yin.*
German translation.
Hamburg: Albrecht Knaus Verlag, 1979.

*The Lonely Man in Beijing.*
Japanese translation by Minoru Takeuchi.
Tokyo: Asahi-Simbunsha, 1979.

II.  Secondary Sources

A.  Criticism in Chinese

Bai Xianyong 白先勇 [Pai Hsien-yung]. "Wutuobang de zhuixun
yu huanmei" 乌托邦的追寻与幻灭 ("The Pursuit and Dis-

solutionment over Utopia"). *Zhongguo shibao* 中国时报 (November 1, 1977).

Cai Danye 蔡丹冶. "Yichu Gaishou zuzhou de beiju: Ping Chen Ruoxi de 'Jingjing de shengri' " 一出该受诅咒的悲剧·评陈若曦的〈晶晶的生日〉 ("A Condemned and Cursed Tragedy: On Chen Ruoxi's 'Jingjing's Birthday' "). *Lianhebao* 联合报 (May 20-21, 1976).

Chun Ren 纯人. "Renxing, huigui yu chaoyue: Du Chen Ruoxi de *Zhihun*" 人性，回归与超越·读陈若曦的〈纸婚〉 ("Humanism, Repatriation, and Beyond: On Chen Ruoxi's *Paper Marriage*"). *Wenyi pinglun* 文艺评论, no. 2 (1988): 87-89, 99.

Lan Yu 蓝雨. "Dengdai Guotuo: Tan Chen Ruoxi de xingzuo, *Zhihun*" 等待果陀·谈陈若曦的新作〈纸婚〉 ("Waiting for Godot: On Chen Ruoxi's New Novel, *Paper Marriage*"). *Zhongbao* 中报 (December 28, 1987).

Li Yong 李勇. "Guo Zijia de gushi" 郭字加的故事 ("The Story of Guo Zijia"). *Zhongyang ribao* 中央日报 (October 12-14, 1977).

Lin Shicun 林适存. "Wo du Chen Ruoxi de xiaoshuo" 我读陈若曦小说 ("Reading Chen Ruoxi's Short Stories"). *Lianhebao* 联合报 (February 29, 1976).

Liu Shaoming 刘绍铭 [Joseph S. M. Lau]. "Chen Ruoxi de gushi" 陈若曦的故事 ("The Story of Chen Ruoxi"). In *Xiaoshuo yu xiju* 小说与戏剧 (*Fiction and Drama*), 83-98. Taipei: Hongfan shudian, 1977.

Lu Yaodong 逯耀东. "Chen Ruoxi he tade lishi yanyu" 陈若曦和她的历史言语 ("Chen Ruoxi and Her Historical Rhetorics"). *Zhonghua wenhua fuxing yuekan* 中华文化复兴月刊, no. 9 (1977): 59-71.

_____. "Chen Ruoxi yu Lao Duan" 陈若曦与老段 ("Chen Ruoxi and Her Husband, Duan Shiyao"). *Lianhebao* 联合报 February 29, 1976).

Luo Qing 罗青. "Lun Chen Ruoxi de 'Didao' " 论陈若曦的〈地道〉 ("On Chen Ruoxi's 'The Tunnel' "). *Lianhebao* 联合报 (February 26-29, 1978).

_____. "Tan fangong wenxue de chuangzuo" 谈反共文学的创作 ("On the Creation of Anti-Communist Literature"). *Zhongyang ribao* 中央日报 (April 30, 1976).

Mo Lingping 莫灵平. "Kulian yu wenti" 苦恋与问题 ("Bittersweet Love and Inquiry"). *Taiwan shibao* 台湾时报 (July 29, 1981), Section II.

Ni Luo 尼洛. "Jiushi nayang fanfu wuchang: Ping Chen Ruoxi de 'Jen Xiulan'" 就是那样的反复无常: 评陈若曦的‹任秀兰› ("Always so Capricious: On Chen Ruoxi's 'Jen Xiulan' "). *Qingnian zhanshibao* 青年战士报 (July 29-30, 1977).

_____. "Qingliangshan de fangke: Ping Chen Ruoxi de *Yin xianzhang quanji*" 清谅山的访客: 评陈若曦的‹尹县长全集› ("Visitor from the Cold Mountain: Criticism on Chen Ruoxi's Complete Collection of *The Mayor Yin*"). *Zhongyang ribao* 中央日报 (July 5-6, 1977).

_____. "*Yin xianzhang* de shehui beijing" ‹尹县长›的社会背景 ("The Sociological Backgrounds of *The Mayor Yin*"). *Mingdao wenyi* 明道文艺, no. 38 (May 1979): 79-83.

Pan Yandun and Wang Yisheng 潘严墩·汪义生. "Chen Ruoxi de changpian xinzuo, *Er Hu*" 陈若曦的长篇新作‹二胡› ("On Chen Ruoxi's New Novel, *The Two Hus*"). *Scholars Book Club* (July 1986): 58-61.

Sima Sangdun 司马桑敦. "Fang Chen Ruoxi" 访陈若曦 ("Interview with Chen Ruoxi"). *Lianhebao* 联合报 (December 16, 1976).

Wei Ziyun 魏子云. "Xuelei zhengyan: Du Chen Ruoxi zhuanji" 血泪证言: 读陈若曦专集 ("Bloody Witness: Reading Chen Ruoxi's Special Collection"). *Zhongguo shibao* 中国时报 (March 17, 1976).

Wu Dayun 吴达云. "Zizhu yu chengquan: Lun Chen Ruoxi xiaoshuo zhong de nüxing yishi" 自主与成全: 论陈若曦小说中的女性意识 ("Independence and Fulfillment: Feminist Consciousness in Chen Ruoxi's Fiction"). *Wenxing* (February 1988): 100-108.

Xia Zhiqing 夏志清 [C. T. Hsia]. "Chen Ruoxi de xiaoshuo" 陈若曦小说 ("The Fiction of Chen Ruoxi"). In *Chen Ruoxi zixuan ji* 陈若曦自选集 , 1-31. Taipei: Lianjing chuban gongsi, 1976.

Xiang Qing 项青 . "Kongju yu zhengzha: Du Chen Ruoxi duanpian xiaoshuoji, *Yin xianzhang*" 恐惧与挣扎:读陈若曦短篇小说集‹尹县长› ("Horror and Struggle: Reading about Chen Ruoxi's Short Story Collection, *The Mayor Yin*"). *Shuping shumu* 书评书目 (May 1976): 34-37.

Xiao Jingmian 萧锦绵 . "Yuankan *Yuanjian*" 远看‹远见› ("An Objective Analysis of *Foresight*"). *Chuban yu dushu* 出版与读书 (March 25, 1984): 1-2.

Xin Wu 心吾 . "Du Chen Ruoxi" 读陈若曦 ("Reading About Chen Ruoxi"). *Mingdao wenyi* 明道文艺 , no. 2 (May 1976): 153-57.

Yan Huo 彦火 . "Suxie Chen Ruoxi" 速写陈若曦 ("Brief Portrayal of Chen Ruoxi"). In *Haiwai huaren zuojia lüeying* 海外华人作家略影 (*Brief Interviews with Chinese Writers Overseas*), 54-71. Hong Kong: Joint Publishing Co., 1984.

Yan Yuanshu 颜元叔 . "Ping Chen Ruoxi de *Laoren*" 评陈若曦的‹老人› ("Critical Review of Chen Ruoxi's *The Old Man*"). *Zhongyang ribao* 中央日报 (March 17, 1980).

Yang Hanzhi 杨汉之 . "Xuerou ninglian de qishou: Lun Chen Ruoxi de xiaoshuo" 血肉凝炼的匕首:论陈若曦的 小说 ("The Dagger Sharpened by Flesh and Blood: On Chen Ruoxi's Fiction"). *Zhongguo shibao* 中国时报 (March 4, 1976).

Ye Jingzhu 叶经柱 . "Tan Chen Ruoxi de shu" 谈陈若曦的书 ("Discussion of Chen Ruoxi's Fiction"). *Zhongyang ribao* 中央日报 (June 17-18, 1976).

Ye Weilian 叶维廉 [Wai-lam Yip]. "Chen Ruoxi de lucheng" 陈若曦的路程 ("The Journey of Chen Ruoxi"). *Lianhebao* 联合报 (November 7-10, 1977).

Zhan Hongzhi 詹宏志 . "Yuanze yu liyi: Ping Chen Ruoxi de 'Lukou' " 原则与利益:评陈若曦的‹路口› ("Principles and

Benefits: On Chen Ruoxi's 'The Crossroads' "). *Shuping shumu* 目评书目 (July 1980): 11-21.

Zhang Cuo 张错 [Dominic Cheung]. "Guopo shanhe zai: Haiwai zuojia de bentuxing" 国破山河在: 海外作家的 本土性 ("Divided Nation, Undivided Land: On Overseas Chinese Writers' Nativism"). *Lianhe wenxue* 联合文学 (Unitas) 7, no. 3 (January 1991): 24-28.

Zheng Yungxiao 郑永孝. *Chen Ruoxi de shijie* 陈若曦的世界 ("The Fictional World of Chen Ruoxi"). Taipei: Shulin chubanshe, 1985.

Zhu Xining et al. 朱西宁等. "*Chengli chengwai* huiping" ‹城里城外›会评 ("Review Committee Report on Chen Ruoxi's *In and Outside the Wall*"). *Lianhebao* 联合报 (January 9-11, 1980).

B.  Criticism and Reviews in English

Berstein, Richard. "Mao's Misfits." *Times* (June 26, 1978): 60, 64.

Cohen, Mark. "Three Literary Works on the Cultural Revolution." *Journal of the Chinese Literature Teachers Association*, no. 5 (1982): 127-35.

Dinsdale, Douglas. "Cultural Revolution Revisited." *San Francisco Review of Books* (November and December 1980): 8-9, 15.

Duke, Michael S. "Personae: Individual and Society in Three Novels by Chen Ruoxi." In *Modern Chinese Women Writers: Critical Appraisals*, edited by Michael S. Duke, 53-57. New York: M. E. Sharpe, 1989.

Dunn, Joe P. "In Search of China." *Air University Review* (May-June 1980): 129, 133.

Dolezalova, Anna. Review of *Two Writers and the Cultural Revolution: Lao She and Chen Jo-hsi*. *Asian and Africa Studies* 18 (1982): 238-40.

Echevarria, Evelio. Review of *Two Writers and the Cultural Revolution: Lao She and Chen Jo-hsi*. *Modern Fiction Studies* (Summer 1981): 399-400.

Eichwald, Bethea. "A Novelist of the Chinese Revolution." *Chicago Literary Review* (June 1981): 22-23.

Goldman, Merle. "Dissent in China." *Problems of Communication* (March-April 1982): 58-59.

Hsu, Kai-yu. "A Sense of History: Reading Chen Jo-hsi's Stories." In *Chinese Fiction from Taiwan: Critical Perspectives*, edited by Jeannette L. Faurot, 206-302. Bloomington: Indiana University Press, 1979.

Kern, William Alfred. "Tales Evoke China's Cultural Revolution." *News Sentinel* (Fort Wayne, Indiana) (October 8, 1984).

Lattimore, David. "Chinese Samizdat." *New York Times Book Review* (July 30, 1978): 10-11, 20-21.

Lee, Leo Ou-fan. "Dissent Literature from the Cultural Revolution." *Chinese Literature: Essays, Articles, Reviews*, no. 1 (1979): 59-79.

Leys, Simon. An "Introduction" to *The Execution of Mayor Yin and Other Stories from the Great Proletarian Cultural Revolution*, translated by Nancy Ing and Howard Goldblatt, xii-xxviii. Bloomington: Indiana University Press, 1978.

Light, Timothy. Review of *The Execution of Mayor Yin and Other Stories from the Great Proletarian Cultural Revolution. Chinese Literature: Essays, Articles, Reviews*, no. 1 (1979): 131-34.

Mc Dougall, Bonnie S. Review of *The Execution of Mayor Yin and Other Stories from the Great Proletarian Culural Revolution. Harvard Journal of Asiatic Studies 39, no. 2 (1979): 469-74.*

Pai Hsien-yung. "The Wandering Chinese: The Theme of Exile in Taiwan Fiction." *Iowa Review* 7, nos. 2-3 (Spring-Summer 1976): 205-12.

Rexroth, Kenneth. "Examination of Two People's Republic Writers." *Los Angeles Times* (November 6, 1980), part v: 35.

Tang Jong See. "First Writer to Throw the Book at Mao's Gang." *The Strait Times* (June 9, 1982): 1.

Wakeman, Jr., Frederic. "The Real China." *New York Review of Books* 25, no. 12 (July 20, 1978): 9-17.

# Yu Lihua 於梨华

## I. Primary Sources

A. Novels

*Sanren xing* 三人行 *(Walking among Three)*.
Hong Kong: Tiandi tushu, 1980, 1982.
Beijing: Youyi shudian, 1984.

*Fujia de ernumen* 傅家的儿女们 *(The Fu Family)*.
Hong Kong: Tiandi tushu, 1978, 1978, 1981, 1983.

*Kaoyan* 考验 *(The Task)*.
Taipei: Dadi chubanshe, 1974, 1975.
Beijing: Renmin wenxue chubanshe, 1982.

*Yan* 焰 *(The Flame)*.
Taipei: Huangguan chubanshe, 1969.

*Youjian zonglu, youjian zonglu* 又见棕榈·又见棕榈
*(Again the Palm Trees, Again the Palm Trees)*.
Taipei: Huangguan chubanshe, first edition, 1967; tenth edition, 1980. Fujian: Fujian renmin chubanshe, 1982.
Beijing: Youyi shudian, 1984.

Bian 变 (The Change).
Taipei: Chengwen chubanshe, 1965.

*Menghui Qinghe* 梦回青河 *(Recollections of Qing River)*.
Taipei: Huangguan chubanshe, 1962; tenth edition, 1980.

B. Short Stories, Novellas, Essays

*Xiangjian huan* 相见欢 *(The Joy of Reunion)*.
Short stories.
Taipei: Huangguan chubanshe, 1989.

*Xun* 寻 *(The Search)*. Short stories.
Hong Kong: Joint Publishing Co., 1986.

*Xin Zhongguo de nüxing* 新中国的女性
*(New Chinese Women).* Short stories and essays.
Hong Kong: Qishi niandai, 1977, 1978.
Hong Kong: Tiandi tushu, 1980.

*Huichang xianxingji* 会场现形记
*(When the Scholars Met).* Short stories.
Taipei: Zhiwen chubanshe, 1972.

*Baiju ji* 白驹集 *(The White Colt).* Short stories.
Taipei: Xianrenzhang chubanshe, 1969.

*Xuedishang de xingxing* 雪地上的星星
*(Stars on a Snowy Night).* Short stories.
Taipei: Huangguan chubanshe, 1966.

*Gui* 归 *(Homecoming).* Short stories.
Taipei: Wenxing chubanshe, 1966.

*Yeshi qiutian* 也是秋天 *(Autumn Again).* Novella.
Taipei: Wenxing chubanshe, 1964.

C. Works Written in English by the Author

"Sorrow at the End of the Yangtze River"
扬子江头几多愁
*UCLA Review* (March 1957): 1-13.

D. Works Translated into English by Others

"Nightfall," translated by Vivian L. Hsu and Julia Fitzgerald. In *Born of the Same Roots,* edited by Vivian L. Hsu, 194-209. Bloomington: Indiana University Press, 1981.

"In Liu Village," translated by C. T. Hsia and the author. In *Chinese Stories from Taiwan: 1960-1970,* edited by Joseph S. M. Lau, 101-42. New York: Columbia University Press, 1976.

"Glass Marbles Scattered All over the Ground," translated by Hsiao Lien-jen. In *An Anthology of Contemporary Chinese Literature Taiwan: 1949-1974,* Vol. II, edited by Chi Pang-yuan et al., 157-73. Taipei: National Institute for Compilation and Translation, 1975.

E.  Works Written or Translated into Chinese by the Author

*Flowering Judas and Other Stories* 盛开的犹大花 ，
by Katherine Ann Porter. Co-translator.
Hong Kong: USIS, 1970.

*A Roman Holiday* 罗马假期 , by Edith Wharton.
Taipei: Huangguan chubanshe, 1968.

"Edith Wharton" 伊德丝华顿其人 . Selected from *Seven Modern American Novelists*, edited by William Van O'Connor, 15-45.
Hong Kong: Jinri shijie chubanshe, 1967.

## II.  Secondary Sources

A.  Criticism in Chinese or English

An Li 安丽. "Guoneiren tan *Fujia de ernumen*" 国内人谈‹傅家的儿女们› ("Chinese on the *Fu Family*"). *Qiaobao* 侨报 (July 31, 1980).

An Ran 安然 . "Ping *Yeshi qiutian*" 评‹也是秋天› ("On *Autumn Again*"). *Gongjiaobao* 公教报 (October 24, 1969).

Chen Ruiwen 陈瑞文 . "Yu Lihua de changpian xiaoshuo: *Bian zhong de renwu ji zhufubing*" 於梨华的长篇小说:‹变›中的人物及妇女病 ("Yu Lihua's Novel: Discussion of Characterizations and Female Problems in *The Change*"). *Zhongwai wenxue* 中外文学 , no. 12 (May 1974): 30-42.

———. "Yu Lihua de <Liujiazhuang shang>" 於梨华的‹柳家庄上› ("On Yu Lihua's 'In the Liu Village' "). *Qiaofeng yuekan* 蕉凤月刊 (February 1974): 79-82.

Feng Zusheng 封祖盛 . "Xiaotan Yu Lihua de tansuo" 小谈於梨华的探索 ("On Yu Lihua's Search"). *Zhongshan daxue xuebao* 中山大学学报 , no. 1 (1981): 32-41.

Hu Po 琥泊 . "Mantan Yu Lihua de xiaoshuo" 漫谈於梨华的小说 ("Overview of Yu Lihua's Fiction"). *Xiangyata wai* 象牙塔外 , no. 4 (December 1975): 9-12.

Ouyang Yinzhi 欧阳莹之 . "Guowang de xinyi: Boxi meiyou gen de yiqun" 国王的新衣:剖析没有根的一群 ("Emperor's New

Clothes: Analysis of the Rootless Generation"). *Nanbeibao yuekan* 南北报月刊 , no. 95 (April 16, 1978: 53-58.

Pai Hsien-yung 白先勇 . "The Wandering Chinese: The Theme of Exile in Taiwan Fiction." *Iowa Review* 7, nos. 2-3 (Spring-Summer 1976): 205-12.

Ting Ling 丁玲 . "Yu Lihua" 於梨华 ("On Yu Lihua"). *Tianjin shibao* 天津时报 (February 1983).

Wang Jingshou 汪景寿 . "Yu Lihua" 於梨华 ("On Yu Lihua"). In *Taiwan xiaoshuo zuojia lun* 台湾小说作家论 , 122-48. Beijing: Beijing University Press, 1984.

Xia Zhiqing 夏志清 [C.T. Hsia]. "Ping Yu Lihua de *Youjian zonglu, youjian zonglu*" 评於梨华的‹又见棕榈,又见棕榈› ("Analysis of Yu Lihua's *Again the Palm Trees, Again the Palm Trees*"). Reprinted. A "Preface" for *Youjian zonglu, youjian zonglu* 又见棕榈,又见棕榈, 7-24. Taipei: Huangguan chubanshe, 1967.

Yan Huo 彦火 . "Yu Lihua yu liuxuesheng wenxue" 於梨华与留学生文学 ("Yu Lihua and Overseas Chinese Literature"). In *Haiwai huaren zuojia lueying* 海外华人作家掠影 (*Brief Interviews with Chinese Writers Overseas*), 32-53. *Hong Kong: Joint Publishing Co., 1984.*

Ye Ruxin 叶如新 . "Yu lihua de daolu" 於梨华的道路 ("The Literary Path of Yu Lihua"). *Taiwan zuojia xuanji* 台湾作家选集 , 115-27. Taipei: Zhongliu chubanshe, 1966.

Yin Di 隐地 . "<Xuedishang de xingxing>" 雪地上的星星 ("On 'Stars on a Snowy Night' "). In *Yin Di kan xiaoshuo* 隐地看小说 , 57-64. Tiapei: Dajiang chubanshe, 1970.

_____. "*Youjian zonglu, youjian zonglu*" 又见棕榈,又见棕榈 ("On *Again the Palm Trees, Again the Palm Trees*"). In *Yin Di kan xiashuo* 隐地看小说 , 177-84. Taipei: Dajiang chubanshe, 1970.

_____. "Yu Lihua de <Deng> " 於梨华的‹等› ("On Yu Lihua's 'Waiting' "). In *Yin Di kan xiaoshuo* 隐地看小说 , 1-6. Taipei: Dajiang chubanshe, 1970.

_____. "Yu Lihua ji qi *Yan*" 於梨华及其‹焰› ("Yu Lihua and Her Novel *The Flame*"). *Shuping shumu* 书评书目 (March 1970): 259-72.

Yin Yongpeng 殷允蓬. "Youjian Yu Lihua" 又见於梨华 ("Again Yu Lihua"). *Zhongguoren de guanhuai ji qita* 中国人的关怀及其他, 107-24. Taipei: Zhiwen chubanshe, 1969.

Zhang Xiuya 张秀亚 et al. "Yu Lihua nüshi de zuopin" 於梨华女士的作品 ("On Yu Lihua's Works"). *Xiandai xueyuan* 4, 现代文学苑, no. 9 (September 1967): 363-66.

Zhong Meiyin 锺梅音. "Xiaotan Yu Lihua de *Kaoyan*" 小谈於梨华的‹考验› ("Brief Discussion of Yu Lihua's *The Task*"). *Zhongguo shibao* 中国时报 (April 13, 1975).

# Nie Hualing 聂华苓

## I.  Primary Sources

A.  Novels

*Qianshan wai, shui changliu* 千山外，水长流
*(Lotus/Far Away, A River).*
Sichuan: Renmin chubanshe, 1984.
Hong Kong: Joint Publishing Co., 1985.

*Sangqing yu Taohong* 桑青与桃红
*(Mulberry and Peach \ Two Women of China).*
Hong Kong: Youlian chubanshe, 1976, 1982.
Beijing: Zhongguo qingnian chubanshe, 1980.
Hong Kong: Huahan wenhua shiye gongsi, 1986.

*Shiqu de jinlingzi* 失去的金铃子 *(The Lost Golden Bell).*
Taipei: Xuesheng chubanshe, 1960.
Taipei: World Book Co., 1964, 1965.
Taipei: Dalin shuju, 1977.
Beijing: Renmin wenxue chubanshe, 1980.

*Geteng* 葛藤 *(Creeper).* Novella.
Taipei: Free China Magazine, 1953.

B. Short Stories, Prose, Essays

*Renzai ershi shiji* 人在二十世纪
*(People, 20th Century)*. Essays.
Teaneck, New Jersey: Global Publishing Co, 1990.

*Heise, heise, zui meili de yanse* 黑色，黑色，最美丽的颜色
*(Black, Black, the Most Beautiful Color)*. Prose.
Hong Kong: Joint Publishing Co., 1983, 1986.

*Aihehua zhaji: Sanshinian hou* 爱荷华札记：三十年後
*(Notes from Iowa: After Thirty Years)*. Prose.
Hong Kong: Joint Publishing Co., 1981, 1983.

*Taiwan yishi* 台湾轶事 *(Taiwan Stories)*. Short stories.
Beijing: Beijing chubanshe, 1980.

*Wang Danian de jijian xishi* 王大年的几件喜事
*(The Several Blessings of Wang Danian)*. Short stories.
Hong Kong: Haiyang wenyishe, 1980.

*Menggu ji* 梦谷集 *(The Valley of Dream)*. Prose.
Hong Kong: Chengwen chubanshe, 1965.

*Yiduo xiaobaihua* 一朵小白花
*(A Little White Flower)*. Short stories.
Taipei: World Book Co., 1963.

*Feicui mao* 翡翠猫 *(Emerald Cat)*. Short stories.
Taipei: Minghua shuju, 1959.

C. Works Translated into Other Languages by Others

*Mulberry and Peach.* Novel in English translation.
Boston: Beacon Press, 1988.

*Mulberry and Peach.* Novel in Dutch translation.
Amsterdam: Uitgeverij An Dekker, 1988.

*Mulberry and Peach.* Novel in English translation.
London: Twomen's Press, 1986.

*Two Women of China.* Novel in English translation.
Beijing: New World Press, 1981.
New York: Lee Publishers Group, 1981.

*Two Women of China.* Novel in Hungarian translation.
Artisjus, Hungary: 1986.

*Two Women of China.* Novel in Croatian translation.
Zagreb, Yugoslavia: Globus Publishers, 1985.

*The Purse.* Short stories in Portuguese.
Brazil: 1965.

D.  Works Translated into Chinese by the Author

*Selected American Stories*  美国短篇小说集 , by William
Faulkner, Stephen Crane, Willa Cather, Sherwood Anderson,
F. Scott Fitzgerald, and others.
Taipei: 1960; Beijing, 1981.

*Madame de Mauves*  德莫福夫人 , by Henry James.
Taipei: 1959; Shanghai, 1980.

E.  Works Written or Translated into English by the Author

*Literature of the Hundred Flowers.* Two volumes.
New York: Columbia University Press, 1981.

*Poems of Mao Tse-tung.*
Co-translator with Paul Engle.
Simon and Shuster: 1972.
England: Wildwood Press, 1974.
Paris: Pierre Seghers, 1974.

*A Critical Biography of Shen Ts'ung-wen.*
Boston: Twayne Publishers, 1972.

*Eight Stories by Chinese Women.*
Hong Kong: Heritage, 1963.

*The Purse.* Short stories in English.
Hong Kong: Heritage, 1959.

## II. Secondary Sources

A. Criticism in Chinese or English

Chen Shixiang 陈世骧 . "Cong 'Wang Danian de jijian xishi' tanqi" 从‹王大年的几件喜事›谈起 ("Beginning with 'The Several Blessings of Wang Danian' "). In *Wang Danian de jijian xishi* 王大年的几件喜事 , 264-68. Hong Kong: Haiyang wenyi chubanshe, 1980.

Li Yi 李怡 . "Fang tuixiu qian de Nie Hualing" 访退休前的聂华苓 ("An Interview with Nie Hualing before Her Retirement"). *Jiushi niandai* 九十年代 (May 1988): 98-101.

Link, Perry. Review of *Literature of the Hundred Flowers. Chinese Literature: Essays, Articles, Reviews*, no. 6 (1984): 185-91.

Nazareth, Peter. "An Interview with Chinese Author Hua-ling Nieh." *World Literature Today* 55, no. 1 (Winter 1981): 10-18.

_____. A Review of *Two Women of China: Mulberry and Peach. World Literature Today* 56, no. 2 (Spring 1982): 403-4.

Pai, Hsien-yung 白先勇 . "The Wandering Chinese: The Theme of Exile in Taiwan Fiction." *Iowa Review* 7, nos. 2-3 (Spring-Summer 1976): 205-12.

Xiang Yang 向阳 "Xiongyongzhe de penquan: Du Nie Hualing xiaoshuo *Shiqu de jinlingzi*"汹涌着的喷泉: 读聂华苓小说‹失去的金铃子› ("Bubbling Fountain: Reading Nie Hualing's *The Lost Golden Bell*"). In *Shiqu de jinlingzi* 失去的金铃子 , 265-79. Taipei: Linbai chubanshe, 1987.

Yan Huo 彦火. *"Nie Hualing de gushi"* 聂华苓的故事 *("Nie Hualing's Story"). In Haiwai huaren zuojia lüeying* 海外华人作家掠影 *(Brief Interviews with Chinese Writers Overseas), 5-31. Hong Kong: Joint Publishing Co., 1984.*

Ye Weilian 叶维廉 [Wai-lam Yip]. "Ping *Shiqu de jinlingzi*" 评‹失去的金铃子› ("On *The Lost Golden Bell*"), 1962. Reprinted. In *Xin wenxue luncong* 新文学论丛 , no. 4 (1980): 194-97.

————. "Tuchu yishun de tuibian: Celun Nie Hualing" 突出一瞬
的蜕变:侧论聂华苓 ("Epiphany in Nie Hualing's Fiction").
In *Wang Danian de jijian xishi* 王大年的几件喜事,
269-85. Hong Kong: Haiyang wenyi chubanshe, 1980.

# Li Li 李黎

## I.  Primary Sources

### A.  Novellas, Short Stories

*Daishu nanren* 袋鼠男人 *(The Kangaroo Man)*.
Taipei: Lianjing chuban gongsi, 1992.

*Fushi* 浮世 *(The Floating World and Other Stories)*.
Taipei: Hongfan shudian, 1991.

*Qingcheng* 倾城 *(The Remembrance of the City)*.
Taipei: Lianjing chuban gongsi, 1989.

*Tiantangniao hua* 天堂鸟花 *(Bird-of-Paradise Flowers)*.
Taipei: Hongfan shudian, 1988.

*Li Li zixuan ji* 李黎自选集 *(Selected Works by Li Li)*.
Zhejiang: Zhejiang wenyi, 1988.

*Zuihou yeche* 最後夜车 *(The Last Subway Train)*.
Taipei: Hongfan shudian, 1986.
Beijing: Zhongguo wenlian chuban gongsi, 1989.

*Xijiang yue* 西江月 *(The Moon of the West River)*.
Beijing: Zhongguo qingnian chubanshe, 1980.

### B.  Prose, Essays

*Beihuai shujian* 悲怀书简 *(Remembering Remembrances)*.
Taipei: Erya chubanshe, 1990.

*Biehou* 别後 *(After Departure)*.
Taipei: Yongchen wenhua gongsi, 1989.

*Dajiang liu riye* 大江流日夜 *(Forever the Flowing River)*.
Hong Kong: Joint Publishing Co., 1985.

C. Editing Work

*Haiwai huaren zuojia xiaoshuo xuan* 海外华人作家小说选
*(Selected Short Stories by Overseas Chinese Writers).*
Hong Kong: Joint Publishing Co., 1983.
Canton: Huacheng chubanshe, 1986.

D. Translation

*Meili xinshijie* 美丽新世界 . *A translation based on Brave New World,*
by Aldous Huxley. Taipei: Zhiwen chubanshe, 1969.
Canton: Huacheng chubanshe, 1987.

## II. Secondary Sources

A. Criticism in Chinese or English

Chen Ye 陈烨. "Yongheng de xiangchou: Ping Li Li *Tiantangniao hua*" 永恒的乡愁: 评李黎‹天堂鸟花› ("Eternally Longing
for Homeland: Review of Li Li's *Bird-of-Paradise Flowers*").
*Lianhe wenxue* 联合文学 *(Unitas)* 5, no. 3 (March 1989):
200-201.

Chen Yingzhen 陈映真. "Diaoyun de fenghua yu choujie: Du Xue
Li xiaoshuo ji *Zuihou yeche* suixiang" 钓运的风化与愁结: 读薛
荔小说集 ‹最後夜车›随想 ("Dissolution of the Diaoyutai
Movement and Its Emotional Complex: Thoughts after Reading *The Last Subway Train*"). Included in *The Last Subway Train*
最後夜车 , 1-12.

Ku Ling 苦苓 . "Ping *Zuihou yeche*" 评最後夜车 ("Review of *The
Last Subway Train*"). *Wenyi yuekan* 文艺月刊 , no. 209 (November 1986): 68-71.

Li Ziyun 李子云 . "Jiebukai de 'Zhongguo qingyi jie' "解不开的‹中
国情 意结› ("The Unsoluble 'Chinese Knot' "). In *The Last
Subway Train* 最後夜车 , 1-13. Beijing: Zhongguo wenlian
chuban gongsi, 1989.

_____. "Zai huangyan yu qiwang zhong xunqiu zhenli" 在谎言
与欺妄中寻求真理 ("In Search of Truth amid Lies and Decep-
tion"). In *Jinghua rende xinling* 净化人的心灵 *(Purification of
the Human Mind)*, 49-63. Hong Kong: Joint Publishing Co., 1984.

Liu Binyan 刘宾雁 . "Li Li, ta buduan chaoyue ziji" 李黎, 她不断 超越 自己 ("Li Li, She Constantly Surpasses Herself"). A "Preface" to *Bird-of-Paradise Flowers* 天堂鸟花 , 1-8. Taipei: Hongfan shudian, 1988.

Ouyany Zi 欧阳子 . "Renxing de jiushu" 人性的救赎 ("Redemption of Human Nature"). In *The Last Subway Train* 最後 夜车, 245-63. Taipei: Hongfan shudian, 1986.

Wang Dewei 王德威 . "Jie 'jie' hanxu xi 'jie' ren: Ping *Zuihou yeche*" 解·结·还需系·结·人:评〈最後夜车〉 Criticism of *The Last Subway Train*. *Lianhe wenxue* 联合文学 (*Unitas*) 3, no. 8 (June 1987): 213-14.

Wang Jinmin 王晋民 . "Lun zuijin liangnian Taiwan wenxue fazhan de xintedian, xinqushi" 论最近二年台湾文学发展的新 特点 新趋势 ("New characteristics and Trends in the Development of Taiwanese Literature, 1981-1983"). *Dangdai wenxue yanjiu* 当代 文学研究 (*Contemporary Chinese Literature*), no. 1 (1984): 53-55.

Xue Renwang 薛人望 . "Li Li yu *Daishu nanren*" 李黎与〈袋鼠男人〉 ("Li Li and the *Kangaroo Man*"). *Lianhe wenxue* 联合文学 (*Unitas*) 8, no. 5 (1992); 106-12.

# Zhong Xiaoyang 锺晓阳

I.  Primary Sources

A.  Novels

*Tingche zan jiewen* 停车暂借问
*(Halt! May I Ask...).*
Taipei: Sansan shufang, first edition, 1982; thirtieth edition, 1984.
Hong Kong: Tangdai wenyi, 1983.

B.  Short Stories

*Aige* 哀歌 *(The Mourning Song).*
Taipei: Sansan shufang, 1987.
Hong Kong: Tiandi tushu, 1987.

*Aiqi* 爱妻 *(My Beloved Wife)*.
Taipei: Hongfan shudian, 1986.
Hong Kong: Tiandi tushu, 1987.

*Liunian* 流年 *(The Fleeting Years)*.
Taipei: Hongfan shudian, first edition, 1983;
thirteenth edition, 1987.

*Zhong Xiaoyang xiaoshuo xuan* 锺晓阳小说选
*(Selected Stories by Zhong Xiaoyang)*.
Hong Kong: Nushen chubanshe, no date.

C.  Prose, Poetry, Essays

*Zouguo* 走过 *(To Pass By)*.
Hong Kong: Nushen chubanshe, 1984.

*Chun zai luwuzhong* 春在绿芜中
*(Spring in the Lüxuriant Green)*.
Hong Kong: Tamuzhi banyuekan, 1983.
Hong Kong: Tiandi tushu, 1987.

*Xishuo* 细说 *(In Reminiscence)*.
Taipei: Sansan shufang, first edition, 1983;
ninth edition, 1984.

II.  Secondary Sources

A.  Criticism in Chinese or English

Chung, Ling. "Perspective and Spatiality in the Fiction of Three
Hong Kong Women Writers." In *Modern Chinese Women Writers: Critical Appraisals*, edited by Michael S. Duke, 217-35. Armonk: M. E. Sharp, 1989.

Sima Zhongyuan 司马中原. "Feishang zhitou cai chun hui" 飞
上枝头采春回("Bringing Spring Back from the Tree Branch").
Preface to *Xishuo* 细说, 1-5. Taipei: Sansan shufang, 1983.

Zhang Huijuan 张惠娟. "Zhong Xiaoyang zuopin qianlun" 锺晓
阳作品浅论("Brief Analysis of Zhong Xiaoyang's Works"). In
*Chungwai wenxue* 中外文学, no. 4 (September 1987): 155-68.

Zhang Lele 张乐乐 . "Zhong Xiaoyang de shijie" 锺晓阳的世界 ("The Literary World of Zhong Xiaoyang"). Included in *Tingche zan jiewen* 停车暂借问 , 219-27. Taipei: Sansan shufang, 1982.

# Part Two: General Studies

## I.  Literary Journals

### A.  Chinese Sources

| | |
|---|---|
| *Baogao wenxue (Pao-k'ao wen-hsueh)* | 报告文学 |
| *Beifang wenxue (Pei-fang wen-hsueh)* | 北方文学 |
| *Beijing wenyi (Pei-ching wen-i)* | 北京文艺 |
| *Caoyuan (Ts'ao-yuan)* | 草原 |
| *Chuangshiji (Ch'uang-shih-chi, Epoch Poetry Quarterly)* | 创世纪 |
| *Chuban yu yanjiu (Ch'u-pan yu yen-chiu)* | 出版與研究 |
| *Chun wenxue (Ch'un wen-hsueh)* | 纯文学 |
| *Dahua fukan (Ta-hua fu-k'an)* | 大华副刊 |
| *Dangdai (Tang-tai, Contemporary Literature)* | 当代 |
| *Guangchang (Kuang-ch'ang, Square Quarterly)* | 广场 |
| *Huaxi [Guiyang] (Hua-hsi, [Kui-yang])* | 花溪 (贵阳) |
| *Jintian (Today)* | 今天 |
| *Liangan (Liang-an)* | 两岸 |
| *Lianhe wenxue (Lien-ho wen-hsueh, Unitas)* | 联合文学 |
| *Mingbao (Ming-pao)* | 明报 |

Mingya (Ming-ya)                                                                明芽

Nüzuojia (Nü-tso-chia)                                                          女作家

Qinghua xuebao (Ch'ing-hua Journal of Chinese Studies)                          青华学报

Qingxi (Ch'ing-hsi)                                                             青溪

Renjian fukan (Jen-chien fu-k'an)                                              人间副刊

Renmin wenxue (Jen-min wen-hsueh, People's Literature)                         人民文学

Shandong wenxue (Shang-tung wen-hsueh)                                          山东文学

Shanghai wenxue (Shang-hai wen-hsueh)                                           上海文学

Shouhuo (Shou-huo)                                                             收获

Shuping shumu (Shu-p'ing shu-mu, Book Review
and Bibliography)                                                             书评书目

Taibei pinglun (Tai-pei p'ing-lun)                                            台北评论

Taiwan wenyi (Tai-wan wen-i, Taiwan Literature)                                台湾文艺

Tansuo (T'an-so)                                                               探索

Wenji (Wen-chi, Literary Quarterly) [Early issues                              文季
entitled Wen-hsueh chi-k'an, and Wen-hsueh shuang-yueh k'an]

Wentan (Wen-t'an)                                                             文坛

Wenxing (Wen-hsing)                                                           文星

Wenxue pinglun (Wen-hsueh p'ing-lun)                                          文学平论

Wenxue zazhi (Wen-hsueh tsa-chih, Literary Magazine)                          文学杂志

Wenxun (Wen-hsun, Literary Bimonthly)                                         文讯

Wenyi chuangzuo (Wen-i ch'uang-tso)                                           文艺创作

*Xiachao (Hsia-ch'ao, The China Tide)*　　　　　　　　　　夏潮

*Xiandai wenxue (Hsien-tai wen-hsueh, Modern Literature)*　现代文学

*Xiandaishi (Hsien-tai shih, Modern Poetry Quarterly)*　　现代诗

*Xianggang wenxue (Hong Kong wen-hsueh,*　　　　　　　香港文学
Hong Kong Literary Journal)

*Xin wenyi (Hsin wen-i)*　　　　　　　　　　　　　　　新文艺

*Xiziwan (Hsi-tze-wan)*　　　　　　　　　　　　　　　西子湾

*Youshi wenyi (Yu-shih wen-i)*　　　　　　　　　　　幼狮文艺

*Zhongguo qingnian (Chung-kuo ch'ing-nien)*　　　　中国青年

*Zhongguo shibao (Chung-kuo shih-pao, China Times)*　中国时报

*Zhongshan (Chung-shan)*　　　　　　　　　　　　　　锺山

*Zhongwai wenxue (Chung-wai wen-hsueh, Chung-wai Literary*　中外文学
Monthly)

*Ziyou fukan (Tzu-yu fu-k'an)*　　　　　　　　　　　自由副刊

*Ziyou zhongguo (Tzu-yu chung-kuo, The Free China Fortnightly)* 自由中国

B.　Non-Chinese Sources

*Bulletin of Concerned Asian Scholars* (Charlemont, Massachusetts)

*Chinese Literature: Essays, Articles, Reviews* (Madison, Wisconsin)

*Chinese Literature: Fiction, Poetry, Art* (Beijing, China)

*The Chinese Pen* (Taipei,Taiwan)

*Comparative Literature* (Eugene, Oregon)

*Comparative Literature Studies* (Urbana, Illinois)

*Harvard Journal of Asiatic Studies* (Cambridge, Massachusetts)

*Journal of Asian Studies* (Ann Arbor, Michigan)

*Literature East and West* (Austin, Texas)

*Modern China* (Beverly Hills, California)

*Modern Chinese Literature* (Boulder, Colorado)

*Renditions: A Chinese-English Translation Magazine* (Hong Kong)

*Tamkang Review* (Tamsui, Taiwan)

*World Literature Today* (Norman, Oklahoma)

II.  Anthologies and Collections of Modern Chinese Fiction

Berninghausen, John, and Ted Huters, eds. *Revolutionary Literature in China: An Anthology.* White Plains: M. E. Sharpe, 1976.

Birch, Cyril, ed. *Anthology of Chinese Literature.* Vol. 2: *From the Fourteenth Century to the Present Day.* New York: Grove Press, 1972.

Carver Ann C., and Sung-sheng Yvonne Chang, eds. *Bamboo Shoots after the Rain: Contemporary Stories by Women Writers of Taiwan.* New York: The Feminist Press, 1990.

Cheung, Dominic, and Michelle Yeh, eds. *Exiles and Native Sons: Modern Chinese Stories from Taiwan.* Taipei: National Institute for Compilation and Translation, 1992.

Chi Pang-yuan, ed. and comp. *An Anthology of Contemporary Chinese Literature: Taiwan, 1949–1974.* 2 vols. Taipei: National Institute for Compilation and Translation, 1975.

Duke, Michael, ed. *Contemporary Chinese Literature: An Anthology of Post-Mao Fiction and Poetry.* Armonk: M. E. Sharpe, 1985.

Goldblatt, Howard, ed. *Chinese Literature for the 1980s: The Fourth Congress of Writers and Artists.* Armonk: M. E. Sharpe, 1982.

Hsia, C. T., ed. *Twentieth Century Chinese Stories*. New York: Columbia University Press, 1971.

Hsu, Kai-yu, ed. *Literature of the People's Republic of China*. Bloomington: Indiana University Press, 1980.

Hsu, Vivian L., ed. *Born of the Same Roots: Stories of Modern Chinese Women*. Bloomington: Indiana University Press, 1981.

Huang Ziping, ed. *Zhongguo xiaoshuo, 1989 (Selected Chinese Short Stories of 1989)*. Hong Kong: Joint Publishing Co., 1990.

Huang Ziping, and Li Tuo, eds. *Zhongguo xiaoshuo, 1988 (Selected Chinese Short Stories of 1988)*. Hong Kong: Joint Publishing Co., 1989.

Ing, Nancy, ed. *New Voices: Stories and Poems by Young Chinese Authors*. Revised edition. Taipei: Chinese Materials Center, 1980.

_____. *Winter Plum: Contemporary Chinese Fiction*. Taipei: Chinese Materials Center, 1982.

Issacs, Harold R., ed. *Straw Sandals: Chinese Short Stories, 1918–1933*. Cambridge: Massachusetts Institute of Technology Press, 1974.

Jenner, W. J. F., ed. *Modern Chinese Stories*. Oxford: Oxford Papers, 1970.

Lau, Joseph S. M., ed. *Chinese Stories from Taiwan: 1960–1970*. New York: Columbia University Press, 1976.

_____. *The Unbroken Chain: An Anthology of Taiwan Fiction since 1926*. Bloomington: Indiana University Press, 1983.

Lau, Joseph S. M., C. T. Hsia, and Leo Ou-fan Lee, eds. *Modern Chinese Stories and Novellas: 1919–1949*. New York: Columbia University Press, 1981.

Lee Yee, ed. *The New Realism: Writings from China after the Cultural Revolution*. New York: Hippocrene Books, 1983.

Li Li, ed. *Haiwai huaren zuojia xiaoshuo xuan (Selected Short Stories by Overseas Chinese Writers)*. Hong Kong: Joint Publishing Co., 1983.

Link, Perry, ed. *People or Monsters? And Other Stories and Reportage from China after Mao*. Bloomington: Indiana University Press, 1983.

_____. *Roses and Thorns: The Second Blooming of the Hundred Flowers in Chinese Fiction.* Berkeley: University of California Press, 1984.

_____. *The Stubborn Weeds: Popular and Controversial Chinese Literature after the Cultural Revolution.* Bloomington: Indiana University Press, 1983.

Liu Shaoming (Joseph S. M. Lau) et al. *Shijie zhongwen xiaoshuo xuan (The Commonwealth of Modern Chinese Fiction: An Anthology).* 2 vols. Taipei: Shibao wenhua, 1987.

Liu, Xinhua, et al. *The Wounded: New Stories of the Cultural Revolution, 77–78.* Translated by Geremie Barme and Bennett Lee. Hong Kong: Joint Publishing Co., 1979.

Liu, Xinwu, et al. *Prize-winning Stories from China, 1978–1979.* Beijing: Foreign Languages Press, 1981.

Munro, Stanley R., ed. and trans. *Genesis of a Revolution: An Anthology of Modern Chinese Short Stories.* Singapore: Heinemann Educational Books, 1979.

*The Muse of China: A Collection of Prose and Short Stories.* 2 vols. Taipei: Chinese Women Writers' Association, 1974.

Nieh, Hua-ling, ed. *Eight Stories by Chinese Women.* Taipei: Heritage Press, 1963.

_____. *Literature of the Hundred Flowers.* Vol. 2: *Poetry and Fiction.* New York: Columbia University Press, 1981.

Research Centre for Translation Committee, eds. *Contemporary Women Writers. Renditions,* nos. 27–28 (Spring–Autumn 1987). Hong Kong: Chinese University of Hong Kong, 1987.

Roberts, R. A. and Angela Knox, trans. *One Half of the Sky: Stories from Contemporary Women Writers of China.* New York: Dodd, Mead, 1988.

*Seven Contemporary Chinese Women Writers.* Beijing: Panda Books, 1982.

Tai, Jeanne, ed. *Spring Bamboo: A Collection of Contemporary Chinese Short Stories.* New York: Random House, 1989.

Wang, Chi-chen. *Contemporary Chinese Stories.* Westport, Conn.: Greenwood Press, 1976.

Yip, Wai-lim, and William Tay, eds. *Chinese Women Writers Today.* Occasional Papers/Reprint Series in Contemporary Asian Studies, no. 4. College Park: University of Maryland, School of Law, 1979.

Zheng Qingwen and Li Qiao, eds. *Taiwan dangdai xiaoshuo jingxuan* (*Collection of Contemporary Taiwanese Fiction*). 4 vols. Xindian: Xindi wenxue, 1990.

Zheng Shusen (William Tay), ed. *Bashi niandai zhongguo dalu xiaoshuo xuan* (*Short Story Collection of the 1980s from PRC*). Taipei: Hongfan, 1990.

————. *Xiandai zhongguo xiaoshuo xuan* (*Collection of Modern Chinese Fiction*). 5 vols. Taipei: Hongfan, 1989.

*Zhongguo dangdai nüzuojia wenxuan* (Collection of Contemporary Chinese Women Writers). Hong Kong: New Asia Cultural Foundation, 1987.

*Zhongguo nüzuojia xiaoshu xuan* (Short Story Collection of Chinese Women Writers). 2 vols. Edited by Yu Ming et al. Jiangsu: Renming, 1981.

### III. General Criticism and Studies

Abel, Elizabeth, Marianne Hirsch, and Elizabeth Langland. Introduction to *The Voyage In: Fictions of Female Development,* edited by Elizabeth Abel, Marianne Hirsch, and Elizabeth Langland, 3–19. Hanover, N.H.: University Press of New England, 1983.

Ahmad, Aijaz. "Jameson's Rhetoric of Otherness and the 'National Allegory.' " *Social Text* 17 (1987): 3–25.

Anderson, Perry. "Components of the National Culture." *New Left Review* 50 (1968): 3–58.

Antin, Mary. *The Promised Land.* 1912. Reprint. Boston: Houghton Mifflin Sentry Edition, 1969.

Arieli, Yehoshua. *Individualism and Nationalism in American Ideology.* Baltimore: Penguin Books, 1966.

Aschheim, Steven E. *Brothers and Strangers.* Madison: University of Wisconsin Press, 1983.

Basso, Keith. "Speaking with Names." *Cultural Anthropology* 3 (1988): 99–130.

Benstock, Shari. "Expatriate Modernism: Writing on the Cultural Rim." In *Women's Writing in Exile,* edited by Mary Lynn Broe and Angel Ingram, 19–40. Chapel Hill: University of North Carolia Press, 1989.

Bercovitch, Sacvan. "The Rites of Assent: Rhetoric, Ritual, and the Ideology of American Consensus." In *The American Self: Myth, Ideology, and Popular Culture,* edited by Sam B. Girgus. Albuquerque: University of New Mexico Press, 1981.

Berger, Peter, Brigitte Berger, and Hansfried Kellner. *The Homeless Mind: Modernization and Consciousness.* New York: Vintage Books, 1974.

Brodsky, Joseph. "The Condition We Call Exile." *New York Review of Books* (January 21, 1988): 16, 18, 20.

Broe, Mary Lynn, and Angela Ingram. *Women's Writing in Exile.* Chapel Hill: University of North Carolina Press, 1989.

Brooks, Cleanth. "The Modern Writer and the Burden of History." *Tulane Studies in English* 22 (1977): 155–68.

Brown, Wayne. "On Exile and the Dialect of the Tribe." *Sunday Guardian* (Trinidad), no. 8 (November 1970): 19.

Cai Yuanhuang. *Cong langman zhuyi dao houxiandai zhuyi (From Romanticism to Postmodernism).* Taipei: Dianya, 1987.

Chang, Sung-sheng Yvonne. "Three Generations of Taiwan's Contemporary Women Writers: A Critical Introduction." In *Bamboo Shoots after the Rain: Contemporary Stories by Women Writers of Taiwan,* ed. Sung-sheng Yvonne Chang and Ann C. Carver, xv–xxv. New York: The Feminist Press, 1990.

Chen Xinyuan. "Dalu de wenxue xungen re" ("The Search for Roots Fever in PRC Literature"). In his *Cong Taiwan kan dalu dangdai wenxue (Taiwanese Perspectives on Contemporary PRC Literature)*, 57–61. Taipei: Yeqiang, 1989.

Cheung, Dominic, trans. and ed. *The Isle Full of Noises: Modern Chinese Poetry from Taiwan*. New York: Columbia University Press, 1986.

Chung Ling. *Xiandai Zhongguo miusi (Modern Chinese Muse)*. Taipei: Lianjing chuban gongsi, 1989.

Clifford, James, and George Marcus, eds. *Writing Culture: The Poetics and Politics of Ethnography*. Berkeley: University of California Press, 1986.

Cong Shu. "Liufang" (On Exile). In her *Zhongguoren, shengqi ba! (Get Angry, Chinese!)*, 68–73. Taipei: Sita, 1978.

*Dangdai wenxue shiliao yanjiu congkan (A Compendium of Contemporary Chinese Literary Materials)*. Vol. 4: *Taiwan wenxue yanjiu (Research on Taiwanese Literature)*, edited by Lin Haiyin et al. Taipei: Dangdai wenxue shiliao yanjiushe, 1990.

Dimont, Max I. *The Jews in America: The Roots, History, and Destiny of American Jews*. New York: Simon and Schuster, 1978.

Duke, Michael S., ed. *Modern Chinese Women Writers: Critical Appraisals*. Armonk, N.Y. : M. E. Sharpe, 1989.

DuPlessis, Rachel Blau. *Writing beyond the Ending: Narrative Strategies of Twentieth-Century Women Writers*. Bloomington: Indiana University Press, 1985.

Eagleton, Terry. *Exiles and Emigres: Studies in Modern Literature*. New York: Schocken Books, 1970.

––––––. "The Subject of Literature." *Cultural Critique* 1 (1985–1986): 95–104.

Faurot, Jeannette L., ed. *Chinese Fiction from Taiwan: Critical Perspectives*. Bloomington: Indiana University Press, 1980.

Fine, David M. *The City, the Immigrant, and American Fiction, 1880–1920*. Metuchen, N.J.: Scarecrow Press, 1977.

Fixler, Michael. "The Redeemers: Themes in the Fiction of Isaac Bashevis Singer." *Kenyon Review* 26 (1964): 371–86.

Friedman, Susan Stanford. "Modernism of the 'Scattered Remnant': Race and Politics in H.D.'s Development." In *Feminist Issues in Literary Scholarship*, edited by Shari Benstock, 208–32. Bloomington: Indiana University Press, 1987.

Gao Tiansheng. *Taiwan xiaoshuo yu xiaoshuojia (Taiwanese Novels and Novelists)*. Taipei: Qianwei, 1985.

Goldblatt, Howard, ed. *Worlds Apart: Recent Chinese Writing and Its Audience*. Armonk, N.Y.: M. E. Sharpe, 1990.

Gurr, Andrew. *Writers in Exile: The Identity of Home in Modern Literature.* Brighton: Harvester Press, 1981.

Hong Weiren. *Huigui xiangtu, huigui chuantong (Return to Native, Return to Tradition)*. Taipei: Zili wanbaoshe, 1986.

Hsia, C. T. "The Continuing Obsession with China: Three Contemporary Writers." *Review of National Literatures* 6 (1975): 76–99.

Hu Juren, "Xungen de mingzu beiju" ("The Human Tragedy of the Search for Roots"). *Shijie ribao (July 22 1991): 71.*

Jameson, Fredric. *The Political Unconscious: Narrative as a Socially Symbolic Act.* Ithaca: Cornell University Press, 1981.

_____. "Postmodernism, or the Cultural Logic of Late Capitalism." *New Left Review* 146 (1984): 53–93.

_____. "Third-World Literature in the Era of Multinational Capital." *Social Text* 15 (1986): 65–88.

Jennings, Francis. *The Invasion of America: Indians, Colonialism, and the Cant of Conquest.* New York: Norton, 1975.

Katz, Jacob. *Emancipation and Assimilation: Studies in Modern Jewish History.* Farnborough: Greggs, 1972.

Ke Qingming. *Xiandai Zhongguo wenxue piping shulun (Essays on Modern Chinese Literary Criticism)*. Taipei: Da'an, 1988.

Kolodny, Annette. *The Lay of the Land: Metaphor as Experience and History in American Life and Letters*. Chapel Hill: University of North Carolina Press, 1975.

Kotker, Norman. "New Found Land." *Nation* (April 12, 1980).

Krupat, Arnold. *The Voice in the Margin: Native American Literature and the Canon*. Berkeley: University of California Press, 1989.

Lagos-Pope, Maria-Ines. *Exile in Literature*. London: Associated University Presses, 1988.

Lau, Joseph S. M. "How Much Truth Can a Blade of Grass Carry?: Ch'en Ying-chen and the Emergence of Native Taiwan Writers." *Journal of Asian Studies* 32 (1973): 623–38.

_____. "The Tropics Mythopoeticized: The Extraterritorial Writing of Li Yung-p'ing in the Context of the *Hsiang-t'u* Movement." *Tamkang Review* 12 (Fall 1981): 1–26.

Lee, Grace Farrell. *From Exile to Redemption: The Fiction of Isaac Bashevis Singer*. Carbondale: Southern Illinois University, 1987.

Lee, Leo Ou-fan. "Dissent Literature from the Cultural Revolution." *Chinese Literature: Essays, Articles, Reviews* 1 (1979): 59–79.

Lessing, Doris. "Flavours of Exile." 1957. Reprinted in *African Stories*, 575–82. New York: Popular Library, 1965.

Li Ziyun. *Dangdai nüzuojia sanlun (On Contemporary Chinese Women Writers)*. Hong Kong: Joint Publishing Co., 1984.

_____. *Jinghua rende xinling (Purification of the Human Mind)*. Hong Kong: Joint Publishing Co., 1984.

Liao Binghui. "Fangzhuo yu zhengzhi" (On Exile and Politics). *Lianhe wenxue* 7, no. 3 (January 1991): 34–37.

Ling, Amy. *Between Worlds: Women Writers of Chinese Ancestry*. New York: Pergamon Press, 1990.

Liu Shaoming (Joseph S. M. Lau). "Tangrenjie de xiaoshuo shijie" (The Fictional World of Chinatown Writings). In his *Shangdi, muqin, airen (God, Mother, and the Beloved)*, 97–121. Taipei: Siji, 1981.

Lu Xiulian. *Xinnüxing zhuyi (New Feminism)*. Taipei: Dunli, 1986.

Lung Yingtai. *Lung Yingtai ping xiaoshuo (Lung Yingtain on Chinese Fiction)*. Taipei: Erya, 1985.

McCarthy, Mary. "Exiles, Expatriates and Internal Emigres." *The Listener* 86 (1971): 705–8.

Miller, Lucien. "Introduction." In his *Exiles at Home: Short Stories by Ch'en Ying-chen*, 1–26. Ann Arbor: Center for Chinese Studies, University of Michigan, 1986.

Miller, Nancy K. "Men's Reading, Women's Writing: Gender and the Rise of the Novel". In *Displacements: Women, Tradition, Literature in French*, edited by Joan DeJean and Nancy Miller, 37–54. Baltimore, Md.: The Johns Hopkins University Press, 1991.

Mitchell, W. J. T., ed. *The Politics of Interpretation*. Chicago: University of Chicago Press, 1983.

Moi, Toril. *Sexual/Textual Politics: Feminist Literary Theory*. London: Methuen, 1985.

Mudge, Bradford K. "Exile as Exiler: Sara Coleridge, Virginia Woolf, and the Politics of Literary Revision." In *Women's Writing in Exile*, edited by Mary Lynn Broe and Angel Ingram, 199–224. Chapel Hill: University of North Carolina Press, 1989.

Murray, Michele. "Internal Emigrations." *Women's Studies* 7 (1980): 210–11.

Niven, Alastair, ed. *The Commonwealth Writer Overseas: Themes of Exile and Expatriation*. Brussels, 1976.

*Nüxing zuyi, nüxing yishi zhuanhao (Feminism and Feminist Consciousness)*. Special issue. *Zhongwai wenxue* 17,no. 10 (March 1989).

Paul, Ilie. *Literature and Inner Exile*. Baltimore, Md.: The Johns Hopkins University Press, 1980.

Pearce, Roy Harvey. "From the History of Ideas to Ethnohistory." *Journal of Ethnic Studies* 2 (1974): 86–92.

Pomerantsev, Igor. "Lost in a Strange City." *Times Literary Supplement* (June 26, 1987): 695.

Potts, Willard, ed. *Portraits of the Artist in Exile: Recollections of James Joyce by Europeans.* Seattle and London, 1978.

Qi Bangyuan (Chi Pang-yuan). *Qiannian zhilei (Tears of Thousand Years).* Taipei: Erya, 1990.

Rowbotham, Sheila. *Woman's Consciousness, Man's World.* London: Penguin, 1973.

Said, Edward. *Orientalism.* New York: Vintage, 1979.

_____. *The World, the Text, and the Critic.* Cambridge, Mass.: Harvard University Press, 1983.

Scott, Bonnie Kime, ed. *The Gender of Modernism.* Bloomington: Indiana University Press, 1991.

Seidel, Michael. *Exile and the Narrative Imagination.* New Haven: Yale University Press, 1986.

Shi Shuqing. "You gudian, you xiandai" ("Again Classical, Again Modern"). In her *Wentan fansi yu qianzhan (Reflection and Anticipation in the Literary Arena),* 172–88. Hong Kong: Mingbao, 1989.

Showalter, Elaine. *The Female Malady: Women, Madness and English Culture, 1830–1980.* New York: Random House, 1985.

Shweder, Richard, and Robert LeVine, eds. *Culture Theory: Essays on Mind, Self and Emotion.* Cambridge: Cambridge University Press, 1984.

Smith, Valerie. *Self-Discovery and Authority in Afro-American Narrative.* Cambridge, Mass.: Harvard University Press, 1987.

Spivak, Gayatri Chakravorty. "The Politics of Interpretations." In *In Other Worlds: Essays in Cultural Politics,* 118–33. New York: Methuen, 1987.

Stern, Fritz. *The Politics of Cultural Despair: A Study in the Rise of Germanic Ideology.* Berkeley: University of California Press, 1974.

Suleiman, Susan Rubin, ed. *The Female Body in Western Culture.* Cambridge, Mass.: Harvard University Press, 1986.

Wang Dewei (David D. W. Wang). *Zhongsheng xuanhua: Sanshi yu bashi niandai de Zhongguo xiaoshuo (Heteroglossia: On Chinese Fiction of the 1930s and the 1980s).* Taipei: Yuanliu, 1988.

Wang Tuo. "Shi xianshi zhuyi wenxue, bushi xiangtu wenxue" ("It Is Realism, Not Nativism"). In *Zhonghua xiandai wenxue daxi, 1970–1989 (A Comprehensive Anthology of Contemporary Chinese Literature in Taiwan, 1970–1989).* Criticism vol. 1, edited by Li Ruiteng et al., 131–52. Taipei: Jiuge, 1989.

*Wenxue de nüxing, nüxing de wenxue (Feminism in Literature, Feminist Literature).* Special issue. *Zhongwai wenxue* 18, no. 1 (June 1989).

Williams, Robert C. *Culture in Exile: Russian Emigres in Germany, 1881–1941.* Ithaca, N.Y.: Cornell University Press, 1972.

Yan Huo. *Haiwai huaren zuojia lüeying (Brief Interviews with Chinese Writers Overseas).* Hong Kong: Joint Publishing Co., 1988.

Ye Shitao. "Wenxue laizi tudi" ("Literature Comes from the Soil"). *Lienhe wenxue* 7, no. 3 (January 1991): 12–17.

Ye Yunyun, ed. *Liangan jiechu yu bijiao (Communication and Comparison between the Two Sides of China).* Taipei: Renjian, 1988.

Yeh, Michelle. *Modern Chinese Poetry: Theory and Practice since 1917.* New Haven: Yale University Press, 1991.

Yip, Wai-lim. "Aesthetic Consciousness of Landscape in Chinese and Anglo-American Poetry." *Comparative Literature Studies* 15, no. 2 (June 1978): 211–41.

_____. "Crisis Poetry: An Introduction to Yang Lian, Jiang He, and Misty Poetry." *Renditions* (Spring 1985): 120–30.

Yu Tiancong, ed. *Xiangtu wenxue taolun ji (Collected Essays on Nativist Literature).* Taipei: Yuanliu, 1978.

_____. "You piaobo dao xungen" ("From Drifting to the Search for Roots"). In *Zhonghua xiandai wenxue daxi, 1970-1989 (A Comprehensive*

*Anthology of Contemporary Chinese Literature in Taiwan, 1970–1989).*
Criticism vol. 1, edited by Li Ruitent et al., 93–112. Taipei: Jiuge, 1989.

Zhang Cuo (Dominic Cheung). *Cong Shashibiya dao Shangtian Qiucheng:*
*Dong Xi wenxue piping yanjiu (From Shakespeare to Ueda Akinara:*
*Research of East-West Literary Criticism).* Taipei: Lianjing, 1989.

_____. 'Guopo shanhe zai: Haiwai zuojia de bentuxing" ("Divided
Naton, Undivided Land: On the Nativism of Chinese Overseas
Writers"). *Lianhe wenxue* 7, no. 3 (January 1991): 24–28.

Zhang Ning. "Xungen yizu yu yuanxiang zhuti de bianxing: Mo Yan,
Han Shaogong, Liu Heng de xiaoshuo" ("The Thematic Metamor-
phosis of the Search for Roots and Homeland Longing"). *Zhongwai*
*wenxue* 18, no. 8 (January 1990): 155–66.

Zheng Shusen (William Tay). *Wenxue lilun yu bijiao wenxue (Literary*
*Theory and Comparative Literature).* Taipei: Shibao, 1986 edition.

Zhong Ling (Ling Chung). *Xiandai Zhongguo miusi: Taiwan nüshiren*
*zuopin xilun (Modern Chinese Muses: Studies of Women Poets of Tai-*
*wan).* Taipei: Lianjing, 1989.

*Zhongguo wenxue piping ziliao huibian (A Compendium of Chinese Literary*
*Criticism).* Edited by Ye Qingbing et al. 11 vols. Taipei: Chengwen, 1978.

*Zhongguo xiandai wenxue shi (A History of Modern Chinese Literature).* 2
vols. Reprint. Shanghai: Fudan daxue, 1980.

Zi Wanyu, ed. *Fengqi yunyong de nüxing zhuyi piping (Trials and Turbu-*
*lence of Modern Chinese Feminist Criticism).* Taipei: Gufeng, 1988.